THE ACCOUNTABILITY DEFICIT

How ministers and officials evaded accountability, misled the public and violated democracy during the pandemic

**MOLLY KINGSLEY   ARABELLA SKINNER
BEN KINGSLEY**

Copyright © Molly Kingsley, Arabella Skinner and Ben Kingsley, 2023

The moral right of the authors has been asserted.

All rights reserved.

No part of this publication may be reproduced, stored in a retrieval system, or transmitted, in any form or by any means, without the prior permission in writing of the publisher, nor be otherwise circulated in any form of binding or cover other than that in which it is published and without a similar condition including this condition being imposed on the subsequent purchaser.

Design, typesetting and publishing by UK Book Publishing

www.ukbookpublishing.com

ISBN: 978-1-916572-44-7

THE ACCOUNTABILITY DEFICIT

How ministers and officials evaded accountability, misled the public and violated democracy during the pandemic

Special thanks to *Leila*, *Kieran* and *Alan* for scrambling to our aid with research when we needed it, and to *Jenny*, *Jane*, *Marta*, *Pru* and *Dawn* for keeping everything else going.

Thank you also to *Danny Kruger MP* for his courageous afterword.

TABLE OF CONTENTS

FOREWORD	1
PART 1	**6**
THE LEGACY OF OUR PANDEMIC RESPONSE	7
SETTING THE SCENE	11
PART 2	**17**
STEAMROLLERED: COVID PASSES	18
90 MINUTES TO REWRITE HUMAN RIGHTS: THE CARE HOME WORKERS VACCINATION REQUIREMENT	31
ETHICALLY CONTENTIOUS AND PROCEDURALLY UNORTHODOX: THE COVID VACCINE PROGRAMME FOR CHILDREN	45
SUPPRESSION AND CENSORSHIP	67
PROPAGANDA	86
ETHICS DENIED: THE MORAL AND ETHICAL ADVISORY GROUP	105
A GRIEVOUS POLICY CHOICE: SCHOOL CLOSURES	124
PART 3	**158**
TAKING STOCK	159
AN UNFETTERED EXECUTIVE	160
INDUSTRY INFLUENCE AND A REGULATORY DEFICIT	189
WHERE IS THE PARLIAMENTARY BACKBONE?	217
PART 4	**231**
CURRENT THREATS	232
RECONCILIATION AND REFORM	242
AFTERWORD BY DANNY KRUGER MP	251
ENDNOTES	263

FOREWORD

"There comes a point when we need to stop just pulling people out of the river. We need to go upstream and find out why they are falling."

Bishop Desmond Tutu

UsForThem started life in May 2020, six weeks into the initial round of school closures in the UK. Founded originally by three parents, over the next two years, tens of thousands of parents, grandparents, experts and those who cared about children joined our campaigning group as we fought to ensure that children were considered front and centre in the policy decisions impacting them.

What started as a single-issue campaign to press for the reopening of schools, bled into other campaigns against enforced social distancing for children, against the closure of playgrounds and children's sport, against the 'bubble and isolation' policy which by June 2021 had resulted in one million healthy children being kept out of school, challenging the compulsory masking of children in classrooms, and to question the ethics and clinical necessity of the roll-out of Covid-19 vaccines to children. Neither seasoned campaigners nor, even, with any formalised organisation for much of our first year, in each case the ferocity of our campaigning was matched only by the passivity of the majority of the incumbent children's organisations and charities whose raison d'être was to advocate for children.

It has been a three year long fight which has seen us despair as the Government repeatedly burdened children with — in some cases — life defining strictures without, it seemed, having paused to reflect on the question of harms. It led us to threaten the Government with formal legal proceedings not once, but three times; and caused us initially to self-censor, then eventually find the strength to speak out, again as a lone voice among children's organisations, about what we perceive to be one of the most misguided and unethical public health policy decisions of modern times — the manipulative, propagandised roll-out to healthy children at very low risk of serious illness of a novel medical intervention with no long term safety data.

By November 2022, we found ourselves proudly working with the then Chair of the Education Select Committee, Robert Halfon MP, to introduce a bill to Parliament that would legally define schools as the 'essential infrastructure' they are;[1] and by March 2022 it led us to hold our heads in our hands as the UK's Covid Inquiry,[2] the mechanism under which children and the public had been promised accountability, failed to include the words 'child' or 'children' anywhere in its terms of reference. We campaigned successfully to change those terms of reference.

For our troubles we have been subject to a three year smear campaign; we have been cancelled more than once; and we now understand that for the majority of our campaigning life our comments have been monitored by the Government's censorship unit, the CDU. That is despite the fact that, to the best of our knowledge, we have never propagated either mis- or disinformation and that without exception our campaigning positions have been guided exclusively by the welfare and wellbeing of children.

In the course of this journey what has really become clear is that the fight isn't about public health restrictions, or about cost/benefit analyses, or — even — about how a country responds to a pandemic. It is a battle about deep deficits in our ways of government, governance and democracy, and about the shape of the future we wish to bequeath to our children.

With life ostensibly returning to 'normal' but a huge array of harm flowing from pandemic policies persisting, and with the UK's official Covid Inquiry crawling at a pace inconsistent with the need for urgent answers, six months ago we started to examine in detail for ourselves how key pandemic decisions had been formed. This work documents that research.

However obvious it might have been to us from early in the pandemic that children had been overlooked by a response that failed even to consider let alone balance their needs, the failings we uncovered in what follows extend beyond children and have implications for us all.

They include:

- ineptitude to an extent which at times was reckless, if not worse;

- the deliberate circumvention of truth on an industrialised scale by means of suppression of dissent and the deployment of propaganda that oscillated between outrageously optimistic and manipulatively dangerous;

- an institutionalised disregard for ethics, integrity and – at times – fundamental precepts of dignity and morality; and

- more prosaically but as important, a two year long refusal to evaluate the harms of policy decisions against the benefits.

Sitting behind many of these failings is a pharmaceutical industry primed and resourced to capitalise on the opportunities presented by those failings.

And what of the ultimate bastion of ethical and transparent democratic decision-making, Parliament? As we show in the chapters which follow, notwithstanding the efforts of a few courageous parliamentarians, our Parliament failed us: seduced, deceived, bamboozled or swerved by an errant unfettered Executive which accorded it neither respect nor due regard; nor — at times — even truth.

Although our analysis has been centred around key decisions in the pandemic response, we believe the deficits of governance and ethics which so marred the period of the pandemic was and is symptomatic of deeper maladies affecting our country's democratic institutions and safeguards.

The result is that our community infrastructure, from schools to libraries, swimming pools, parks, transport hubs and hospitals, is crumbling — literally in some cases; our national debt is skyrocketing and we have already mortgaged the futures of our next generation to pay for the ruinous policy decisions of the pandemic; our ever-unhealthier population has succumbed to a public health dogma which, tainted by excessive corporate influence, captivates our people and politicians with quick fix medicalised interventions in lieu of taking greater individual responsibility for our own good health.

We reject this model of government and democracy for ourselves and we reject the future it implies for our children. While our purpose in writing this account is not, primarily, to apportion blame, a society that endeavours to bury these failures can only repeat them.

We publish what follows in the hope that by helping to illuminate how we reached this nadir, we can chart a better course for the sake of our children, and indeed for all of us.

October 2023

A practical note

Many of our footnote references link to website pages hosted by the UK Government or other public bodies. These links can occasionally become redundant if the relevant organisation reorganises its website materials or hosting systems. If you are a journalist or researcher seeking to check any of our source materials and you experience this phenomenon, please contact us if you are unable to find the new location of that source material.

Attribution etc

The views we express are our own, as are any errors. Danny Kruger MP's afterword reflects his views alone, and likewise he is not responsible for the views we have expressed.

About the authors

Molly is a founder of UsForThem, having originally trained and worked as a lawyer. She writes on political and social issues in a number of newspapers and magazines and regularly appears as a commentator in print and broadcast media. Molly co-authored *The Children's Inquiry: How the state and society failed the young during the Covid-19 pandemic* (Pinter & Martin, 2022).

Arabella is a director at UsForThem. She regularly appears as a commentator in print and broadcast media. She holds a MSc in psychology and previously had a career in business and marketing strategy across Unilever, BBC and in consultancy.

Alongside writing and campaign advocacy, Ben coordinates the strategic legal aspects of UsForThem's campaigns, having completed a career as a partner in the law firm Slaughter and May advising on regulatory, financial crime and commercial law.

PART 1

THE LEGACY OF OUR PANDEMIC RESPONSE

The UK is not in good health.

Our children are unhappier[3] and unhealthier[4] than ever before. Their life chances are materially worse today than before the pandemic.[5] Unexpected deaths are more than 10% higher than the pre-pandemic average,[6] predominantly attributed to heart problems and diabetes, with experts warning of *"a catastrophe of equal proportion to the pandemic itself"*.[7] The backlog of NHS procedures for England alone is running at more than 7.75 million, up from 4.2 million at the start of the pandemic.[8]

The country is experiencing a sharp economic downturn, with inflation running hot, interest rates rising rapidly and UK public sector net debt standing at 99% of GDP,[9] a level last seen more than 60 years ago. Official figures estimate the total direct cost of the pandemic response as between £310 billion to £410 billion,[10] much of it met with quantitative easing. For comparison, in 2019 the UK's annual healthcare expenditure was £225 billion,[11] the Department for Education spent more than £100 billion,[12] and the Ministry of Defence spent £38 billion.[13]

Public capital that in the future might have been invested to nurture research, to stimulate private sector economic activity, to support public sector modernisation and to improve children's health and education has been mortgaged and the proceeds spent.

Consequently our ability over the longer term to innovate and educate has been materially compromised.[14] A two year period in which education was severely disrupted has devalued schooling in the eyes of pupils and parents: in 2022, 1.7 million children missed more than 10% of their schooling and 140,000 children were missing from school completely,[15] a pronounced increase on the pre-pandemic years.[16]

Throughout society, the most disadvantaged have been most affected.[17] [18] For the vulnerable, policy choices have contributed to loss of life, loss of dignity and treatment that at times has been degrading and inhumane.[19] [20] [21] [22] Social Mobility, already struggling in 2019, has only worsened as a result of the pandemic.[23] [24]

Public officials have lost the confidence of the public they serve, and the public's trust in public health has suffered as a result. 57% of people in the UK (including 72% of 18 to 25 year olds) now think that Ministers were dishonest about the necessity of Covid restrictions.[25]

Perhaps worst of all, cornerstone ethical principles – principles that are intended to protect the vulnerable and to safeguard human rights we regard as inalienable – have been compromised,[26] most seriously in relation to children.[27]

The origin of the UK's current ill health is not a cave in Yunnan Province or a lab in Wuhan. It is the period of two years from March 2020 to March 2022, during which the creeping abnormality of an 'ad libbed' and increasingly authoritarian response trampled cornerstone principles of human rights and medical ethics, and at times subverted a foundational pillar of our representative democracy — the public scrutiny and accountability functions of Parliament.

We contend that the UK's response to the pandemic has been an economic, social, medical, ethical and safeguarding disaster. Our thesis is that the causes of this disaster lie in serious deficits – of ethics, of governance, of truth and integrity, of transparency and ultimately of accountability. We have examined those deficits, and we undertake to evidence their extent and severity. Our aim is to trigger the public reflection and reconciliation that we believe is necessary to allow us then to chart a better way.

At the core of this economic, social, medical, ethical and safeguarding disaster was a series of terrible decisions, examined in detail in the chapters which follow, that led to outcomes measurable on a scale between bad and catastrophic. As we shall show, different factors contributed to those avoidable outcomes:

1. Governance structures and safeguards were weakened, sidelined or outright abandoned by key decision-makers, enabling decisions to be made without the beneficial rigour and discipline, testing and challenge, that formal governance could have provided.

2. The public's understanding and acceptance of the Government's decision-making was skewed by a fanatical official consensus, cultivated by propaganda which consistently sought to emphasise the potential benefits of Government interventions and to under-play the risks and harms.

3. The Government, with the encouragement of Parliament, excessively locked down the public square and used State apparatus and co-opted social media to suppress critical and dissenting voices.

4. The pharmaceutical industry seized the commercial opportunities presented by the pandemic and the Government's

chaotic governance and, in the absence of a regulatory brake, monetised the public health emergency.

5. Parliament's attempts to apply scrutiny and accountability to decisions and decision-making were at times inadequate and were variously evaded, deflected and disregarded by Ministers and senior officials.

Our motivations

From our very first campaign in Spring 2020 it seemed apparent that harms of interventions – at that time school closures – had not been weighed against the anticipated benefits. As we continued, so this failure to consider harms was repeated and repeated, but also aggravated by, seemingly, ever more serious deviations from principles of good governance, ethics and integrity.

As outsiders looking in at some of the Government's key pandemic decisions, and experiencing ourselves and with our families the impacts, we had a strong sense that something was going very wrong with policy-making. In the Spring of 2023, with the official Covid Inquiry underway – and underwhelming – we decided that we had to dig into the evidence ourselves. As we did so, we began to understand the depths of the deficits in pandemic decision-making.

Our aim is to bring that evidence to life. Before we do that, a brief scene set is needed.

SETTING THE SCENE

More than three years on from the start of the pandemic, it is easy to forget that a virus that was presented to the public as a potential existential threat was at first seen through sober eyes.

The earliest data evidenced that Covid was a discriminating virus, disproportionately affecting the elderly and those with comorbidities. This was acknowledged by the UK's Chief Medical Officer, Professor Chris Whitty, when he answered questions in Parliament on 5 March 2020, the day after Italy had shocked Europe by closing all of its schools, and as the UK experienced its first official Covid-related death:

> *"I have a reasonably high degree of confidence that 1% is at the upper limit of what the mortality rate is, to be clear"*, and *"I think it's easy to get a perception that if you are older and you get this virus then you're a goner – absolutely not, the great majority of people will recover from this virus, even if they are in their 80s"*.[28]

The scientific grounding of Professor Whitty's commentary was evident – opinion based on informed understanding, recognising the possibility of differences and disagreements, and conditioned by the transparent acknowledgement of uncertainties. *"Here was a man willing to treat the country as adults and didn't feel the need to lie about the severity of the situation"*, reported one mainstream political commentator later that day.[29]

Professor Whitty at this time appeared equally moderated on the range of possible interventions that might be necessary to combat the virus:

"We are trying to say really clearly that in this country there is a range of things we could do, ranging from those with almost no economic impact and high efficacy—top of the range being washing your hands and second being covering your mouth with a tissue when you cough —all the way down to those that have major societal impact, such as closing schools, which obviously affects children but also parents, potentially employment and particular sectors of the economy. It is very easy to choose a package of measures that is quite dramatic but has relatively little impact on the epidemic. We are very keen to avoid that, so we are modelling out all the combinations that we can because people's livelihoods depend on it".[30]

Apparently implying an intention – sensible in our view – to adhere to the pre-existing pandemic policy of Contain, Delay, Research and Mitigate, Matt Hancock, the Health Secretary, had just a few days earlier emphasised to Parliament the need for proportionality in the UK's response to the emerging situation: *"Another important consideration is that overreaction has economic and social costs too. We have to keep the public safe, but we need to act in a way that is proportionate…"*, adding that *"schools should stay open, with no blanket ban, unless there are specific reasons for them not to".*[31]

The steps by which the UK travelled from this sober state to a state of fear and frenzy have by now been well documented,[32] and to some extent revisited by the official Covid Inquiry. Within a few short days, concerns about restrictions being imposed in neighbouring countries grew,[33] the WHO declared that Covid had become a pandemic (Director General, Dr Tedros Ghebreyesus, alarmingly called for all possible action to be taken: *"Not testing alone. Not contact tracing alone. Not quarantine alone. Not social distancing alone. Do it all")*,[34] and the temperature among key policy-makers in Westminster rose further when, on 16 March, a pandemic modelling team from Imperial College London, led by

SETTING THE SCENE

Professor Neil Ferguson, presented its Covid modelling report to Downing Street.

Ferguson's paper predicted over 500,000 deaths in the UK if no steps were taken to mitigate the virus, and that 260,000 would die if the moderate measures which had already been implemented were retained, mortality figures which would overwhelm the NHS and devastate the economy. The report concluded that *"epidemic suppression is the only viable strategy at the current time"*, i.e. a blanket national lockdown.[35]

In the week that followed, the Government's rhetoric escalated. Foreshadowing what was to come, Matt Hancock reported to Parliament that the Government would introduce a 14 day quarantine for those infected by the virus, mandate a general cessation of social contact, require widespread working from home, and impose a 12 week period of shielding for the most vulnerable.

Seeking support from all parties for the Government's plan, Hancock described it as *"a war against an invisible killer"*,[36] having noted that the Government would very soon be asking Parliament for new powers of intervention: *"Some of those measures will be very significant and a departure from the way that we do things in peacetime"*.

The following day, while announcing this first tranche of draconian restrictions on national television, Prime Minister Boris Johnson invoking the authority of *"scientific advice"* explained that the public would be asked to submit to these measures because *"'This is a disease that is so dangerous and so infectious that without drastic measures to check its progress it would overwhelm any health system in the world"*.[37]

On 20 March, the Prime Minister continued his escalation, evoking a vision of imminent preventable deaths across all age groups: *"Bit*

13

by bit, day by day, by your actions, your restraint and your sacrifice, we are putting this country in a better and stronger position, where we will be able to save literally thousands of lives, of people of all ages, people who don't deserve to die now. People whose lives can, must, and will be saved".[38]

Then finally, on 23 March, in his televised address to announce that the whole of England was to be locked down, the Prime Minister described Covid as *"... the biggest threat this country has faced for decades ... All over the world we are seeing the devastating impact of this invisible killer"*.[39]

From then on daily televised briefings and wall-to-wall media coverage further served to fuel the growing sense among the public – and parliamentarians – of a siege. What was not apparent to the public at the time, but with hindsight appears to have been known by at least some senior policy-makers and officials, was the following.

First, at this defining moment which set the tone for the entire pandemic response, the Government's communications were both founded on and fuelling an exaggerated understanding of risk. Images of overrun hospitals in Italy dominated the media for a few days – images that were later found to have been contrived.[40] Lockdowns – which had never before been part of any WHO or national pandemic plans – were starting to be described as *"effective"* by the media,[41] and the WHO congratulated China on its brutal yet apparently effective response in Wuhan.[42]

Indeed on the 13 March, a meeting had taken place among infectious disease experts from across the UK to discuss, among other topics, whether Covid should remain classified as a High Consequence Infectious Disease[43] (in January 2020 there had been an interim recommendation to classify Covid as a HCID on the

SETTING THE SCENE

basis of early data).[44] The minutes of the meeting of the Advisory Committee on Dangerous Pathogens (ACDP) record that the experts *"unanimously agreed that this infection should not be classified as a HCID"*,[45] and that advice was communicated the same day to Jonathan Van Tam, Deputy Chief Medical Officer for England at the DHSC.[46] This ostensibly positive news was not, however, published by the NHS until 19 March[47] and appears not to have been expressly communicated to Parliament.[48]

Second, a behavioural science team, SPi-B, which had been working at the heart of the Government at that time, had produced, on 22 March, a paper on the options for increasing the public's adherence to social distancing measures which warned Ministers that *"[a] substantial number of people still do not feel sufficiently personally threatened"* and, appearing explicitly to acknowledge the heavily age-stratified nature of the viral threat: *"it could be that they are reassured by the low death rate in their demographic group"*. SPi-B therefore recommended that *"[t]he perceived level of personal threat needs to be increased among those who are complacent, using hard-hitting emotional messaging"*.[49]

With hindsight the Government's failure to contextualise its public presentation of the viral threat with the age-based risk stratification that was clearly well understood in private at the most senior levels[50] appears conspicuously alarmist or at the very least reckless. As Mark Woolhouse pointed out in his evidence to the Covid Inquiry, *"...we knew from very early on in the pandemic that there was a relatively small subset of the population that were at tremendously enhanced risk, tremendously enhanced, and...these were the elderly, the infirm and the frail. They were at far more risk from this virus. And a statistic that sums it up is that someone over 75 was at 10,000 times more likely to die of a Covid-19 infection than a 15-year old. 10,000 times. This is a massive difference...the average age of a Covid death is older than - was older than - than the average age of death"*.[51]

Third, the exaggeration of risk and the apparently deliberate stoking of fear among the public marked a significant departure from the UK pandemic plans in place when the pandemic struck.[52] A key element of those plans was documented in a Cabinet Office pandemic management ethical framework produced in 2007 and updated in 2011. This urged that *"those responsible for providing information will neither exaggerate or minimise the situation and will give people the most accurate information that they can"*. It included a 'reasonableness requirement'; and noted that decisions should be *"rational; not arbitrary; based on appropriate evidence; the result of an appropriate process..."*; and with respect to the principle of proportionality, that *"decisions on actions that may affect people's daily lives, which are taken to protect the public from harm, will be proportionate to the relevant risk and to the benefits that can be gained from the proposed action"*.[53]

A pandemic policy response founded on a strategy of fomenting public fear and exaggeration of risks of harms from Covid[54] both ignored existing planning assumptions and crossed ethical lines even before any substantive policy decisions were made; and yet in the UK this cynical and at times perhaps arrogant approach to managing the public's health set the scene for the pandemic, and the series of ethically-compromised policies which followed.

* * *

Arrogance feels an apt description for the Government's approach across the Autumn and Winter of 2021 to the hotly contested topic of Covid vaccination status passes, or Covid passports. As we shall see this became a paradigm example of the Government attempting to steamroll a legally, ethically and morally contentious policy through Parliament.

PART 2

STEAMROLLERED: COVID PASSES

"This is no longer really a debate about whether masks work or who should have a vaccine. It is about who we are and what kind of society we are creating for our children. Do we really care about the freedoms that we all took for granted before 2020? People roll their eyes when Conservatives and libertarians start talking about civil liberties and freedoms, but freedom is not an abstract ideology.

Freedom is what enables my constituents to see their family, comfort the dying, go to school and go to work. That is what freedom looks like. After 20 months in and out of restrictions, we have to accept that there has been a permanent change in the understanding of what liberty is in this country, which is why I cannot support these measures. I urge the Government to return to a society of freedom and responsibility. Our constituents deserve that and they will rise to the challenge".[55]

Miriam Cates MP, Parliamentary debate on mandatory masks, the NHS vaccine mandate and Covid passes, 14 December 2021

The debate that took place in Parliament on 14 December 2021 represented a moment of profound significance for liberty and human rights in the UK. At stake was our collective understanding of what it means to live in a free society – to work, to move about, and literally to breathe, free from Government interference.

In a functioning democracy governmental interventions as fundamental as these would have received focussed and extensive scrutiny in Parliament, in the media and among the public.

Instead, on the day of the vote itself and across the days immediately before the vote, with Parliament and the media engulfed by sniping and intrigue over the Owen Patterson and Partygate scandals, the Government saw fit to combine a vote on Covid passes – an intervention which could fundamentally rebase the liberties and rights of the UK's population – combined into one session with votes on three other highly controversial interventions.[56] Consequently, scrutiny of the proposals was threadbare.

A controversial idea seeded

As Miriam Cates alluded, for a country which cherishes its role as the modern world's most mature liberal democracy it is hard to conceive of a more lightning-rod policy than the deceptively titled 'vaccine passport', combining as it does two significant State infringements on individual liberty: a requirement to carry papers (or a digital equivalent) and a requirement to accept a medical treatment to access essential aspects of public life – transport, places of work, restaurants, entertainment venues, shops even.

In early September 2020 the Prime Minister's innocuous use of the word 'passports',[57] as a proxy for demonstrating proof of a negative test result to gain access to theatres and sports venues, was shot down almost immediately by SAGE, which indicated the money spent on mass testing could be better deployed elsewhere.[58] Just three months later, at the end of November and before any vaccine products had been approved for use in the UK, the Vaccines Minister was threatening that normal life could soon be denied to those who could not show proof of inoculation via a smartphone-based vaccine status app[59] – a proposition that was vocally denounced by

Marcus Fysh, a backbench Conservative Party MP, who described himself as *"100 per cent against this ignorant authoritarianism"*.[60]

Conflicting messages

The very next day, Michael Gove, the senior Cabinet Minister in charge of the Covid operations task force, ruled out the possibility of vaccination passes, saying *"I certainly am not planning to introduce any vaccine passports, and I don't know anyone else in government who is"*,[61] apparently unaware that Dido Harding, the head of the Government's Test and Trace programme, had just told an event hosted by the Health Service Journal that her team were working on creating a *"single record"* for immunity testing for vaccines and those self-administering tests at home. *"We are working very closely with the vaccine team"*, she had stressed.[62]

The Vaccines Minister, apparently having suffered a change of heart, over the festive period, by early February 2021 was describing the possibility of health-based passes for domestic use as *"discriminatory"*,[63] emphasising that he believed testing was the best way to control transmission.[64]

That brief period of apparent clarity was shattered again on 22 February, when the Government announced a formal review of its plans for reopening the economy, including the role that Covid passes could play.[65]

Public resistance

As the review proceeded, a group of more than 70 senior cross-party MPs and peers wrote to the Prime Minister to say that they would vote against vaccine passports, describing it as *"dangerous, discriminatory and counterproductive"*;[66] the Leader of the Official Opposition, Sir Keir Starmer MP, subsequently came out against the idea for Covid vaccine passports, saying that *"there will be a British sense that we don't actually want to go down that road"*; [67]

Over the three month period from December 2020 to March 2021 a public petition titled *'Do not rollout Covid-19 vaccine passports'* attracted over 375,000 signatures,[68] and the UK's Equality and Human Rights Commission warned soon after, in mid-April, that introducing any form of Covid vaccination status certificate could create a *"two-tier society whereby only certain groups are able to fully enjoy their rights"*.[69]

A stitch up?

Less publicly, but arguably more materially, in December 2020 a group of experts called the Moral and Ethical Advisory Group (MEAG) – a group that features prominently in a later chapter – met to discuss the possibility of a Covid pass. MEAG had been formed at the end of 2019 by the Department for Health and Social Care specifically for the purpose of advising Ministers and senior officials on the moral, ethical and faith aspects of decision-making. Officials from the DHSC attended that meeting as observers.

The official summary of the meeting[70] records that the group had raised a number of serious ethical concerns were expressed about any requirement for vaccine status certificates or passes; specifically, that human rights considerations had not yet been given adequate attention, that the public lacked sufficient understanding of the science behind the Covid vaccines that had been developed, and the fact that semi-coercive policies were known to affect trust in public health.

As far as we have been able to find that advice was not shared with Parliament let alone communicated to the public.

Then in February of 2021, we now know that Boris Johnson sent a series of messages into a Whatsapp group including his aide Henry Cook which suggest the Government by then was looking to gather evidence to buttress a policy decision which had already been taken. They included *"when would we announce that we were going to have vaccine passports and on what basis? by when do we expected we will have the evidence we need? march 29? April 12? this will make a big difference to people's thinking about nightclubs etc"*. Henry Cook replied *"Good questions PM, and I think we have at least serviceable answers to them"*.[71]

Then in May, on the same day that Michael Gove MP had told the House of Commons that the Government was reviewing whether Covid status could be used to help facilitate major events such as Premier League matches, it was reported that the Government had, in fact, already signed a number of vaccine passport contracts with terms of a number of years,[72] a disclosure which prompted outrage from backbench MPs: *"The Government appears to have decided to introduce Covid-status certification — a two-tier checkpoint Britain — by stealth, without a vote in Parliament"*, decried Steve Baker MP.[73]

Parliamentary rejection

The Public Administration and Constitutional Affairs Committee (PACAC) of the House of Commons then published on 10 June a report following its own review of the possibility of a Covid pass.[74] That report concluded that the Government had not made a case for the introduction of status certification on the basis either of science or the public interest, and lamented the contradictory nature of Government communication around the idea for Covid passes, which it considered was due either to duplicity or to incompetence but *"either way, the Government's approach to certification has risked damaging trust in government and in the measures put in place to tackle the pandemic"*.[75]

In its summary the PACAC's report commented:

"Given the significance and seriousness of introducing such a Covid-status certification system, the Committee was surprised at the lack of consideration by the Government of a number of issues and concerns with their suggested approach, in particular the scientific case for that system. And the Committee was struck by the fact that the best assessment the Minister could make in favour of certificates was to say that it was a 'finely balanced judgment'".[76]

As if that rebuke was not sufficiently unambiguous, the report later added:

"The Committee finds that there is no justification for engaging in what is likely to be a significant infringement of individual rights by introducing a Covid-status certification system and given the absence of convincing scientific case and the large number of uncertainties that remain, we recommend that the Government abandon the idea of using a Covid-status certification system domestically".[77]

The PACAC is the Select Committee of Parliament with responsibility for constitutional matters. It is an important committee. The Committee's unambiguous rejection should have been the end of the matter.

However, soon after, on 21 June 2021, and before the Government's review of the possibility of a Covid pass had been concluded, the NHS launched an unannounced Covid Pass facility in an overnight update to its App[78] which was then promptly flagged by Big Brother Watch: *"Covid passports are being rolled out before the Gove review is published - all after [the PACAC] found there was 'no justification' for them".*[79]

Government defends the proposition

On 5 July 2021, the Government published just six pages of commentary, in oversized font, as the output of its four month review process.[80] The call for public evidence associated with that review had prompted 52,450 responses, most of which were reported by the Government to have expressed strongly negative views on the concept of certification.

The conclusion of the review was that *"Having considered a wide range of evidence as part of the review, the Government has concluded that it will not mandate the use of COVID-status certification as a condition of entry for visitors to any setting at the present time".*[81]

Perhaps in recognition of the fact that the NHS had pre-emptively launched the Covid Pass through its App a few weeks earlier, the Government concluded that *"The Government believes that to ban certification in domestic settings would, in most cases, be an unjustified intrusion on how organisations choose to make their premises safe. Essential settings should not use certification, but others can decide to use it at their own discretion in compliance with legal obligations. ... [and so] the Government will make the NHS COVID Pass, accessed via the NHS app, available so that individuals can prove their status".*[82]

Curiously, in light of the strong objections raised by MEAG in December 2020, the report also claimed that *"Ethical, moral and equality considerations of certification have been explored through extensive engagement with ethicists, academics and a range of specialists and representatives including from faith, race and disabilities groups"*, and that *"Many ethicists saw a clear case for certification"*, yet without even a footnote to explain the identity or provenance of those ethicists, academics and specialists.[83]

A fortnight later, on 19 July, the Prime Minister signalled in a televised address to the country that vaccination status passports were firmly on his agenda, albeit not yet on a mandatory basis: *"... I would remind everybody that some of life's most important pleasures and opportunities are likely to be increasingly dependent on vaccination. ... I should serve notice now that by the end of September - when all over 18s will have had the chance to be double jabbed – we are planning to make full vaccination the condition of entry to nightclubs and other venues where large crowds gather".*[84] Surprisingly in the very same speech he acknowledged that *"even if [people] have been vaccinated there is a significant risk that they can still pass the disease on"*, seemingly under-cutting any purported public health justification for certifying vaccine status.

On 12 August, the Government responded to the PACAC to address the negative conclusions of its June 2021 report,[85] but the response lacked any meaningful substance.

For example: the Government claimed to have carried out a review of the cost and benefits of COVID-status certification as part of its earlier review process – but that claim was belied by the absence of anything that could reasonably be described as an evidence-based public health evaluation in the six pages of report produced by the Government following that review (as we shall see, is a recurring theme).

In response to the PACAC's comment that it was *"highly regrettable"* that the Government had committed to, but had not yet, provided costings for the proposal, and that *"Full costings must be provided alongside any announcement in regards to Covid-status Certification"*, the Government replied somewhat fatuously that *"The cost of certification will differ depending on the final model used for certification"*.

Finally, in response to the PACAC's conclusion that *"the Committee does not think the Government has made a case for any form of domestic Covid-status certification system"* the Government simply referred back to its six page July report, stating that *"the Government believes that certification would provide a public health benefit"*.

Almost comically for a Government which had just overseen the longest closure of schools in Europe, save for Italy, its devotion to certification appears to have been driven in part by the fact that *"a number of countries have been forced to close their nightclubs after a surge of cases, which we want to avoid"*.[86]

Notably, as part of its formal response to the PACAC, the Government committed to facilitate *"appropriate parliamentary scrutiny"* ahead of any roll-out of Covid status certification.[87]

Public consulted but not heard

At the end of September the Government issued another call for evidence on its proposal for mandatory COVID certification in a 'Plan B' scenario. Plan B referred to a package of measures proposed earlier in the year for a tightening of Covid restrictions over the winter period which also included mandatory face masks in most indoor settings, working from home and daily testing. That call for evidence remained open for two weeks.

Despite the Governmental Code on Public Consultations requiring the Government to provide a summary of consultation responses before taking further action (including the laying of legislation before Parliament),[88] there does not appear to have been any published output from that call for evidence, so it is not possible to know how many responses were received.

In any event, according to a House of Commons briefing paper, the evidence received was still being analysed when the vote on mandatory Covid passes took place in Parliament on 14 December 2021.[89]

Against the backdrop of a crescendo of distractions – the Owen Patterson scandal, the Partygate scandal which had broken in November and the *"very mild"* Omicron variant emerging from South Africa triggering legislation to mandate face coverings in indoor settings,[90] tension was rising between the Government and parliamentarians: *"… again we see the Government's immediate assumption that what it should reach for is new controls, new compulsion, new rules that will be inflicted on the British people. And I think we need to move away from that, move back to a world where we trust people".*[91]

On 7 December 2021 there were further revelations in the media about the Partygate scandal, including a highly damaging video in which the Prime Minister's press secretary was seen to be joking about officials in Downing Street having known that a party held the previous year had breached lockdown rules in force at the time.[92] The next day, the Prime Minister confirmed that he was activating Plan B in England: *"The Prime Minister has today confirmed that England will move to Plan B following the rapid spread of the Omicron variant in the UK … Parliament will debate the measures next week, with a vote expected to take place on Tuesday 14 December".*[93] At the Prime Minister's press conference there was virtually no scrutiny of the restrictions; almost all of the media questions focused on Partygate.

A raucous Parliament has its say, rebels wound the PM but the measures pass

Finally, on 14 December 2021, during a chaotic debate in the House of Commons, votes on four measures were called: on mandating face coverings for retail premises and public transport, on daily testing, on Covid passes and on an NHS staff vaccine mandate as part of 'Plan B' restrictions. The legislative instruments which reintroduced face coverings across public venues and the requirements for daily testing of close contacts had already come into force before the debate.[94] The instrument under which mandatory Covid passes would be introduced for entry into large venues and events had been laid before Parliament only the day before,[95] leading Labour Party MP Justin Madders to comment: *"two of these sets of regulations were published only at 3 pm yesterday, less than 24 hours before this debate began"* for which there was *"no excuse"*.[96]

At times the debate descended into farce:[97]

> *"Repeatedly, the Government have refused to do a cost-benefit analysis on the impact of their policies. We have before us now a number of statutory instruments without impact assessments"*, complained Graham Stringer MP. *"In fact, I can see the Vaccines Minister waving impact assessments at me"*, Wes Streeting MP, the Shadow Health Secretary, interjected. Then Graham Stringer MP, again: *"the Under-Secretary of State for Health and Social Care, Maggie Throup was waving a sheet about, which may or may not have been the impact assessment"*.

Sir Peter Bottomley MP:

> *"To those who have said an impact assessment has not been made, I say that it has and it has been published; those who invigilate [impact] assessments do not think it is adequate, but that is a side point"*.

A number of backbench MPs spoke forcefully against both the substance of the proposals and the manner in which they had been brought before the House. Richard Drax MP, for example, gave this impassioned short speech:

> *"Previous speakers have asked whether these further laws will be effective. Whether they are or not is not as much of an issue for me as how we as a nation want to live our lives. Do we want to fear more restrictions every time a new variant appears, as it will? No is my answer.*

> Do we want to damage our economy and all within it every time a new variant appears? No is my answer. Is working from home when I can enter a packed pub the right approach? [To cheers from the chamber of: "No!"] No is my answer. Do we want to shut down schools and universities and further ruin young people's lives? [Other members: "No!"] No is the answer. Do we want to restrict people's movement and tell them what they can and cannot do when there is no evidence to suggest this would work? [Cheers: "No!"] No is the answer.
>
> Do we want to see hundreds of thousands of NHS patients waiting, some in agony, because their operations have been delayed again? [Cheers: "No!"] No is the answer. Do we want to see the hospitality and retail sectors collapse because we keep instilling the fear of God into their customers? [Cheers: "No!"] No is the answer. Do we want to go on spending taxpayers' money on this eye-watering and unaffordable scale? [Cheers: "No!"] No is the answer.
>
> Finally … do we want the state to give us back our lives and freedom? A monumental yes is the cry from many a heart".

Tim Loughton MP followed on:

> "Yesterday I was asked in an interview whether I was plotting to revolt, and indeed I have seen my name on various lists of rebels today. Let me make it clear that I have not been plotting, I am not rebelling and I am certainly not revolting. What I am doing, in three minutes, is trying to scrutinise a really important piece of legislation affecting all our constituents—a duty that Labour [Party MPs] seem to have completely abrogated by giving the Government a blank cheque here today. They have been here only in single figures for most of this debate".

All four of the measures debated were passed. Media attention focused on the fact that the measure was subject to the second biggest Parliamentary rebellion since World War Two (all of the Liberal Democrat MPs voted against it, plus 8 Labour MPs and 99 Conservative MPs), and it was reported as a huge blow for the Prime Minister in the midst of Partygate – indeed it may well be that the fallout from more than 100 MPs voting against Covid passes was a turning point for the Prime Minister's Parliamentary authority. Certainly the episode sparked speculation about whether the Prime Minister retained the confidence of his party.

Of greater constitutional significance, however, Parliament had been treated with stunning disregard at a critical moment for human rights and freedom in the UK. Ironically, Covid passes proved to be a short-lived policy. From 15 December 2021 they became mandatory for entry to nightclubs, unseated indoor events with 500 or more attendees, unseated outdoor events with 4,000 or more attendees and any event with 10,000. Just five weeks later, the Government terminated that mandate.

Another high-profile example of the Government having cynically pushed through a legally, ethically and morally dubious policy which ultimately failed – the care homes vaccination mandate of Summer 2021 – is the subject of our next chapter. As the Prime Minister's official spokesperson put it in February 2021, *"Taking a vaccine is not mandatory and it would be discriminatory to force somebody to take one"*.[98]

90 MINUTES TO REWRITE HUMAN RIGHTS: THE CARE HOME WORKERS VACCINATION REQUIREMENT

"We could perhaps have a painting next to me of Munch's 'The Scream' to get a sense of how I feel about the conduct of Government business in this House. The Government are treating this House with utter contempt: 90 minutes on a statutory instrument to fundamentally change the balance of human rights in this country is nothing short of a disgrace."

William Wragg MP (Conservative), Chair of the Public Administration and Constitutional Affairs Committee in Parliament

By February 2021 it was reported that 3 in 10 care home workers had yet to receive a first dose of the vaccine.[99] By March of that year, over a third of Covid deaths were recorded as taking place in care homes and the Government remained under fire for its earlier handling of care homes which it was said to have *"left out to dry"*.[100]

Having ruled out universal mandatory vaccinations in February 2021, the Prime Minister was by 21 February asking advisers within No 10 *"what are we doing to insist on vaccination of care workers?"*.[101] By March senior Ministers including the Prime Minister had begun to actively plan for a care home worker mandate,[102] despite official denials[103] and despite apparent warnings in a report prepared for a Cabinet committee that the move would force many social care workers to leave the sector, and result in successful legal claims against the Government.[104]

At the end of that month, a group of DHSC officials gave a presentation on mandates to the Government's expert moral and ethical advisory group, MEAG, after the Prime Minister had earlier said that there would be *"deep and complex"* ethical issues in any mandate scheme.[105] The official summary of that meeting records that MEAG's experts expressed concerns about the ethical basis for mandating vaccination, the resourcing consequences for the care home sector and *"a lack of evidence that mandating vaccinations will be effective at increasing uptake"*.[106]

The following day, on 1 April, the Italian government passed an emergency decree mandating vaccination for all healthcare and pharmacy workers – the first such mandate in Europe.[107]

Support sought

On 14 April 2021, the Government launched a public consultation on its proposal to make vaccination a condition of access to care homes for staff and service providers in England – effectively a 'no jab, no job' mandate.[108] That consultation was predicated on an assertion of evidence that vaccination would reduce transmission, and invoked epidemiological advice from Sage that *"an uptake rate of 80% in staff and 90% in residents in each individual care home setting would be needed to provide a minimum level of protection against outbreaks of COVID-19"*.[109] Notably the consultation document made no reference to the deep and complex ethical considerations to which the Prime Minister had earlier alluded.

The Government reported the outcome of the consultation on 16 June 2021.[110] Overall, 41 per cent of respondents to the consultation were supportive of compulsory vaccination but 57 per cent did not support the proposal. Among care home users and their relatives, more than 61 per cent were unsupportive, and among members of the public, more than 77 per cent were unsupportive. Only care home providers showed significant support, with 66% being supportive and a further 10% being rather supportive. Members of the Adult Social Care workforce who responded to the consultation were 51% against and 47% in favour of the mandate.

Despite the majority negative responses, in particular from care home users in whose interests the mandate had been proposed, and that *"respondents were concerned about the potential impact of the policy on staffing levels",*[111] the Government announced that *"in response to the consultation"* and *"to protect all care home residents who are clinically vulnerable to COVID-19"*, it would be publishing legislation to mandate vaccination for staff working inside all registered care homes in England.

NHS statistics show that already by this point more than 80% of care home workers had received a first dose, and more than 70% had received a second dose.[112]

Listened but not heard

In the official press release accompanying the public consultation feedback, Matt Hancock, the Health Secretary at the time, was quoted as saying: *"Through our consultation we have listened to the experiences and concerns of providers and people living and working in care homes to help shape our approach".*[113]

Previewing a probably inevitable discussion of extending the mandate to all healthcare workers, he then added: *"We have a responsibility to do all we can to safeguard those receiving care including in the NHS and so will be consulting further on whether to extend to other health and social care workers".*

On the same day, the council chair of the British Medical Association voiced serious concerns, cautioning that *"Mandatory vaccination for NHS staff is an incredibly complex issue that raises many ethical, legal and practical questions"* and *"Compulsion is a blunt instrument to tackle a complex issue".*[114]

Mandatory Impact Assessment goes missing

The statutory instrument for effecting the mandate was published in draft form on 22 June 2021.[115] As a draft statutory instrument (as opposed to an Act of Parliament) this draft legislative measure could be either adopted or rejected by MPs but could not be amended, and the parliamentary debate for the measure in the House of Commons would be limited to 90 minutes.

Nevertheless, as a legal matter the Government was obliged to produce a full impact assessment for the legislation. Despite the dry description, impact assessments are an essential tool for good law and policy-making. They require the costs, risks and benefits of legal, regulatory and policy proposals to be quantified and weighed, and for that assessment then to be published. When MPs vote on new laws, many look to the impact assessment to quantify in real terms the effects of the texts on which they are being asked to vote. *"An impact assessment is not an optional extra"*, as one veteran parliamentarian stressed during a debate.[116] Without them, Parliament is flying blind.

The documentation laid before Parliament suggested that the impact assessment was included with the draft instrument but it was not in fact included. In our view this should have immediately blocked the vote from going ahead; but it did not.

Scrutiny frustrated

On 8 July, the House of Lords Secondary Legislation Scrutiny Committee, whose role is (as the name suggests) to scrutinise all secondary legislation proposals, published its assessment of the draft legislation.[117] Serious procedural issues were immediately evident to the Committee including a lack of clarity and practical detail about how the legislation would operate; the absence of any assessment of the impact on the care home workforce and care homes in general; a confusing analysis of current vaccination levels in the sector, and the absence of any clear explanation of the policy choices made. This made *"effective scrutiny of the instrument impossible"*.[118]

The Committee also then roasted the evidence base for the legislation:[119]

> *"For many years we have made clear to departments that it is not acceptable to present legislation for scrutiny without all the explanatory material. [...] Equally, we have consistently made clear our view that all key definitions and criteria on which decisions that might affect a person's welfare or livelihood will be made, should be included in legislation and not put in guidance that is not subject to Parliamentary scrutiny or approval. DHSC has laid this instrument with neither".*[120]

Unusually, in its concluding remarks, the Committee recommended that the Parliamentary debate should be postponed until the necessary supporting evidence and the missing impact assessment was made available.[121]

The Committee also demanded that a Minister appear to give oral evidence. Nadhim Zahawi, the Vaccines Minister, and two senior DHSC officials appeared before the Committee on 13 July – the same day that the House of Commons debate and vote took place. In his opening remarks the Chair, Lord Hodgson of Astley, wryly set the scene: *"... the committee recognises the extraordinary and very special pressures which the pandemic has put on the Government, the importance of keeping our fellow citizens safe, and how difficult it is to strike the right balance. Equally, Minister, you will be aware of the phrase, 'The road to hell is paved with good intentions'".*[122]

A week later the Committee published a second report reflecting on that oral evidence.[123] It appears the Committee had not felt convinced about the quality of the evidence given by the Minister and senior officials:

> *"We asked why legislation was necessary at all. Given the extensive NHS vaccination programme, which has been prioritising care workers, we would have expected to see some sort of analysis of the reasons why SAGE's recommended levels of first dose vaccination for 90% of residents and 80% of staff had not yet been achieved. [...] It became evident that the DHSC are trying to target this legislation on particular groups of people, but DHSC had not explained this or provided a sufficient explanation of who those people are".*[124]

In yet another example of a Minister talking up the viral threat to justify a policy decision, Zahawi had told the Committee that Covid was *"the most contagious respiratory aerosol transmitted virus that mankind has experienced"*. The Committee seemed unmoved by his dramatics, quoting back to him evidence that it had received from one of the largest commercial groups operating in the care home sector which had reported that just 2 of the 955 deaths registered in its care home over the previous 18 weeks (a rate of 0.2%) had been specifically attributable to Covid.[125]

Though the Committee lacked powers to force the Government to produce satisfactory formal evidence in support of the legislation, to produce the promised impact assessment, or to delay the passage of the measure through Parliament, in a final withering assessment of the Government's conduct the Committee concluded that *"It is a long-established principle that, to enable Parliamentary scrutiny, all the explanatory material to support the policy set out in an instrument should be laid before Parliament at the same time as the instrument itself. DHSC has failed to do this, leaving us unsighted about several aspects of the policy intention and its implementation. We regard this as an example of particularly poor practice"*.[126]

Parliament affronted

On 13 July 2021, the House of Commons approved the adoption of the draft mandate legislation into law following a debate that had been capped at just 90 minutes. The measure passed without the support of the Labour and the Liberal Democrats parties, and in the face of 33 Conservative MPs who rebelled against the Government.

The debate bears reading in full, as evidence of the fury among so many experienced Parliamentarians.[127] The rate of interventions during the Minister's opening statement alone betrays the strength of feeling. The Minister presenting the measure, Helen Whateley, was persistently pressed on the absence of an impact assessment but could offer no answer, save to say that it was *"being worked on"*.[128] On a number of occasions during the debate the Minister was accused, implicitly and explicitly, of having provided misleading information to the House.[129]

One of the first to speak was the veteran parliamentarian, Sir Christopher Chope MP, whose scathing assessment speaks for itself:

"I must say that this was probably the most depressing performance from a Minister that I have listened to in this House. She showed a cavalier disregard for the conventions and courtesies of this House, and, as she has admitted to, she completely breached

> the rules under the Government's better regulation framework [by failing to produce an impact assessment], which is designed to inform decision making for regulations that affect businesses and individuals in this country. When criticised, the Minister's response is best described as dumb insolence, and that is just not good enough.[...]
>
> The Minister has not explained what has happened to [the impact assessment], whether it ever existed, and whether it contained information that she found embarrassing and has therefore been suppressed".[130]

A chorus of condemnation not only of the substantive proposal for a mandate but also of the Government's failure to produce an impact assessment for the policy followed from MPs of all parties around the chamber:

> **Dr Rosena Allin-Khan MP (Labour), a practising medic:** "Forcing carers to choose between losing their job and taking a vaccine that they are afraid of is inhumane. [...] We have a moral imperative not to force people to take a vaccine that they are afraid of, so I urge the Government to listen to our care workforce. Surely they deserve at least that after the last year".[131]
>
> **Mark Harper MP (Conservative):** "The proposals will have a very significant impact on hundreds of thousands of people and many thousands of businesses ... and it is frankly offensive that it is being debated in a 90-minute statutory instrument debate in the House. The second point is that if the information is available, even if it is imperfect ... it is the Minister's duty, if she has that information ... to put what she has in front of the House. She should sign it off ... and allow us to see it before we are asked to vote on the regulations. I am afraid it is an abuse of the House to ask us to vote without that information".[132]

Munira Wilson MP (Liberal Democrats): *"Coercion is not an effective way to overcome hesitancy. Compulsory vaccination is a blunt tool for a complex issue…"*.[133]

William Wragg MP (Conservative), Chair of the Public Administration and Constitutional Affairs Committee in Parliament: *"We could perhaps have a painting next to me of Munch's 'The Scream' to get a sense of how I feel about the conduct of Government business in this House. The Government are treating this House with utter contempt: 90 minutes on a statutory instrument to fundamentally change the balance of human rights in this country is nothing short of a disgrace. It is a disgrace, too, that no impact assessment exists. [...] I believe that 1898 was the last time vaccination was mandated in this country, and following that mandate, the rates of vaccination fell. That should tell us all we need to know. We will give succour to lunatics and crackpots who advance ridiculous theories about vaccination if we mandate vaccination. [...] This instrument is an abomination. It should be withdrawn, and <u>the Government should stop treating this House with contempt</u>"*, (emphasis added).[134]

The Regulatory Policy Committee is an independent regulatory scrutiny body the purpose of which is to assess the quality of evidence and analysis included in an impact assessment and used to inform government legislative and regulatory proposals. On the day of the Commons debate it published this short statement which we suggest was as constitutionally significant as it was ostensibly bland; significant because it records the exceptional contempt shown by Ministers when they denied Parliament the information it wanted and needed to be able to make an informed decision on this highly contentious policy:

"The [care home mandate regulations] were debated in the House of Commons today, 13th July 2021. The Department

of Health and Social Care (DHSC) has not yet submitted an appropriate impact assessment (IA) to the RPC for us to assess and provide an opinion on. As a qualifying regulatory provision, an IA should have been produced by the Department, submitted to the RPC for independent scrutiny, seen by ministers and presented to Parliament. We remain open to the DHSC submitting an appropriate IA for RPC scrutiny to allow us to provide an opinion on whether it is fit for purpose or not fit for purpose".[135]

This was not only contemptuous, but a deeply undemocratic way for an elected Government to behave. One week later, the House of Lords debated a 'motion to regret' on the care home mandate legislation.[136] This is a mechanism for the second chamber of Parliament officially to record its dissent to the passage of legislation which it does not have powers to halt or modify.

The mandate comes into effect

The House of Lords debated the legislation on 22 July 2021, after which the measure was voted through but only after the inclusion of a note in the documentation recording the notable absence of an impact assessment. The measure was signed into law that day by Helen Whateley, the DHSC Minister who had presented the draft in the Commons.[137]

The mandate did not become operational, however, until 11 November 2021; from that date anyone unvaccinated was barred from entering a care home, unless they could satisfy limited exemptions.[138]

An impact statement providing a preliminary analysis of the implications of the mandate is recorded as having been provided to Parliament just a few days before the House of Lords debate.

The official Impact Assessment which accompanies the legislation is dated 20 July 2021, but was not in fact signed off by a Minister until 8 November 2021, three days before the mandate eventually came into force.[139]

When it eventually appeared, the official Impact Assessment recognised that the mandate policy was likely *"to have a significant impact on staffing in the short- to medium-term"* [140] and estimated the cost to social care providers of recruiting replacement workers as £94m on a centralised 'best' estimate. It acknowledged *"a high degree of uncertainty on the reactive response of the affected workforce to the introduction of the policy"*.[141]

Although it was unable to quantify the benefits of imposing a mandate, the Impact Assessment repeated the Government's assertion that intervention was necessary to sustain *"high levels of staff vaccination now and in the future"* so as to *"minimise risk of outbreaks"*.[142] Less fearful care home residents and staff was cited as an additional 'non-monetised' benefit, notwithstanding this appeared to be at odds with the responses to the public consultation from members of those groups.

Even before the mandate took effect, the care home sector was suffering staff shortages, with the top two causes attributed to stress and low pay. In a survey conducted in late October 2021 by Unison, one of the two largest unions in the UK, representing care home workers, the vaccination requirement was identified as a material aggravating factor, with 14% of those care workers who were thinking of leaving the sector giving it as their reason.[143] Meanwhile the media were by then reporting that the NHS was facing a beds crisis as care homes closed their doors to new patients, and that care workers were leaving in droves to work in the hospitality and tourism sectors.[144]

Another short-lived policy

On 31 January 2022 the Government announced plans to revoke the mandate following a brief consultation.[145] In its subsequent press statement conceding its reversal of the policy, the Government confirmed that more than 90,000 responses had been received during the one week consultation period – an enormous volume of responses – and admitted that *"90% of responses supported the removal of the legal requirement for health and social care staff to be double jabbed"*, while continuing to insist that *"the clinical evidence [had] weighed heavily in favour of introducing the requirement in order to protect patients and the people who receive care and support"*.[146] On 15 March 2022, the care homes vaccination requirement was revoked.

Subsequently, a June 2023 study by the University of Nottingham concluded that between 14,000 and 18,000 unvaccinated staff left their jobs in the care home sector in England as a result of the mandate policy.[147] Contrary to the Government's assertions that the mandate would save lives and hospitalisations, the study found *"no evidence that the mandate saved any lives at all"*.[148]

Two controversial policies impacting thousands of people

We have started our tour of pandemic failures with the examples of Covid passes and the care home vaccination requirement because they exemplify how Ministers came to treat parliamentarians, and thus also the public, with condescension and contempt.

By effectively forcing vaccination onto those care home workers who needed to keep their jobs, while stripping others of their employment rights, the care home mandate impacted directly and in some cases catastrophically not only on the provision of care to the elderly, but most seriously on the livelihoods and right to bodily autonomy of care workers. Covid passes in a sense went a step further, by combining that authoritarian incursion into rights of bodily autonomy with the notion of a 'papers please' society. The signing of vaccine passport supply contracts with rolling terms inspired no confidence that this was to be only a temporary interference.[149]

By pushing through these two controversial measures Ministers threatened to rebase our understanding of cornerstone human and civil rights.

On any objective standard, these were consequential decisions. Yet, as we have sought to document, Parliamentary and press records of these two episodes evidence numerous examples of Ministers obscuring critical information, exaggerating threats and risks and downplaying the significance of the interventions.

"We don't want to inhibit spontaneity, we just want to work with those who organise venues and activities which are so important to our life to make sure they are as safe as possible",[150] Michael Gove had said in May 2022, evidencing a paternalistic public health approach which, by claiming that the downside of these measures lay simply in a threat to spontaneity, significantly understated their true implications. As Baroness Shami Chakrabarti, former director of advocacy group Liberty, had said, *"This is the biggest shift in civil liberties in the history of the United Kingdom. Why is it OK for this to happen by stealth?"* [151]

After a general lack of clarity and contradictory messages given in relation to the Covid pass scheme, it appeared Ministers remained less than forthright in revealing their intentions for the care home mandate: again it was presented as only an emergency, temporary measure, but the House of Lords Secondary Legislation Scrutiny Committee had flagged in July 2021 that the Government's consultation on the measure had *"made it clear that this legislation is not just intended as a pandemic measure but is both permanent, and only a first step",* (emphasis added).[152]

As well as eroding public trust, such contradictory and confused messaging appears to have had a poisonous impact on the relationship between the Government and Parliament. This is summarised by an exchange in September 2021 when Nadhim Zahawi, as Vaccines Minister, responded to an urgent question in the House:

> "I will begin by saying to the House that no one in this Government, and certainly not this Prime Minister—it is not in his DNA—wants to curtail people's freedoms or require people to show a piece of paper before they enter a nightclub ... The reason we are moving forward on this is that we have looked at what has happened in other countries, where nightclubs were opening and then shutting again, and opening and then shutting again, and we want to avoid that disruption and maintain sectors that can add to people's enjoyment of life and dance ... We want them to be able to do that sustainably".[153]

In a response met with universal outrage, we give the last word to William Wragg MP, Chair of the PACAC:

> "What a load of rubbish. I do not believe that my hon. Friend believes a word he just uttered, because I remember him stating very persuasively my position, which we shared at the time, that this measure would be discriminatory. Yet he is sent to the Dispatch Box to defend the indefensible. ….. to go down this route, which is overtly discriminatory, will be utterly damaging to the fabric of society".

In relation to both Covid passes and the care homes mandate, that the Government's behaviour undercut the ability of Parliament to perform its constitutional role requires no further explanation. Yet despite the evident fury of parliamentarians of all parties, ultimately no Minister was held accountable by Parliament for any element of this subversion of the democratic process.

ETHICALLY CONTENTIOUS AND PROCEDURALLY UNORTHODOX: THE COVID VACCINE PROGRAMME FOR CHILDREN

In the beginning…

In October 2020, as it became clear that one or more vaccines were likely to become available for use in the UK, Kate Bingham, the head of the UK Vaccine Taskforce, made an unambiguous statement: *"There's going to be no vaccination of people under 18. It's an adult-only vaccine, for people over 50"*,[154] a sentiment reiterated by Matt Hancock, the Health Secretary, when he gave a statement to Parliament in November 2020: *"this is an adult vaccine, for the adult population"*.[155]

That seemed to make good sense, and other medical experts agreed, for even in that early stage of the pandemic, the available evidence showed that the vast majority of children were at negligible risk of suffering serious harm from the virus; this has been born out in the longer term.

In ethical terms, for a vaccine to be rolled out to a population (or a section of the population) not at significant risk from Covid, it would need to be shown to be very safe, a point acknowledged by the CMO Chris Whitty when he had said in a WhatsApp message directed to Matt Hancock and Dominic Cummings, the Prime Minister's most senior adviser, in February 2020, *"the rate limiting steps [for vaccine development] are late clinical trials for safety* and efficacy, and then manufacturing. For a disease with a low (for the sake of argument 1%) mortality a vaccine has to be very safe so the safety studies can't be shortcut. So important for the long run".[156]

…by the end

Less than a year later, with no fundamental change to either the severity of the virus or the susceptibility of children, and the vaccines in use in the UK having been fast-tracked through to temporary authorisations, the Pfizer vaccine was not only being offered to children aged 12 to 15, but persistently pressured onto them. By February 2022, the same vaccine was being offered to 5 to 11 year olds, a cohort at such low risk from Covid that by the JCVI's own calculation under some scenarios four million doses would need to be given to two million children to avert a single intensive care unit admission.[157]

While it is understandable that government policies and positions might change as the pandemic unfolded, one must question how such a stark reversal of position took place within a relatively short period of time when the clinical risk posed by the virus to children appeared not to have changed, and indeed to this date has not materially altered.

We cannot know all of the discussions and decisions that took place within the Government during that period, but we can observe the evolution of attitudes and policies based on public statements and transcripts of hearings and debates.

The middle

By as early as February 2021, having started at the baseline that only older adults would ever need to be immunised against the virus, some members of the Government's scientific advisory group, SAGE, had started to call for children to be vaccinated *"as fast as we can"*, on the basis that this would keep children in school. The Prime Minister was asking his aides *"why can't we vaccinate children? teenagers? is that the plan? we used to have a flu jab at school.. bloody useless it was too"*.[158] The Health Secretary echoed those calls, suggesting that *"...the value, the importance of vaccinating children is to try to stop the spread of the disease and obviously that's something - the impact of the vaccine on stopping transmission is something - that we have early evidence of"*.[159]

As the narrative of vaccinating children to reduce transmission and educational disruption took hold, though, other respected figures raised concerns about the possibility of children being vaccinated. In May of that year Professor Anthony Harden, the Deputy Chair of the JCVI, in an interview with the BBC raised concerns about the ethical aspects of vaccinating children against a virus which posed them only a negligible risk of harm:

> *"From an ethical, scientific or any other perspective, we cannot start immunising children for the indirect protection of adults, which is what we would be doing, because we know it is a much more benign illness in children, until we are absolutely sure that it is safe and that it reduces transmission"*.[160]

Professor Andrew Pollard, then Chair of the JCVI and also a director of the Oxford University group which would go on to develop the AstraZeneca Covid vaccine, speaking before an All-Party Parliamentary Group hearing also in May 2021, expressed his concerns that children had *"near-to-zero risk"* of severe disease or death from coronavirus, yet many older people in other countries would not have access to vaccines. Vaccinating children would be *"morally wrong"*, he said, while global vaccine inequity is *"plain to see"*.[161]

At around the same time, however, Matt Hancock, continued his advocacy for children to be vaccinated, principally on the basis that this would help reduce transmission of the virus albeit he believed that it could also mitigate the widespread disruption to schooling that children were suffering: *"The number one epidemiological reason to vaccinate children is to reduce the risk of transmission to others"*.[162] The largest union for secondary school heads signalled its support for the use of peer pressure to increase vaccination rates among children, despite no safety approval having been given: *"The peer pressure of seeing that your friends are lining up to do it is likely to make the overall numbers taking up the vaccine higher"*.[163]

The Health Secretary also announced at that time that the UK had just acquired sufficient vaccine doses from Pfizer to be able to immunise all children aged 12 and over.[164] That significant purchase order predated the official regulatory approval of the Pfizer vaccine for use with children in the UK by more than two weeks, and came four months before an exceptionally unorthodox decision of Chief Medical Officers in the UK's four nations to offer the vaccine to children in the 12 to 15 years age group.

The MHRA then granted an authorisation for the Pfizer vaccine to be used with 12 to 15 year olds on 4 June 2021, stating that the benefits of vaccination outweighed the risks for those children. Matt Hancock immediately called for the vaccine to be deployed to those children as soon as August, notwithstanding that the JCVI had yet to make a recommendation for that age group.[165]

Presumably to the disappointment of many in Government, when the JCVI met on 1 July 2021,[166] it declined to advise that children aged 12 and over should be offered vaccination. On 19 July that advice was made public with an explanation that from a clinical perspective the benefits did not outweigh the risks: *"The health benefits in this population are small. And the benefits to the wider population are highly uncertain. At this time, JCVI is of the view that the health benefits of universal vaccination in children and young people below the age of 18 years do not outweigh the potential risks".*[167] This was an unambiguous statement consistent with established principles of medical ethics.

The minutes of a subsequent JCVI meeting, which took place on 22 July 2021, noted that the committee had previously given its advice declining to recommend the vaccination of children and young people on 2 July *"but there had been a relatively long delay in the statement being accepted and announced publicly by DHSC"*; and that the committee had now been asked by the CMO to accelerate a second planned review of that advice for children and young people, which appears then to have taken place soon after that 22 July meeting.[168]

To inform that second review, the committee had received a safety data presentation from Pfizer during the meeting, and in particular *"The Committee heard an update from Pfizer on myocarditis. Those data were unpublished and commercially sensitive and are not recorded in the Minutes"*. JCVI members apparently also asked *"if there was an update on the serious adverse events that were included in the published study of COVID-19 vaccination in adolescents. Pfizer did not have the data to hand but agreed to respond via email"*.[169]

The same minutes for that 22 July meeting go on to say that the committee considered that any potential harms from vaccination could impact negatively on the vaccination programme and could also reduce confidence in other vaccine programmes,[170] including the important meningococcal and HPV programmes for the same group:

> *"Members commented that there would need to be clear benefit to offer vaccination to this cohort. It was raised that young people, while capable of independent decisions, could be easily influenced, therefore the committee needed to be clear that their safety was a priority in the decision process. Members raised that it would*

not be ethical to vaccinate young people in order to protect other people who had the option to get vaccinated themselves".

The latter comment – on ethics – appears significant in light of Matt Hancock's earlier comment that *"The number one epidemiological reason to vaccinate children is to reduce the risk of transmission to others"*.[171]

Nevertheless, having met to discuss the matter a third time exactly one week later (29 July 2020),[172] with political and media pressure having intensified,[173] the JCVI agreed to give new advice to the Government in which it had reversed its earlier position in relation to 16 and 17 year olds, and clinically vulnerable children, though it held firm in declining to recommend that 12 to 15 year olds be offered a jab. That advice was then made public on 4 August.[174]

This was despite the committee having noted in its official statement (under the heading 'Benefits of vaccination') that:

- "[t]he incidence of severe outcomes from COVID-19 in children and young people is very low";

- "estimates of vaccine effectiveness [against 'long Covid'] are not available";

- "[t]he extent to which vaccination may mitigate the mental health and educational impacts of COVID-19 on children and young people is difficult to quantify";

- "[f]ollowing disruptions in routine immunisation programmes because of the pandemic, there is an urgent need to catch-up on non-COVID-19 school immunisations";

- "[the] health benefits from these various non-COVID-19 school-based immunisation programmes are well established" and "further deferral of the delivery of these immunisation programmes may be associated with permanent decreases in uptake of these vaccines in affected school age cohorts";

- "[d]elivery of a COVID-19 vaccine programme for children and young people is likely to be disruptive to education in the short-term, particularly if school premises are used for vaccination"; and

- "[c]onsiderable additional resource will be required to minimise the operational impacts of a COVID-19 vaccine programme on the wider health of children and young people".[175]

As parents reading that litany of caveats it is exceptionally difficult to understand what genuine benefit the JCVI could have comfortably relied on to justify the reversal of its position of just three weeks before. The only other benefit referenced in that official statement is that *"Modelling from the University of Warwick and from Public Health England indicate that vaccinating children and young people could have some impact on hospitalisations and deaths in older adults. The extent of such benefits is highly uncertain"*, (emphasis added).[176]

The minutes of the JCVI's meeting itself do not make for particularly comforting reading either. They record what appears to have been an extensive discussion of the risk of cardiac issues associated with mRNA vaccinations, including myocarditis and pericarditis, particularly for younger males, including a comment that *"the evidence presented at the meeting showed that the myocarditis risk was real and potentially serious"*.[177]

Particularly notable from an ethical perspective, the minutes also recorded that *"The Committee agreed that public communications would need to be clear especially in relation to the myocarditis and long-term effects risk compared to the benefits, to ensure that informed consent is gained"*,[178] yet the Government's official statement published on 4

August included only a brief mention of *"extremely rare"* reports of myocarditis and pericarditis having been reported, and nothing more explicit about long-term effects risk compared to benefits.

Immediately after the JCVI statement was published on 4 August, the Prime Minister in a Sky TV interview emphatically stated his confidence in the *"extremely expert"* JCVI's judgment: *"I would just urge all families ... to listen to the JCVI [...] they know what's safe and I think we should listen to them and take our lead from them"*.[179]

Perhaps inevitably, the JCVI's rapid change of position provoked alarm, particularly among parents, and questions about whether Ministers or senior Government officials had pressured the committee, something the committee explicitly denied. The Guardian newspaper then noted, perhaps with some scepticism, that the JCVI had *"moved to 'refresh' the membership of its Covid subcommittee in recent weeks, with one prominent critic of Covid jabs for children, Prof Robert Dingwall, leaving the body"*.[180]

On 3 September, despite a clear hunger within Government for the green light to be given for 12 to 15 years olds, and similar clamour from the Official Opposition, the JCVI declined to recommend a roll out for that age group:

> *"Overall, the committee is of the opinion that the benefits from vaccination are marginally greater than the potential known harms (tables 1 to 4) but acknowledges that there is considerable uncertainty regarding the magnitude of the potential harms. The margin of benefit, based primarily on a health perspective, is considered too small to support advice on a universal programme of vaccination of otherwise healthy 12 to 15-year-old children at this time. As longer-term data on potential adverse reactions accrue, greater certainty may allow for a reconsideration of the benefits and harms. Such data may not be available for several months"*.[181]

The JCVI noted, however, that while it had expressed a clinical opinion, it would be open to the Chief Medical Officers to take account of a broader range of factors before deciding whether to go ahead with a roll-out *despite* the JCVI's advice. This 'second bite' approach had never been taken before, and has not occurred since.

The day after the JCVI's decision, and more than a week before the CMOs eventually gave their advice, the BBC reported that *"the Government believes there is a strong case for giving jabs to healthy kids as it awaits advice from the CMOs"*.[182]

Nadhim Zahawi, at that time the Vaccines Minister, was quoted as saying that 12 to 15 year olds would be able to overrule their own parents on decisions about whether to receive the Covid vaccine, presumably in anticipation of the CMOs recommending that they be made available.[183]

Perhaps unsurprisingly given the background, on 13 September the CMOs agreed to override the JCVI's clinical advice by concluding that vaccinating young teenagers would have broader educational benefits:

> *"Overall however the view of the UK CMOs is that the additional likely benefits of reducing educational disruption, and the consequent reduction in public health harm from educational disruption, on balance provide sufficient extra advantage in addition to the marginal advantage at an individual level identified by the JCVI to recommend in favour of vaccinating this group. They therefore recommend on public health grounds that ministers extend the offer of universal vaccination with a first dose of Pfizer-BioNTech COVID-19 vaccine to all children and young people aged 12 to 15 not already covered by existing JCVI advice.*

> *[...]*
>
> *In recommending this to Ministers, UK CMOs recognise that the overwhelming benefits of vaccination for adults, where risk-benefit is very strongly in favour of vaccination for almost all groups, are not as clear-cut for children and young people aged 12 to 15. Children, young people and their parents will need to understand potential benefits, potential side effects and the balance between them".*[184]

The 'vaccinate to prevent school disruption' argument was not without controversy at the time.

David Paton, Professor of Industrial Economics at Nottingham University, writing in September 2021 noted that on the basis of the core modelling scenario used by the CMOs, vaccinating teenagers would save just 15 minutes of missed school per child (*"less than the time that it is going to take them to have the vaccine"*, as was pointed out by Caroline Johnson MP).[185]

Indeed, some six months later, the JCVI, in the context of the decision about 5 to 11 year olds, subsequently confirmed that *"the benefits of vaccinating [children] in preventing school absences were indeterminate"*,[186] apparently confirming the views of many others at the time that the protection of education was an artificially inflated benefit. A group of MPs writing to the Health Secretary in September 2021 reiterated that education disruption was a policy decision rather than an inevitable clinical consequence.[187]

The Minister for Prevention, Public Health and Primary Care, Jo Churchill MP, held an all-MP call on the day of that announcement to ensure MPs could be fully briefed and had the opportunity to ask questions[188] – there is no public record of how many MPs attended that call. The following day, the Vaccines Minister submitted a Written

Ministerial Statement to Parliament to explain that the Government would press ahead with vaccinating this age group and to apologise that it *"has not been possible to provide 14 sitting days' notice to consider these issues in advance of the planned vaccination of these groups in the UK"*.[189]

Some MPs were horrified by the unorthodoxy and made their views known, including Marcus Fysh MP, a Conservative Party backbencher:

"I just think it's an outrageous way in which the medical advice has been manipulated. It's actually the DfE that has wanted this and it's looking in the rear view mirror; it's treating us all like we're still in a pandemic where everyone is going to die if we don't do x y and z. We need to make choices now in respect of what's good for the individual. Individual children are not at risk of having a problem from this. They are not at risk of missing tons of education...That is absolutely not a good enough reason".[190]

Perspectives such as this echoed loudly among the thousands of parent and grandparent members of UsForThem at the time. A senior source in the UK vaccines programme was anonymously quoted as having despaired that *"[i]f the JCVI can't agree, how can a child truly make an informed decision? And why the unseemly rush to push this through? It's so scary and unethical"*.[191]

The following week, on 21 September, a debate about the vaccination of children brought by Miriam Cates, a backbench Conservative Party MP, took place in Westminster Hall in which she voiced concerns about the ethics of the CMO's advice:

"That decision is a marked departure from the principle of vaccinating people for their own medical benefit, because those wider issues—educational disruption and concerns around mental health—are the consequences of policy decisions and are

not scientific inevitabilities. Children in the UK have already missed more education than children in almost any other country in Europe, despite comparable death rates. Since January 2020, British children have lost on average 44% of school days to lockdown and isolation. That is not a consequence of Covid infections in children, but rather a result of policy decisions to close schools and isolate healthy children.

According to the Government's modelling, vaccinating children could save 41 days of schooling per 1,000 children between October and March. That equates to an average of just 15 minutes of education saved per child over this period—surely an insignificant amount, and negligible when we account for the time it takes to vaccinate and the subsequent days off school to recover from potential side effects. There is a much simpler way to stop harmful educational disruption, and that is to follow the advice of the Royal College of Paediatrics and Child Health and end the mass testing of asymptomatic children. This unevidenced and unethical policy is costing tens of millions of pounds a week—I would be grateful if the Minister could confirm the exact cost—and is continuing to disrupt education. Even the CMO acknowledges that a vaccination programme alone will not stop school closures".[192]

And Andrew Lewer MP remarked to the newly-appointed Vaccines and Public Health Minister, Maggie Throup MP:

"Throughout the pandemic we have continually been told of the importance of following the science. I warmly welcome my honourable friend [...] to her ministerial position, but will she explain why we are now disregarding the science and the experts who clearly said that it is not necessary nor advisable on the basis of the evidence we have for that cohort to receive a covid-19 vaccine?"

THE COVID VACCINE PROGRAMME FOR CHILDREN

On the following day the Education Select Committee, chaired by Robert Halfon MP, sought to quiz Professors Chris Whitty and Jonathan Van-Tam (Whitty's deputy Chief Medical Officer) and Professor Wei Shen Lim (then Chair of the JCVI Covid-19 sub-committee) on the implications of the CMOs' recommendation.[193]

During that hearing, Tom Hunt MP echoed Miriam Cates' ethical concerns with the CMOs' recommendation when he asked whether that recommendation had been *"solely about the welfare of 12 to 15 year olds in terms of mental health, education and also the threat of the virus, or did it to some extent take into account what is in the best interests of wider society and potentially those in other age groups?"*. Professor Whitty responded definitively, yet apparently in conflict with the JCVI's justification a month earlier for allowing 16 and 17 years olds to be vaccinated,[194] *"that the only evidence [we] would consider was things that directly or indirectly were beneficial or problematic to children aged 12 to 15"*.[195]

In response to a later question from Tom Hunt MP on the process that had led from MHRA granting conditional authorisation in June 2020 for the Pfizer vaccine to be used with teenagers to the CMOs recommending the vaccine be deployed for 12 to 15 year olds, Professor Whitty remarked as follows:

> *"MHRA is starting off with the question, 'Is it safer to have it than not to have it overall?' and if they had said no we would not have got to first base. They have to say yes first ... JCVI have the responsibility then to talk about deployment and ultimately, in this situation, the CMOs are kind of third umpire in this situation".*[196]

Professor Whitty's suggestion that the CMO's act as a third umpire – a tie-breaker in cases where the MHRA has approved a vaccine but the JCVI has declined to recommend its deployment – is curious. As far as we have been able to determine, the CMOs had never before played that role and have not since; and nowhere does it appear to have been documented that it would be an option for the Government to ask the CMOs to do so. At a meeting of the Science and Technology Select Committee in December of that year, Jeremy Hunt MP, then the chair of that committee and latterly the Chancellor of the Exchequer, straightforwardly described the CMOs' recommendation as *"a workaround".*[197]

One might reasonably question whether Professor Whitty's description of the CMOs intervention as akin to a 'third umpire' underplayed the significance of what had happened, or perhaps even whether the comment portrayed to the parliamentarians on the Education Committee a normality in what, in truth, had been a highly unusual – unprecedented even – process.

In any event, by then the Government was already pressing ahead to vaccinate those children as soon as possible. The roll-out for 12 to 15 year olds commenced on 20 September,[198] but already by October, in the face of weak uptake for the vaccine among teenagers, the Health Secretary Sajid Javid and the (by then) Education Secretary Nadhim Zahawi decided to write to the parents of teenagers to urge them to get their children vaccinated:

> *"We know that some of you will be concerned about the health risks to the young people you care for. We want to reassure you that the evidence shows that young people remain at very low risk of serious illness from COVID-19. However, we need to continue to reduce the spread of COVID-19. Young people who get ill will need to miss school or college, and may spread it to others. That is why we are encouraging you all to support your children to get vaccinated and to continue to test regularly. This will help to detect cases early, reduce spread, and keep students in education".*

Without confirming whether parental consent could be overruled by teenagers, that letter encouraged parents to give their consent for vaccinations to take place in school, and noted that *"[t]housands of young people across the country have already taken the opportunity to receive their vaccine. If your child is 12-15 years old, a consent form and information leaflet from the NHS will be sent home allowing you to provide consent for your child to receive their vaccination at school"*.

As 2021 drew to a close, and having crossed a Rubicon by overriding the JCVI's reticence to extend the vaccination program to children, attention turned to the 5 to 11 year olds.

In an interview arranged by the BBC at the end of November and broadcast on 2 December, Dr Albert Bourla, the Chair and Chief Executive of Pfizer, appeared to have been encouraged by the BBC's Health Editor to talk up the benefits of vaccinating children, yet neglected to make any mention, at all, of risks or the relativity of benefits. Dr Bourla commented emphatically about the merits of vaccinating children under 12 years of age, saying *"[So] there is no doubt in my mind that the benefits completely are in favour of doing it"*.

Despite the strength of Dr Bourla's superlative pitch for vaccinating the under-12s, the MHRA would not authorise the vaccine for use with children of that age until the very end of 2021. In a complaint brought by UsForThem, Dr Bourla's promotional comment to the BBC was subsequently held by the UK's Prescription Medicines Code of Practice Authority (PMCPA) — the regulator responsible for policing promotions of prescription medicines in the UK — to have been misleading and incapable of substantiation in relation to the safety of vaccinating that age group.[199]

On 22 December 2021, the MHRA approved the Pfizer jab on a conditional basis for use with children aged 5 to 11.[200] On 16

February 2022, in what was another distinctly unusual decision, while not expressly recommending the vaccine for mass roll-out to 5 to 11 year olds the JCVI advised that 'a non-urgent offer' be made to that age group,[201] and once again this was despite there being no clear clinical benefit for those children.

By the JCVI's own admission if the next wave of the virus was to be more severe, 1 million children would need to have been double-vaccinated to prevent 3 children from being admitted to an ICU; if the next wave was less severe (as turned out to be the case), 2 million children in this age group would need to be double-vaccinated in order to prevent just one child from being admitted to an ICU. The JCVI itself acknowledged that even as regards those figures, *"[t]he extent of these impacts is highly uncertain"*.[202] In any case, and perhaps not surprisingly, the 'non-urgent offer' was resoundingly rejected by the vast majority of parents in the UK.[203]

Procedure and governance bypassed

By the autumn of 2021 and over the months that followed, with the vaccination campaign for adults in full swing, what was already a procedurally unprecedented, irregular and controversial decision to extend the vaccination program to children was further ethically compromised.

When the CMOs exercised their newly-ordained discretion on 13 September 2021 effectively to override the conclusion of the UK's official vaccine experts, they had prescribed conditions with which the roll-out to children would need to comply, not least in order to remain compliant with cornerstone medical ethics.

In particular, the paramount necessity of informed consent was emphasised, including clear explanation of *"potential benefits, potential side effects and the balance between them"*; the voluntary nature of each family's decision for a child to be jabbed was also recorded by Professor Whitty: *"individual choice should be respected".*[204]

Yet once the CMOs' approval was given, the ethical significance of those conditions appears quickly to have faded.

Manipulation and the absence of voluntary and informed consent

As the roll-out started, on 20 September 2021, an NHS press release quote the Deputy Lead for the NHS Covid-19 Vaccination Programme, Dr Nikki Kananai, as saying *"The vaccine is safe and effective and I would urge families to work closely with their schools based vaccination team to get their loved ones vaccinated when they are invited to protect themselves and their families ahead of the winter period"*, and a teenager from Essex was quoted as saying *"I am proud to have had my vaccination [this morning] so that I can remain in school and continue in my education – the jab was quick, easy, and painless".*[205] No sign of clear explanations of potential benefits, potential side effects and the balance between them; and arguably an implication that remaining in school might be conditional on accepting a vaccination.

In December 2021, the Department for Education published an advertisement and accompanying tweet which said *"Vaccines give your children the best possible protection against the virus, and helps keep them in school"*, with no reference to natural immunity (most children were believed to have had the virus by that point), to risk or to possible side effects.[206] An NHS England video published in February 2022 which promoted the vaccine to children had to be withdrawn after it was branded as misleading by medical professionals for claiming that 1% of children with Covid were being hospitalised.[207]

Professor Whitty's statement on the need for consent to be voluntary and free from stigmatisation and pressure[208] immediately preceded a period during which, internationally, the ability to travel freely to popular holiday destinations including Spain and Malta became conditional upon vaccination of teenage children alongside adults;[209] and to encourage uptake the NHS and the Government had been promoting the use of ethically inappropriate incentives for young people to take the vaccine, such as pizza and cinema tickets.[210]

The possibility even of offering straightforward cash incentives was at one point proposed by the then Universities Minister,[211] and one NHS Trust went as far as to send letters addressed directly to young children at their home addresses enclosing promotional materials adorned with bees and flowers and rainbows which evangelised the benefits of vaccination, yet omitted commentary on risk, and included a packet of sunflower seeds to *"bring joy and sunshine into children's lives"*.[212]

If it were needed, concrete evidence that parents were not given sufficient information to understand the circumstances of the offer to children was revealed in an August 2023 survey carried out for UsForThem. This showed that the unconventional role of the CMOs in recommending the rollout to children, and the fact that the JCVI had declined to recommend vaccines for 12 to 15 year olds, was understood by less than a quarter of parents of under-18s. Only one third of those parents who had originally not been aware of that context now say that they would still have agreed to vaccinate their children if they had known at the time that the JCVI had not recommended vaccination for that age group.[213]

We do not suggest here that the failure of communication at the time was with the CMOs – who had published their advice in full[214] by way of a letter sent to, among others, Sajid Javid, the Health Secretary, stressing the importance of informed voluntary consent. Nevertheless, this contextual information of critical significance to an informed decision appears to have been lost or obscured in subsequent official communications, and this raises serious questions about the ability of parents and their children to have given informed consent to that vaccination.

Parental consent

On 26 August 2021, the Telegraph reported a plan for the NHS to vaccinate 12 year olds without requiring parental consent in the week that children returned to school for the new term,[215] relying instead on the concept of 'Gillick competence'. A blazing row followed in which Nadhim Zahawi, the Education Secretary, told Times Radio on 5 September that people in that age range could override their parents' wishes *"if they're deemed to be competent to make that decision, with all the information available"*.[216]

A few days later, though still before the CMOs had recommended the roll-out to 12 year olds, Sajid Javid the Health Secretary prolonged that row by explaining to Sky News that in the event of a disagreement between parent and child, the child's decision on vaccination *"will prevail"* provided that the child is *"competent enough"*.[217]

Then, in the autumn of 2021, with vaccine uptake among teenagers remaining stubbornly low, the Ministers further escalated the debate by toying with the idea of sending letters directly to that age group to ask them to get vaccinated.[218]

All quiet on the front line

For much of the uncomfortable year documented above, UsForThem took a front line role in campaigning on this issue: questioning the clinical need and ethical basis of the intervention for healthy children; challenging manifestly unsubstantiated and in some cases misleading public statements made by those in positions of authority (including, as we have seen, the CEO of Pfizer); and trying, as best we could, to raise awareness of our concerns with Parliamentarians and press. The episode left us profoundly troubled.

For much of that period there was limited appetite among most of the media – print and broadcast – to carry any commentary which questioned the necessity, let alone the ethics, of the Government's push to vaccinate children. Virtually none of the challenges from Parliament to the Government and its medical advisers seemed to be reported.

As far as we can tell, the Westminster Hall debate described above was not reported by national newspapers or broadcast media, and even today the comments made by parliamentarians in that debate can only be found by reviewing the official Hansard debate records.[219]

The majority of parents, therefore, were not able to hear informed critical viewpoints from parliamentarians, including Miriam Cates MP:

> *"That decision is a marked departure from the principle of vaccinating people for their own medical benefit, because those wider issues—educational disruption and concerns around mental health—are the consequences of policy decisions and are not scientific inevitabilities [...] According to the Government's modelling, vaccinating children could save 41 days of schooling per 1,000 children between October and March. That equates to an average of just 15 minutes of education saved per child over this period—surely an insignificant amount, and negligible when we account for the time it takes to vaccinate and the subsequent days off school to recover from potential side effects".*

And Karl McCartney MP, who had noted in that same debate:

"There is no medium or long-term study data. I admire Chris Whitty and his colleagues for many things that they have done in the past 18 months. However, citing educational disruption, or the fear of more of it, as a justification for child vaccination against JCVI advice seems a little desperate, as far as I am concerned".

Likewise, the limited reporting of the Education Select Committee hearing of September 2021 – a key hearing in relation to a topic impacting millions of children and known to be controversial – focussed almost exclusively on comments made by Professor Whitty that *"nearly all children will get Covid if they don't get vaccinated"*.[220] Again, it seems that there was no mainstream reporting of any of the concerns raised by the members of the Select Committee.

Trust was shattered

We saw first hand in real time through UsForThem's network of parents, grandparents and carers of children, how the unethical rush to vaccinate children, the unorthodox process to steamroll it through, and the manipulative cajoling deployed to roll it out, was eroding trust in our public health system, official Government advice and even the traditional childhood vaccination programme.

This seemed obvious to us from our viewpoint as parents and campaigners, but to verify that what we were seeing was representative of broader public sentiment we needed to test it independently; so we commissioned two surveys. Those surveys – carried out in June and August 2023 – confirmed much of what we had expected.

Prior to the pandemic, the UK had high rates of uptake for childhood vaccination programmes; 84% of parents of children under 18 reported that prior to the pandemic they would have given their children all traditional childhood vaccinations available from the

NHS. Yet **only 60%** now said that they would be likely to give their child a vaccine recommended by the Government in the future.[221]

The surveys also confirmed that **less than half of parents (48%)** had been aware that the Covid vaccine had only been granted a provisional MHRA authorisation at the point that it was offered to children in December 2021; **45% said they were unaware.** Less than 1 in 4 parents knew that the JVCI had declined to recommend the vaccine roll-out for 12 to 15 year olds. **60% of parents of children under 18 were unaware** that the JCVI had declined to recommend the roll-out of the vaccine for 12-15 year olds. **Just 1 in 3 parents** of children under 18 said they would still have wanted to get their children vaccinated had they understood this critical context at the time.[222]

This data goes some way to explaining the origins of the public trust deficit that now affects our public health system.

* * *

The Spring and Summer of 2021 was a lonely, anxious period of campaigning for UsForThem. To an extent we were prepared for the 'anti-vax' smears which had tarred anyone attempting to question the Covid vaccination roll-out. Nevertheless the full extent and persistence of those smears was unexpected. The fact that we were advocating for children seemingly was irrelevant. For a time, the labelling certainly achieved its presumed aim – hampering our ability to cut through and stunting our reputation among public sector contacts by associating us with what one political contact described as 'the mad anti-vaxxers'.

It is only later that we have come to understand more about the circumstances in which this had taken place and the extent to which our campaigning might have been held back without our knowledge.

SUPPRESSION AND CENSORSHIP

By the time we formed UsForThem in May 2020 opinions about school closures had already coalesced around a consensus which framed children as vectors for transmission and schools consequently as dangerous places, with the virtuous position cast as accepting, if not supporting, school closures.

UsForThem's early campaigns to get schools reopened set us firmly against that already-cemented mainstream opinion, and the smear campaigns began almost immediately. Across social media those who objected to UsForThem's campaigning sought to intimidate us and relentlessly maligned us as dangerous idiots and 'granny killers', supporters of eugenics or murderers who wanted to kill disabled children.

As the profile of our campaigning grew it drove a noticeable increase in the volume and intensity of the trolling we attracted, and triggered attempts to smear our group and our founders as, variously, a Brexiteer-backed group, a Conservative Party-backed group, (strangely, given our confrontational approach to the Government and its policies) a Government-backed group, a Covid-denial organisation, purveyors of fake news, and with alleged personal connections to prominent Ministers, the former Prime Ministers Boris Johnson and David Cameron, Donald Trump and the Koch Brothers. For the record, none were or are true.

At this point we had no reason to think we were suffering from anything more sinister than the ire of some fanatical online supporters of the main teaching unions and the pro-lockdown zero-Covid wing of the medical community. Though the trolling and smearing at times surprised us in its intensity and its outlandish unsubstantiable claims, it appeared at least to have been organic and was out in the open – we could see it, everyone could see it if they wished.

More insidious, however, was the point in Spring 2021 when, having achieved prominence as a campaign group we started to feel that we were the subject of attacks that we could not see, and thus could not fully understand; and which seemed to be more sophisticated or coordinated. This included:

- unexpected outages and denial of service attacks on our campaign website;

- emails seeming to go missing, or not reaching their destinations;

- new volunteers ostensibly offering their support while seeking access to our core team – what we believed at the time to be attempts at infiltration, though we were unsure by whom.

At the same time, we had official warnings appearing on some of our social media channels that our content was inconsistent with the platform's terms of use and threatening that our posts would be demoted or our account closed outright if we did not remove the flagged content. This was surprising, not least because the flagged content included posts that merely shared articles or papers which had already been referenced by mainstream media sources on topics such as health risks associated with masks. As a campaign group that had come together over social media, it always felt as if there was a sword of Damocles hanging over us: a 'wrong' post or comment could trigger the dreaded *"Admin Violation"* which risked bringing the whole community to an end.

Content touching on vaccination was quite obviously a lightning-rod topic. To avoid a permanent shutdown we had to prohibit any discussion of Covid vaccines for children on our social channels, just as it was becoming apparent that children might – despite at first having been officially off limits for the vaccines – be included in the roll-out. As was doubtless equally true among the general population, many of our members wanted to discuss their concerns, but we could not host discussions on the topic.

As we have just discussed this also coincided with a notable increase of trolling across social media platfoms, denouncing UsForThem as an anti-vax group, despite the founders having adopted a policy decision explicitly not to campaign about the roll-out of the vaccine to children at that point. (This reached a pinnacle when UsForThem later applied for core participant status in the official Covid Inquiry.)

UsForThem first began to question in public the merits and the ethical basis for a roll-out to kids when one of the founders was commissioned to write two articles on proposals for extending the vaccine programme to children.[223] Thereafter, and notwithstanding that our position – that healthy children have never needed the vaccine – was previously recognised by the Health Secretary, by the Government's Vaccines Tsar and by the JCVI, the deplatforming and suppression began.

Print and broadcast outlets which had previously sought regular articles and commentary from us largely stopped calling or returning our messages, and our social media account seemed to be being inexplicably stunted, with follower numbers for both the main campaign accounts and those of our founders flatlining or decreasing despite posts routinely achieving tens of thousands of views and hundreds of repostings. Many other campaigners who questioned pandemic policies have since shared similar experiences with us.

That period of apparent suppression coincided with a period of serious ethical jeopardy for children, reflected in a series of challenging decisions for the Government which should have been subjected to meaningful debate and scrutiny. It felt to us that our voice had been muted at the moment that challenge was most needed.

Little did we know….

Countering fake news

> *"His Majesty's Government (HMG) defines disinformation as the deliberate creation and dissemination of false and/or manipulated information that is intended to deceive and mislead audiences, either for the purposes of causing harm, or for political, personal or financial gain. Misinformation refers to inadvertently spreading false information".*[224]

Already as the pandemic was emerging in February 2020 the Government was alert to the risk that an information pandemic, or infodemic, could undermine global efforts to assess and mitigate the viral pandemic, and understandably it consequently marshalled resources that would enable it to monitor and, hopefully, manage disinformation and misinformation.

Responding to a question on the UK's efforts to battle fake news about Covid, Matt Hancock had told Parliament in February 2020: *"… I have been working on that in the past 24 hours, to ensure that tech companies, social media companies, Google and others promote the right answers to questions about coronavirus. Most of the social media companies—we have* been in contact with them—have behaved in an exemplary fashion, ensuring that information from, for example, the NHS gets promoted".[225]

Then at the beginning of March 2020 the Department for Culture, Media and Sports *"stood up"* a Counter-Disinformation Cell team *"in response to the acute disinformation risks emerging from the Covid-19 pandemic"*.[226] The Cell subsequently became known as the Counter-Disinformation Unit, or CDU.[227]

In correspondence a fortnight later between the Minister responsible for the CDU, Culture Secretary Oliver Dowden MP, and the Chair of the Parliamentary Culture, Media and Sports Select Committee, Julian Knight MP, the Minister reassured that committee: *"The Government takes this issue [false information] extremely seriously, and shares your concerns about the undermining of life-saving factual information at a time of heightened risk to public health. As the Minister responsible for leading the Government's counter-disinformation policy, I am ensuring that the Government is taking all necessary steps to identify and respond to false information relating to COVID-19".*[228]

It appears the Government's aim at this early stage of the pandemic was that the public regard the Government, through its press conferences and website, as the definitive source of pandemic information, with mainstream print and broadcast news outlets – working closely with government – buttressing that official messaging. Appearing before the Culture, Media and Sports Select Committee on 22 April 2020, the Culture Minister appeared to suggest that the CDU was by that stage involved in keeping those trusted news outlets on message:

> *"The starting point with all of this is that people should be going to trusted sources of news in the first place. One of the positive things we have seen during this crisis is more people going to gov.uk, clearly a trusted source, more people going to traditional*

broadcasters ... and more people going to newspapers. ... Of course, we already have ongoing relationships, but the point of stepping up the counter-disinformation unit is a call we took as a Government ... in respect of this unprecedented public health crisis and the risk of misinformation ...".[229]

Social media platforms were asked to collaborate

Dowden also told that Select Committee hearing that the Cabinet Office was at that time leading on the rebuttal of false narratives, but at the same time acknowledged that his own department – in the form of the CDU – was *"principally working with the social media companies both to understand the nature of what is going on and, in the process of that, <u>to occasionally identify false narratives and things that the social media companies will take action to take down</u>"*, (emphasis added).[230]

That the CDU existed and was monitoring social media throughout the pandemic thus was never a secret, though its work was not widely publicised. Nor was it a secret that the CDU was engaging with social media platforms and flagging content for removal. In December 2020, the House of Commons Sub-committee on Online Harms and Disinformation held a hearing to *"focus on 'anti-vax' content carried on social media platforms with Google, Facebook and Twitter invited to attend".*[231] Appearing at that hearing alongside representatives of the social media platforms was Sarah Connolly, Director of Security and Online Harms at DCMS and the head of the CDU, a senior official who had worked previously on counter-terrorism policy at the Home Office.

Connolly talked about the role and activities of the CDU at that time. As well as coordinating across government departments an analysis of dis and misinformation narratives, she explained, *"[the] other big function [the CDU] has is talking to social media platforms and passing information over. It gets information back from them, and*

SUPPRESSION AND CENSORSHIP

encourages that swift takedown... The [CDU] has daily interactions with almost all the platforms. ... For some of them, we have what is called trusted flagger status. If somebody from the [CDU] says, 'We are worried about this,' that goes immediately to the top of the pile. Whoever it is in whatever company then acts on it. It is the same system they have across Government for things like terrorist content".[232]

In other words, the CDU liaised on a daily basis with social media platforms and enjoyed elevated access that would enable it to flag comments or articles for 'action'.[233] Though not stated explicitly, the implication is that action here means removing or suppressing. According to a more recent article published in *The Telegraph*, *"The Government confirmed [...] that social media firms had taken action on more than 90 per cent of the posts referred to them by the CDU during the pandemic, often by deleting them or using algorithms to ensure they were not seen as widely".*[234]

This apparent admission that algorithms were used to suppress content flagged by the CDU clarified our own experience in the latter half of 2021. It also indicates that we were right to be worried about the implication of an *"Admin Violation"* being attached to our social media accounts: an interesting insight into the impact that these warning labels had was revealed in evidence given by Rebecca Stimson, UK Head of Public Policy of Facebook, to the DCMS Select Committee in December 2020. She stated: *"we see a 95% rate of people not clicking through to read content that has had a warning placed on it".*[235]

If this State-coordinated suppression was and remains lawful in the UK it can probably be attributed to the absence of codified free speech rights as embodied, for example, in the First Amendment rights of the US Constitution. Revelations of similar types of collusion having taken place with big tech firms in the US have led to lawsuits.[236] While officially it was not a secret that this activity was underway (and indeed, as we discuss later, was encouraged by

Parliamentarians), many in the UK were shocked by the scale and extent of the monitoring and censorship activity eventually exposed.

The CDU exposed

In early 2023 an investigation by Big Brother Watch[237] revealed that the Government, under the guise of combatting pandemic disinformation, had since 2020 used a number of secretive Whitehall units – including the CDU – to monitor the online activity of critics of the Government and its policies. The target of these units had included MPs, academics, journalists, campaigners and some members of the public.

Inspired by that investigation, we submitted data subject access requests to the Cabinet Office and other government departments. When we received responses to those requests it dawned on us what might have happened in the summer of 2021.

Those documents revealed that the CDU had flagged concerns about some of the public comments of Molly and Arabella, two of UsForThem's directors, starting in September 2020 when Molly wrote a comment piece in a national newspaper criticising the Department for Education's decision to allow schools to enforce differing levels of social restrictions on children as the new school year began.[238]

The commentary and content flagged by the CDU spanned, though, a broad range of pandemic topics. They were typically either opinion pieces, or comments quoted in mainstream news articles, and thus were plainly not in any sense masquerading as official or factual information. Really the only unifying factor was that all of the flagged content expressed positions which were contrary, or at least in contrast, to the official Government narrative. Examples included:

- *"It would be unforgivable to close schools"* (December 2020)

- *"Let children use playgrounds"* (February 2021)

- *"Healthy children don't need the Covid jab"* (May 2021)

- *"We should not be edging towards something that has not been sanctioned by the JCVI. It is building a climate of pressure"* (August 2021)

- *"Schools and councils have to follow the rules rather than making it up as they go along"* (December 2021)

- *"Parents are totally distraught that their children's schools have decided they will continue with masks in class with no end in sight"* (January 2022)

- *"It is indefensible that children's lives [are] still not back to normal when the rest of society is"* (February 2022)

- *"Once again universities are using Covid as an excuse and not putting the educational needs of their students first"* (May 2022)

Even as campaigners on the receiving end of the Government's efforts to curtail discussion of controversial lockdown policies[239] we recognise that there may have been a reasonable public health argument for early efforts to limit the spread of demonstrably false or intentionally harmful information.

At least in the very early days of the pandemic, Ministers seemed to recognise the benefit of listening to a range of viewpoints. On 16 March 2020 when the Health Secretary had first sought Parliament's support for initial restrictive measures, Jonathan Ashworth MP (Labour) articulated well the need to allow for the plurality of opinions that can exist within scientific fields: *"Throughout the outbreak, we have been as one in agreeing that all decisions must be based on science and evidence, but the Secretary of State, of course, will know and understand that different scientists can reach different conclusions, even when presented with the same data and evidence..."*.[240]

Hancock had replied: *"We welcome questioning of the approach, because we are constantly looking for the very best solution for this nation, and the very best way through this, in order to protect life"*.[241]

One might have taken from this comment that the raising of questions and challenges, and the expression of differences of opinion, at this point was not a concern for the Government – perhaps even the opposite of a concern.

Indeed the importance of allowing legitimate questions to surface, and of reasonable challenge and debate to occur, was recognised by the social media groups questioned by MPs in December 2020:

> *"Theo Bertram of TikTok: The real challenge is those people in the middle, who have real concerns. Probably about 50% of us, like me, would take the vaccine straight away, as soon as it is offered. There is probably a smaller group—about 9% to 15%—who do not want to take the vaccine whatever. Then there is that middle group. That middle group have real concerns and questions, and sometimes they post videos that have #antivaccine or something like that, and they do have reasonable concerns"*.[242]

The ability to voice doubts or express scepticism is not only an essential part of the scientific method, but a core element of a functioning democracy.

Another exchange in that same hearing exemplifies the difficulty of identifying commentary or questions definitively as disinformation:[243]

> "John Nicolson MP (SNP): Let me give you an example. Do you know who Olivia Madison is?
>
> Theo Bertram: No, I don't.
>
> John Nicolson: She has 606,000 followers on your platform. I looked her up last night just to see, because I suspected you would tell us you were taking down all these videos. She is very beautiful and what she does is utterly wicked. The first thing I came across that she had to say was, 'Vaccinations contain foetuses', and—I quote her—'I don't believe in injecting a baby with another baby'. She has 606,000 followers and her videos are all still up on your platform".

Nicolson continues, "The point I am making is that if you cannot sort out somebody with 606,000 followers, what chances are there that you are going to get rid of the smaller fry? This woman is just screaming lies as publicly as she possibly can in very professionally produced videos…I am a journalist by profession…If I was writing a story on this, the headline would be, 'TikTok's system not working: anti-vax fanatics everywhere'".

Even this seemingly straightforward instance of 'obvious' disinformation (or at the very least strong misinformation) illustrates a point about the potential dangers of treating anyone questioning the Covid vaccines as a fanatic or extremist. Just six weeks earlier, the Government's advisory group on moral and ethical issues (MEAG) had met to discuss the components used to manufacture vaccines. The summary of that meeting records as follows:

> "There was discussion around the origin of some vaccines being developed from fetal cell lines. Although there are no fetal cells in final vaccine composition, when developed in this way, there are still concerns amongst some members of the public and this can be a barrier to vaccine take up. Those concerns should be taken seriously".[244]

It should be trite to observe that scientific consensus can change over time so that today's misinformation becomes tomorrow's fact; or that one person's dis or misinformation is another's testing of scientific theory.

Regardless of the difficulties in distinguishing mis- and disinformation edge cases, however, it would be incredulous to suggest that opinion pieces and the recounting of real time real life perspectives from the parent and grandparent supporters of UsForThem could reasonably be categorised as *"disinformation narratives"* or *"attempts to artificially manipulate the information environment"*, which were the CDU's declared areas of focus. Consequently the inference we drew from the CDU's laundry list of Molly and Arabella's apparently harmful articles was that essentially any comment or opinion which ran contrary to official messaging could be flagged as misinformation (unintentionally harmful) if not disinformation (intentionally harmful) and acted on accordingly.

Would this have been what most MPs had pictured when, in March and April 2020, Ministers had talked about the need to counter false information? Would they have anticipated that distinguished epidemiologists such as Professor Mark Woolhouse would later tell the official Covid Inquiry that options other than full lockdown were ignored because SAGE *"got caught up in their eagerness to disapprove, not accept the proposal in the Great Barrington Declaration"* or that *"supporting lockdown became a test of virtue. …. It was very, very difficult to say that you didn't support lockdown"*.[245] We suspect probably not, but perhaps this was the unsurprising consequence of a community of suppression and censorship specialists evolving without the guardrails of either public or Parliamentary resistance.

SUPPRESSION AND CENSORSHIP

CDU acting beyond its publicly-disclosed purposes

The Government's fact sheet on the CDU, incidentally published only in June 2023 in response to press revelations that it had been spying on journalists and parliamentarians, reports that *"Its purpose is to understand disinformation narratives and attempts to artificially manipulate the information environment to ensure that the government understands the scope and reach of harmful mis and disinformation and can take appropriate action. Such action can include posting a response on social media rebutting the claim, awareness raising campaigns to promote the facts, and working with social media companies to encourage them to promote authoritative sources of information and consistently enforce their terms of service"*.[246]

Senior civil servant Susannah Storey further explained in a recent witness statement for the UK Covid Inquiry: *"The primary purpose of the CDU is not to monitor for harmful content to flag to social media platforms, but to understand the disinformation landscape which has the potential to impact UK audiences …. [The Government] does not seek to, nor does it have the legal power to compel social media platforms to remove mis and disinformation content. However, when in the course of its work the CDU identifies content which potentially violates platforms' terms of service, including coordinated inauthentic or manipulated behaviour, CDU may decide to escalate the content to the platform. [...] As a matter of principle the CDU does not escalate content to platforms from elected politicians, journalists or established news outlets"*, (emphasis added).[247]

Those anodyne descriptions seem to contradict the evidence given to Parliament at the December 2020 committee hearing described above. The CDU seems quite obviously to have been focussed on monitoring harmful content to flag to social media platforms and indeed it has become clearer, including from the Big Brother Watch investigation and report, that the CDU's attention extended beyond the narrow aims and terms of reference described to Parliament in December 2020 and certainly as described in the CDU fact sheet and the evidence presented to the Covid Inquiry.

For instance, David Davis MP, an elected politician (off limits to the CDU according to Susannah Storey's sworn witness statement[248]) who had been critical of the Imperial College modelling at the outset of the pandemic and continued to express contrarian views during the pandemic, received attention from the CDU. Big Brother Watch describes how in one CDU report Mr Davis was flagged for simply being *"critical of the government"*.[249] So too Big Brother Watch revealed the CDU monitoring and flagging of other prominent commentators – print and broadcast journalists – again supposedly off limits.[250]

The narrow and sanitary description of 'seeking to understand the landscape', in contrast to the policing of content by asking social media companies to act against it, seems flatly to contradict not only Parliament's understanding, but also the expectations of at least two key Ministers.

Nadhim Zahawi, Vaccines Minister, speaking in the House of Commons in February 2021 responded to a question about vaccine disinformation as follows: *"We have been working across Government. In the Cabinet Office, the covid [sic] disinformation unit was set up in March. It works online with the digital platforms to ensure that <u>we identify disinformation and misinformation to them. They should be taking that down immediately</u>. My message to all of them, whether Twitter, Facebook or any of them is this: "<u>You must, must be responsible and play your part in taking this disinformation down as soon as we flag it up to you</u>"*, (emphasis added).[251]

Nadine Dorries, speaking at the time as Secretary of State for the Department of Culture, Media and Sport later confirmed the censorious role of the CDU in January 2022 that *"Daily, we work to remove harmful online content and, particularly when it comes to covid-19 vaccinations, content that provides misinformation and disinformation. Daily, we have contacts with online content providers, and the work is ongoing"*.[252]

MPs hungry for more suppression

In the midst of a public health emergency which had pedestalled vaccination as the exit strategy, a concerted effort to counter 'anti-vaccination misinformation' sounds ostensibly reasonable, and perhaps even a necessity.

Recognising this, Sub-Committee Chair Julian Knight MP had said in a press statement publicising the evidence session held in December 2020 that *"it is very clear that there is a small window of opportunity to crack down now on misinformation put out there about vaccines that are intended to halt the spread of COVID-19"*, and so it is perhaps no surprise that during that hearing the committee of MPs repeatedly stressed their desire for social media companies to pursue and remove anti-vaccine dis and misinformation. Many questions were asked about the approach used to tackle misinformation, and about the results that had been achieved[253] – results in this case being measured with the seductive statistical simplicity of 'numbers of videos taken down'.[254]

The main concern of the committee appears to have been whether sufficient content had been removed: *"why is [it] that there are fewer videos being taken down but more accounts being acted against?"*, asked Knight[255]; and whether the approach to countering anti-vaccine material until then had been sufficiently robust: *"I am not sure that is strong enough, honestly"*, bemoaned Heather Wheeler MP. Another MP raised concerns as to whether social media company staffing levels would be adequate to meet the challenge ahead.

The expansive use of anti-vax labelling

The apparent logic of this strategy disintegrates, however, on contact with the public square where a vast spectrum of viewpoints can interact. We suggest this was a significant issue for the whole narrative control project undertaken by the CDU and its supporters. Suppressing disinformation, including vaccine disinformation, might have seemed ostensibly right, and (for some at least) righteous; but the ethical basis for censoring faltered at the reality that even where questions or comments appeared instinctively false or dangerous to those who cleaved to the official narratives, legitimate nuance could still be found. Are questions about foetal cell lines harmfully misleading or just misguided? Are comments challenging the quality of the Government's official modelling harmful or just harsh? Is it dangerously inaccurate or just inconvenient to opine that the mass vaccination of healthy children at low risk from a virus is unnecessary or unethical?

In any case, it appears that the type of information considered 'within remit' of the CDU was broader still. Responding to a question from MPs in December 2020, Sarah Connolly, head of the CDU, explained the types of 'anti-vax' content considered most problematic:

> "There are broadly three themes, with a fourth. The three that we worry the most about, there is material around speed, the vaccine was done too quickly, it is not safe, those kind of narratives. The second one is around side-effects. <u>The third is around monetary and big business and links to pharma</u>. The fourth is there is, as the Committee pointed out in the previous session, a long history of antivax and in some communities it is quite embedded. From those sometimes you get the slightly outlandish 5G-type conspiracies. Those are broadly the themes that we see", (emphasis added).[256]

We found this to be a startling disclosure. If a particular community is enraptured by a conspiracy theory, censoring otherwise lawful discussion of that theory – however outlandish – seems unlikely to cause that community to change its mind; more likely it will create more theories. Debunking ridiculous claims through counter-explanation is the scientific, democratic, ethical approach. As an experienced politician said recently, *"A government that can censor its critics has licence for every atrocity. It's the beginning of totalitarianism. There's never been a time in history when we look back and the guys who were censoring people were the good guys … Once you start censoring you're on your way to dystopia and totalitarianism"*.[257]

But it seems from these comments that the CDU's censorship operation extended far beyond conspiracy theories. According to Connolly's testimony, the CDU considered any questioning of the unprecedented accelerated approval process for the Covid vaccines to be problematic anti-vax speech; and likewise any concerns raised about the apparent spike in adverse event yellow card reports following deployment of the vaccines. Most surprisingly, Connolly's comments indicate that criticism of the pharma industry and its monetary links may also be off limits.

This expansive use of the anti-vax label is especially concerning given the weaponisation of that term. Through media coverage, and unfortunately even through the comments of parliamentarians,[258] 'anti-vax' has become as personally toxic and professionally fatal a label as the stain of racism, anti-semitism or sexual harassment. The consistent narrative of the pandemic became that those who did not remain fully faithful to the scientific catechism shared by public health officials – particularly as it concerned the safety, effectiveness and necessity of the Covid vaccines – were by definition dangerous apostates: *"The UK has a good record on vaccination and only a small lunatic fringe of antivaxxers"* wrote *The Times* in December 2021.[259]

It cannot seriously be the case that the CDU believes that critical discussion of the pharma industry or its business interests in vaccines and vaccine policy is anti-vax, and thus fair game for the censors.

Nevertheless, for most academics, clinicians, mainstream journalists, broadcasters and commentators, the professional risks associated with any questioning in public of the benefits of Covid mRNA vaccination, or whether the risks or side-effects may have been understated (let alone suppressed), or that universal vaccination may have been unnecessary for low risk age groups, quickly became too great. To voice such thoughts has been to commit heresy of the highest order and consequently self-censorship out of a sense of professional self-preservation has flattened debate.

One example of this was illustrated by comments given to us by broadcast presenter Richard Tice. In January 2023 on his TalkTV show he had interviewed Angus Dalgleish, an expert in immunology and Professor of Oncology at St George's Hospital Medical School in London with over 50 years of medical standing, about concerns based on his own clinical observations of a possible link between mRNA vaccination and cancer regrowths. Professor Dalgleish has written subsequently about the *"unbelievable scorn, scientific ostracism and the ignominy of being 'cancelled' by the MSM as well as by professional colleagues for nearly three years now"* for having aired concerns that some had regarded as unorthodox, including his belief that Covid had originated in a lab-leak[260] (now understood to be a plausible and even the most probable theory).[261]

Very few broadcasters had been willing to discuss Professor Dalgleish's important but uncomfortable observations. Tice told us that he and TalkTV knew they had to be exceptionally careful about discussing harms around the vaccines, but given Dalgliesh's status and experience and the fact that his concerns were based on first hand clinical observations, Tice believed that this was information that the public was entitled to hear and to assess for themselves. Mindful of the febrile environment, however, he felt he had to take the unusual step of holding a pre-interview with Dalgliesh. In Tice's view there is *"no question many broadcasters are terrified of this issue [vaccine harms]"*, and he believes there is *"no doubt that many broadcasters have been put off touching it"*.[262]

The same self-preserving self-censoring tendencies seem equally to have applied to parliamentarians. Matt Hancock was quoted, some months after he left office, as having cause to celebrate that nobody in Parliament had resisted the Government on its vaccination strategy: *"One Nigel Farage-like anti-vax figure in the Commons could have been a real problem. And once it was clear that it was working, almost all the media were onside. … So the counter-narrative [to the anti-vaxxers] was very strong, and ultimately very effective"*.[263]

PROPAGANDA

"The strong emphasis of totalitarian propaganda on the 'scientific' nature of its assertions has been compared to certain advertising techniques which also address themselves to masses."

Hannah Arendt, 1951

Censorship and propaganda are essentially two sides of the same coin. Just as the Government's efforts to limit harmful disinformation appears to have evolved into an enormous censorship operation, co-opting the private sector, so too we can see how official narratives became total narratives.

Scientifically-cloaked narratives

Across the Summer and Autumn of 2020 a series of strong narratives emerged around Government policies, ostensibly shrouded by 'the science', including the efficacy of the rule of 6,[264] and the 'don't kill granny' campaign.[265]

The unethical tactics deployed to turbo-charge these campaigns have been extensively covered elsewhere, most notably in Laura Dodsworth's *State of Fear*,[266] and we do not seek to supplement that account other than to point out that so extreme were the tactics deployed, that it led senior parliamentarian Sir Charles Walker MP later to decry:

"What makes me so angry is the evils and the psychological warfare we deployed against young people and the population, all those behavioural psychologists".[267]

Likewise, we discuss later in this work the disputed basis of much of the science underlying these campaigns, and simply note here that so prevalent was the apparent misuse or misrepresentation of data to support policy decisions that it caused former Prime Minister Theresa May to comment, in what was seen as a highly critical speech, that *"...for many people it looks as though the figures are being chosen to support the policy, rather than the policy being based on the figures"*.[268]

Though this was long before revelations about the CDU surfaced, by Autumn 2020 it was already apparent that experts who raised questions or concerns about the data, the science or the policies were finding themselves unexpectedly sidelined, disparaged or asked to retract their comments.

One such expert, Professor Mark Woolhouse who was a member of SAGE and Professor of Infectious Disease Epidemiology at Edinburgh University, has recounted how, following Sir Patrick Vallance's 'charts of doom' presentation[269] he had contacted the independent Science Media Centre to record that it was highly unlikely that the number of reported cases would reach the levels predicted by Vallance in the presentation (correctly, as it turned out). Shortly after, he was reportedly invited in a message communicated via a colleague to 'correct' his comments and was then later contacted by two senior government scientists expressing concern that he might criticise Sir Patrick's graphics when giving oral evidence to a forthcoming Select Committee hearing. As we now understand, this was simply the most visible tip of an iceberg of broader State-led controlling and suppressive activity, both in the UK and further afield.

We could have chosen any number of the Government's campaigns to ground this chapter, including the discomforting *'Look into their eyes'* campaign of Spring 2021, but we have chosen to focus on the narrative around the mass vaccines roll-out, and in particular the children's vaccination campaign. In many ways that campaign was at the sharpest end of the spectrum of unethical tactics, and yet it has been notably the least covered to date. The explanation for this may lie in the previous chapter.

Vaccine propaganda begins

In December of 2020 the strongest of these scientifically-cloaked narratives of the pandemic began to emerge. Though that particular narrative evolved multiple times as it struggled to keep pace with reality, the absolutist nature of the messaging – and of the information management required to maintain its primacy over all other views and professional opinions – intensified to astonishing levels.

In early October 2020, Kate Bingham, then the Government's Vaccines Tsar, had given an interview to the Financial Times in which she had said that universal vaccination of the UK population was *"not going to happen"*, and that *"[w]e just need to vaccinate everyone at risk"*.[270] Indicating that her comments had not been fully 'on message', subsequently leaked WhatsApp messages revealed a furious Health Secretary, Matt Hancock, disparaging her as a *"totally unreliable"* woman who *"has views and a wacky way of expressing them"*, following on with *"we absolutely need No 10 to sit on her hard"*.[271]

Then in early November as news of Pfizer's '90% effective' vaccine trials broke,[272] optimism inevitably rose. Further leaked WhatsApp messages reveal the fervour among Ministers, and particularly Matt Hancock, to capitalise: *"Pfizer announcement at lunchtime on their vaccine"* (adviser to Hancock) … *"I should DEFINITELY do the [media] round tmrw"* (replied Hancock).[273]

Hancock appeared in Parliament the next day to champion the procurement efforts of the Vaccine Taskforce: *"We in the UK are among the first to identify the promise shown by the vaccine, and we have secured an order of 40 million doses. That puts us towards the front of the international pack, and we have placed orders for 300 million further doses from five other vaccine candidates that have yet to report their phase 3 results, including the Oxford-AstraZeneca vaccine".*[274]

We know that by this point, the Government had already committed £6 billion of public money on vaccine procurement.[275] One might say that the six billion pound question hanging over the Government, and indeed over the UK medicines regulator, for the remainder of that month, was whether the Pfizer vaccine, and the Moderna and AstraZeneca candidates trailing shortly behind, would be declared safe and effective, thus vindicating the Government's high stakes gamble with public money.

Consequently, when on 2 December 2020 that medicines regulator, the MHRA, gave a provisional temporary approval for the Pfizer vaccine to be deployed, Matt Hancock shed tears of joy[276] (reportedly) before refocusing on the media coverage for the jabs programme which he described privately as *"a Hancock triumph".*[277]

The Government then fired the starting pistol on the largest and fastest vaccination campaign in our national history, and on a public messaging and information control campaign of equal scale.

Official narratives became total narratives

From that moment on Ministers could brook no dissent of the Government's vaccination strategy. In a moment of apparently unguarded conceit shortly after his 'Hancock triumph' moment, in response to comments made in Parliament by an opposition MP and the Chair of the Public Accounts Committee, Dame Meg

Hillier MP, in which she commented that as Health Secretary Matt Hancock had been *"somewhat dismissive of an important National Audit Office report that raised serious concerns about the letting of [Covid PPE-related] contracts in Government"* and asked whether in relation to the vaccine roll-out programme he would *"commit to being open and transparent and publishing the contracts and all the paperwork that goes with them?"*,[278] Hancock gaslighted Hillier – an MP of considerable repute and experience – for having aired the question:

> *"Of course I will defend to the end the work that we did to get the PPE roll-out to which the hon. Lady refers. Of course we had priority contracts, because we wanted, when somebody had a good lead, to be able to see if we could make an arrangement as fast as possible, but that was all done through the proper processes, as the NAO report sets out. She asks—I have a lot of respect for the hon. Lady, but really—whether private companies will be involved in the vaccine roll-out. Try Pfizer or BioNTech, the people who came up with and are manufacturing this vaccine. Without them, we would not have a vaccine at all, and a bit of a thank you would do well from the Chair of the Public Accounts Committee".*[279]

Simple and impermeable messaging was needed

The Government and its advisors knew from the outset that official messaging needed to be kept as simple as possible to maximise its effect – as demonstrated by the Downing Street podium triplets such as 'Hands, Face, Space'.[280] Attaching that simplicity to the vaccine roll out, which by this time had already been feted as probably the only viable exit option, was a deliberate communications strategy.

Appearing before the Parliamentary Sub-Committee on Online Harms and Disinformation, in December 2020, James Sorene, the Deputy Director of Covid-19 Vaccine Communications at the Department of Health and Social Care, pinpointed the need to get *"as much clear, quality and proactive information out there as possible"*, and that *"the most important thing that we are trying to get across is that the vaccine is simply the most effective way to combat coronavirus and protect people. That is our number one message"*.[281]

So from the outset the ubiquitous mantras we saw and heard were that the vaccines are the solution to lockdowns; the vaccines are 'safe and effective'. There was no room for nuance or qualification. One only has to look at the instructions for the most simple medications to recognise that there is always nuance and qualification – no medication is without the potential for risks or side effects – but here there was none. Indeed, the Government's unambiguous messaging around safety was expressed in terms that the vaccine manufacturers themselves could not lawfully have used in the UK.[282] By means of a Freedom of Information Act request UsForThem discovered that the Government was treating its public health communications promoting uptake of Pfizer's vaccine to young adults and children as being exempt from the legislative rules governing the promotion of prescription only medicines, on the technical basis that the Government did not consider those communications to have been advertisements.

Private sector co-opted to amplify the official comms strategy

As James Sorene explained in the same hearing, to ensure the success of the Government's communications strategy the DHSC relied on an extended ecosystem of public and private organisations, including the NHS, health charities, royal colleges, local government, academic institutions and of course mainstream media and social media, to amplify its messages: *"There is a very, very big coalition working together to try to get these messages out…"*.[283]

As to how that worked in practice, we gained some insight from the evidence provided to Parliament by the major social media groups. What we see is that the social media platforms were co-opted to feed people 'the right' narrative.

Theo Bertram, Director of TikTok: *"When you create a video and we identify it as a Covid-related video, we put a sticker on it, and that sticker directs people to the Covid hub. This week we are creating a vaccine-specific version; we will direct people to a vaccine-specific hub"*.[284]

In other words, users who sought out Covid or vaccine-related online were redirected to official sources, and particularly the NHS website. This strategy appears to have worked with a significant success rate, and on an industrial scale, as Rebecca Stimson, UK Head of Public Policy at Facebook, explained:

> *"We have driven 3.5 million UK citizens to NHS data sources through our Covid hub and displayed information to 40 million users, which is almost the entirety of our UK usership"*.[285]

This partnership between the Government and social media (and, one can deduce from its uniformly supportive coverage at the time, also involving the mainstream media and the BBC-led Trusted News Initiative) extended more generally to presenting a positive unified front on the vaccination strategy: *"... we are also looking at how we can positively campaign and build public confidence in the vaccine"*, reported Iain Bundred, Head of Public Policy for UK and Ireland at YouTube.[286]

In June 2021, the Government announced a further collaboration with leading social media platforms to support the drive to vaccinate younger adults with unified messaging and the use of social nudges.[287] Vaccines Minister Nadhim Zahawi took the opportunity to reinforce the central narrative of vaccines being our panacea: *"I'm thrilled that some of the leading social media platforms are joining forces to boost vaccine uptake among younger people. ... The vaccine is our way out of this pandemic...".*[288]

Collaborations of this kind to buttress public health messaging are not per se surprising or necessarily objectionable. What becomes concerning, however, are instances of the co-opted members of that ecosystem being held out as independent sources of information, or as expressing non-partisan scientific views. Financial associations with vaccine manufacturers at the very least raise question marks as to the independence of views of some of the individuals and organisations involved in amplifying Government messages,[289] as has opacity around the methodologies of 'fact checking' authorities.[290]

We found it notable that the commercial division of the BBC, for example, whom many around the world will historically have regarded as a scrupulously impartial source of news and information, has received funding measured in millions of dollars from a private organisation with strong ties to the pharma industry and to vaccine manufacturing in particular.[291]

Directly, through partnerships and paid advertorials, and indirectly through relationships with influential intermediaries such as the social media groups, the Government was able to marshall to its cause a huge range of influencers to reinforce its official messaging and, it seems, to 'normalise' the messaging around the vaccination programme:

> *"We are also talking to various partners about how we can drive segmented messages, and how we can seek to normalise things" (Ian Bundred of YouTube).*[292]

The notion that vaccination needed to be normalised gained traction. Though it was not obviously propagandised content, watched with hindsight one can now readily spot the embedded nudges in widely-viewed content such as the segment broadcast on primetime UK breakfast television program 'This Morning' on 8 January 2021 as the vaccine roll-out began, and then republished on YouTube, in which TV medical personality Dr Ranj recounts how easy, slick, painless, free from side effects and apparently uplifting his first Covid jab experience had been.[293]

It was reasonable to expect that if government departments paid for promotional articles – 'advertorials' – in mainstream media, or influencer support on social media, that they would adhere to the standards of transparency expected of promoters and commercial organisations involved in similar product promotion activities. The UK's competition regulator, the Competition and Markets Authority, has issued guidance on advertorials for social media influencers which states that *"it's important that all this content is clearly identifiable as an ad (or advertising)"* and reminds content creators that disguised or subliminal ads may breach both consumer protection law and industry rules on advertising.[294] It goes on to say that *"content must not make false or unsupported statements"* and *"[y]ou should be clear which brands you're advertising for in your post"*.

The Government's strategy of placing advertorials has not however always met these basic standards. For example a paid-for article on the influential parents website Netmums claimed that *"The MHRA (Medicines and Healthcare products Regulatory Agency) has been very cautious when it comes to rolling out the vaccination to children and has only recommended it when there has been extensive safety data and a clear benefit"*,[295] when in fact the JCVI rather than the MHRA is the organisation with responsibility for deciding when to recommend mass roll-out and as we have earlier shown, the JCVI expressly declined to do so for 12 to 15 year olds and for 5 to 11 year olds stopped short of advocating mass roll-out instead advising – in unusual language – only a 'non-urgent offer' (which most parents declined).

An advertorial in the Mirror newspaper meanwhile made claims including that Covid vaccination for children was *"incredibly safe"*.[296] Though the article stated that it was an advertorial, it contained no indication that it was funded by the Government.[297] We are aware that other advertorials have been discovered online without any labelling; corrective statements disclosing that the pieces had been paid for by the Government were only added later, after members of the public raised queries about the nature of the articles.[298]

Comms volume increased as the strategy falters

Even with the force of that huge ecosystem of public and private sector cheerleaders behind it, unable to throw off the adage that no plan survives first contact with the enemy, it was not long before the vaccination comms campaign encountered unexpected resistance in some sectors.

Royal Society for Public Health polling in December 2020[299] suggested that 79% of white adults and as few as 57% of BAME adults would agree to be vaccinated. London was a particular enclave of resistance – a third of its 7 million inhabitants intended to decline the offer as of August 2021.[300] By the end of 2022 only half of Londoners had taken up the option of the 3rd booster.[301]

This was nothing, however, compared to the resistance that was met when plans to vaccinate children were first leaked to the press: first via a Telegraph article on 23 March 2021 – well in advance of the JCVI being asked to consider any potential roll-out to children – which headlined news of the Government's intention to extend the programme to children from August 2021;[302] and then in a follow-on piece in The Daily Mail the next day reporting that *"Children 'will be vaccinated from August with up to 11 million under 18s inoculated by the start of the autumn term' as the government pushes for maximum immunity"*, invoking comments made by the JCVI's

Adam Finn on herd immunity as a justification: *"Children constitute close to a quarter of the population, so even if we could achieve 100 per cent uptake of vaccines across the adult population, it only gets you to 75 per cent coverage"*.[303]

The public comments which quickly attached to that article were almost universally ferocious in their hostility, and perhaps gave someone in the Government communications team an inkling of the extent to which they had misjudged the public's willingness to accept a novel product applied to children after having seen born out the Health Secretary's early confirmation that the risk of healthy children suffering serious illness from the virus was *"very, very low"*.[304]

> *"An irresponsible and unscientific policy"; "Over my dead body"; "If the dark forces in charge think that my grandchildren are being given a vaccine still in the trial phase with a number of reported side effects, despite the denials of vaccine PR central, then they'll have to start bumping us off"; "Forcing these vaccines, still in the trial phase, on people, especially children, for whom Covid poses no risk whatsoever, is unethical"; "An act of pure evil"; "The very definition of madness"; "Never Ever Will my kids be vaccinated with this new type of vaccine .. I would rather go to Prison.... This Government need to look at the Ethics...".*

Indeed a notable thread in the thousands of posted comments is a strong sense that the vaccination of children would be deeply unethical as well as unnecessary.

Desperate measures break free from ethical constraints

As in most other countries, there are strict advertising controls in the UK which in effect prohibit drug manufacturers from marketing their prescription-only products directly to consumers. Non-prescription medicines can be advertised, but such advertisements cannot be directed at children.[305] Across all industries, advertising rules provide an additional layer of protection for children; on this point, the Information Commissioner's guidance explains in plain terms that *"Advertising standards stipulate that marketing targeted directly at or featuring children should not contain anything that is likely to result in their physical, mental or moral harm. For example, adverts must not exploit their credulity, loyalty, vulnerability or lack of experience"*.[306]

Leaving aside the legal question of whether a Government-led campaign to promote a prescription product, including to children, is subject to the same restrictive rules applicable to commercial parties, one might reasonably have expected the Government to subject itself to an equivalent standard of care, especially when dealing with children and with a newly-developed prescription-only medical product which, according to foundational principles of medical ethics, should only ever be given with fully informed voluntary consent.

Even for older cohorts, there is a clear ethical divide between on the one hand raising the profile of a medical product to spotlight its availability, to explain clinical needs, and to evidence the benefit and risk profile of the product; and on the other hand advertising with a view to inducing or coercing a target audience to accept a treatment, whether or not risks or needs have been explained or understood. When dealing with teenagers and children – who are by their nature vulnerable to influence by authority figures, and who cannot be assumed to understand or evaluate the nuance of clinical risks and benefits when that information is not presented to them candidly and transparently – the ethical considerations are heightened.

Yet in our opinion it has been a consistent hallmark of the State-led vaccine campaign in the UK that this ethical line has been repeatedly crossed.

By way of example, The Local Government Association website (an official government website) contains a page on *"Encouraging vaccine take-up among younger people"*, noting that *"Younger generations are more likely to be vaccine hesitant ... partly because they perceive themselves to be at lower risk of developing a severe form of COVID-19"*. Apparently thinking nothing in those circumstances of promoting nudge techniques to get youngsters to accept vaccination, the site continues to explain behavioural insights that *"could be relevant when encouraging younger generations to get vaccinated"*.[307]

These include such ethically dubious tactics as peer pressure *"[s]ince young people tend to be more susceptible to peer influence"*, *"motivat[ing] vaccination through financial incentives"* and stressing the potential for long-term risks to artificially inflate perceptions of seriousness: *"People are more likely to get vaccinated if they believe COVID-19 is serious and if they believe that they risk contracting it ... Since young people are less at risk of developing a lethal form of COVID-19, highlight the potential long-term consequences of the illness"*.[308]

Such techniques were also readily employed even when the target audiences for the campaign were teenagers and children, as demonstrated by the following sample of examples.

In May 2021 a BBC news video presented the exclusively positive comments of teens who had been vaccinated in the United States, explicitly referencing the Pfizer BioNTech product: *"really excited!"*; *"just a little prick, it was really easy"*; *"I don't like getting stabbed, but it's a good thing and I'm still excited for it"*; *"didn't hurt that much"*; and with tantalising upsides: *"I'm actually planning to go back to school on Monday"*; *"[I'll] be able to ride bikes and actually sit close to my friends"*.[309]

Shortly after, the BBC published an article describing, with a somewhat disparaging tone, the *"bribes"* being offered by other countries to encourage uptake of the vaccine among young adults, including free beer, lottery tickets, gym memberships, jewellery, food and electrical items. Susan Michie, a Professor of Health Psychology at University College London and an adviser to the UK government on Covid, is quoted as saying that incentives are an unhelpful distraction, probably counterproductive in the long run, and *"undermine the whole thing"*.[310]

In June 2021, the Government announced that it was teaming up with social media companies to reach younger age cohorts, including a campaign with YouTube taglines 'Let's Not Go Back' with the message that 18 to 34 year olds needed to be vaccinated in order to avoid going back into lockdown,[311] a campaign described enthusiastically by a digital marketing industry publication as *"a pro-Covid jab ad blitz"*.[312]

In July the Prime Minister and Education Ministers floated the idea of making vaccination a precondition for university students to be able to attend lectures or even to enter student accommodation; in other words a vaccine mandate for students at low personal risk. The idea was dropped following deeply negative feedback, but it showed the lengths Ministers were prepared to go.[313]

By August, the Government had reached a new low point as it partnered with businesses to offer an array of 'incentives' (no longer described as 'bribes') for younger people to get vaccinated, including taxi rides, cinema tickets, pizza, supermarket vouchers and leisure centre passes.[314] Professor Susan Michie appears not to have been asked to comment at this time. The possibility of offering straightforward cash incentives was at one point proposed by the Universities Minister, though the idea did not come to pass.[315]

Also in August, shortly after the announcement of the JCVI's u-turn allowing the roll-out to 16 and 17 year olds, 'vaccine buses' were deployed at Premier League football games and music gigs, expressly for the purpose of driving uptake in this age cohort who – crucially – would not need parental consent.[316]

In September 2021, nearly 4 months before the JCVI eventually recommended a 'non-urgent' offer for the 5 to 11 year old cohort, after a survey of more than 27,000 students aged between nine and 18 had suggested that just over a third of nine-year-olds were willing to have the jab and that only around half of 13 year olds would be, celebrity Tik Tok influencers were brought in to *"help boost Covid vaccine uptake among children"*,[317] as described by the i newspaper.

As the roll-out to 16 and 17 year olds, and then to 12-15 year olds, began in the Autumn of 2021, the Government appeared ready to discard any remaining ethical shackles to increase acceptance rates, resorting to both bribery and coercive tactics particularly aimed at young adults, though kids were not spared. The Vaccines Minister even went on record to say that he believed children could overrule their parents on a Covid vaccination decision.[318]

By October, with vaccine uptake among teenagers remaining stubbornly low, Ministers contemplated writing letters directly to 12 to 15 year olds to ask them to get vaccinated. Some in Whitehall called it out as inappropriate and it was quietly dropped.[319]

Then in December 2021, the Department for Education resorted to implying that children and teenagers might be excluded from school if they were not vaccinated. A DfE advertisement and accompanying tweet said *"Vaccines give your children the best possible protection against the virus, and helps keep them in school"*, making no reference to natural immunity (most children were believed to have had the virus by that point), or to any possible side effects.[320]

Even leaving aside the ethics of inducing any part of the population to take part in the vaccines programme by suggesting that the alternative will be a confiscation of liberty or denial of education, or by offering fleeting freebies, particularly given that healthy teenagers and young adults were known not to be at significant risk from any of the virus variants, was it legitimate to pressurise them at all?

Was it legitimate to bribe and coerce teenagers who had reached what one could ordinarily have accepted was a reasonable decision that they did not need a vaccine to protect themselves, because so many had by then acquired natural immunity and were anyway statistically not exposed to any meaningful risk of serious harm?

We now know that this unethical approach has had a disastrous impact on trust in vaccination programmes. A survey carried out for UsForThem in June 2023 confirmed that **more than half of 18 to 25 year olds** in the UK (52%) do not agree with the statement 'The Government has been honest about the risks and benefits of being vaccinated for Covid-19'.[321]

Othering of the unvaccinated

In a sinister evolution of what had already become an oppressive and at times unethical comms strategy, and having almost exhausted its carrots and sticks, we can see how alongside its coercive tactics the Government more overtly sought to denigrate those who remained unvaccinated or supported the right of others to chose.

Matt Hancock was possibly the first Minister to single out unvaccinated hospital patients for criticism in May 2021,[322] but other Ministers and MPs followed his lead over the following months including Cabinet Minister Michael Gove who described it as *"a selfish act … putting other people's lives at risk"*.[323]

In December, after the Prime Minister posited the need for a *"national conversation"* about mandatory vaccinations[324] (whether that conversation would have involved unvaccinated people was not clear) and Health Secretary Sajid Javid said the unvaccinated *"must think about the damage they are doing to society"*,[325] public opinion was surveyed.

The othering appeared to gain some traction with sections of the public. Such was the fear stoked that a survey carried out just before Christmas of 2021 had indicated that one in three people believed the unvaccinated should be put into a lockdown until the pandemic passed, and should not have the same access to hospital treatment as vaccinated people, a finding which London School of Hygiene and Tropical Medicine research fellow Alex de Figueiredo attributed to blaming and othering of the unvaccinated by politicians and journalists, warning that this *"could have profound consequences for trust in the government or public health policies"*.[326]

At its high point, or perhaps low point, this increasingly coordinated effort to blame the unvaccinated for the continuation of pandemic restrictions (ignoring entirely the likely significant effect of natural immunity) the Government briefed The Daily Mail for an article on Christmas Day 2021 which reported that Ministers were planning to send teams armed with vaccine doses to the houses of unvaccinated people, with one unnamed Minister quoted as saying *"The mood in the country is hardening against people who refuse to be vaccinated"*.[327]

With a miserable Christmas and New Year period weighing heavily, the othering of the unvaccinated as the cause of that misery seems to have been too seductive for some.

Conservative MP Tobias Ellwood appeared on Talk TV on 28 December to lament that *"the people filling up our hospitals are those who choose not to get jabbed ... they are causing a burden on the rest of us, it is so irresponsible"*.[328] Meanwhile the Prime Minister gave an interview in which he explained: *"I'm sorry to say this, but the overwhelming majority of people who are currently ending up in intensive care in our hospitals are people who are not boosted... I've talked to doctors who say the numbers are running up to 90% of people in intensive care"*.[329] The reality according to official governmental figures was that in the week when these comments were made, only 25% of patients admitted to hospital with Covid were unvaccinated, and of those admitted to intensive care the proportion was 61% having risen from 47% in October.[330]

An editorial in The Guardian newspaper around the same time recognised that *"A growing sense of frustration with people who have not been vaccinated against Covid has been creeping into the speeches of senior government figures from Sajid Javid to Boris Johnson in recent weeks"*, and appeared possibly to advocate for those choosing not to be vaccinated to carry a social cost.[331]

What happened here, and why?

Though we have insights as to what might have motivated Ministers and senior health officials at certain times, in particular for the period covered by the leaked WhatsApp messages of former Health Secretary Matt Hancock, we may only speculate as to the complex web of causes and effects which fed the evolution of this project of State-led propaganda.

The strength of conviction with which Ministers and officials projected the Government's pandemic narratives and rubbished even the possibility of contrary opinions and alternative options – notably but by no means exclusively in relation to the vaccines programme – seems to have surprised many public health professionals, authors and commentators. Certainly it has surprised us.

We have puzzled over the apparent willingness of so many politicians and scientists and academics of good standing to blur or outright breach well-understood ethical norms by participating in this propaganda project. We do not rule out that in some cases the motivation was an unshakeable certainty of a benevolent purpose – the ends justify the unorthodox means.

It is a sad indictment of how little resistance this unethical propaganda campaign met with that, in March 2022, a series of NHS 'Get vaccinated' advertisements won the Advertising Industry magazine, Campaign's, award for the 'most emotionally effective' advertising campaign of 2021.[332]

And it is doubly concerning that the use of the behavioural tactics of persuasion, bribery, social pressure and – ultimately – outright coercion became so normalised by Ministers and officials that to speak out against it on even just ethical grounds could be portrayed as extremist, or indeed as 'anti-vax'.

As far as the children's vaccine programme is concerned, we know that the UK had aquired *"one of the biggest portfolios [of vaccine doses] per capita in the world"*.[333] In February 2021, the UK had over 400 million doses on order, sufficient to give every person in the UK – adult, child and baby – six jabs. "Our strategy has been to invest early and invest at risk", said Matt Hancock at the time.[334] Is it conceivable that the strength of conviction in the Government's delivery of that vaccine programme was in part a product of earlier spending decisions?

Regardless of the motivations at play, confronted with the fact that ethical lines were seriously and repeatedly crossed, the question is less 'why did this happen', but more pertinently, 'how did this happen?'. Our next chapter provides at least part of the answer.

ETHICS DENIED: THE MORAL AND ETHICAL ADVISORY GROUP

In October 2019 the Department for Health and Social Care established the Moral and Ethical Advisory Group. Its membership comprised approximately twenty experts and leaders drawn from the fields of medicine, ethics, law, social science and religion, and according to its terms of reference its purpose was to *"provide independent advice to the UK government on moral, ethical and faith considerations on health and social care related issues as they occur. This advice will be used to inform management of health related incidents including but not limited to pandemic flu"*.[335]

The group was sponsored by the Director of Emergency Preparedness and Health Protection at the DHSC, and was expected to provide advice to the Chief Medical Officers as well as to Government Departments, Ministers and the Cabinet's civil emergencies committee, COBRA. Formed with an initial fixed term of three years, it was anticipated in its terms of reference that MEAG would *"in the longer term ... advise proactively on issues that might be relevant to emergency preparedness planning more generally"*.[336]

MEAG's last meeting took place in December 2021, and the Group was then stood down in October 2022 at the end of its initial fixed term after a review in September 2022.

The three years of MEAG's existence coincided with a complex pandemic response which included: lockdown, mass school closures, mass testing, the Covid vaccine roll-out and related passports, and the vaccination of children. It is trite to note that each of these policy decision points involved ethical considerations, navigating complex webs of rights and benefits, duties and burdens with outcomes that would have profound consequences for the lives, livelihoods and life chances of millions of people.

One might have expected the Government's advisory group on ethical issues to play a central role during this period; and for it to have been vocal, and instrumental in setting ethical guardrails for legally and ethically robust policy decisions.

This chapter draws heavily on the official summaries of MEAG meetings. We have also spoken to former members of MEAG for background purposes to help us to corroborate certain aspects of our reading of the official summaries.[337]

An optimistic start

MEAG was first brought together on 10 March 2020, at the outset of the pandemic response in the UK. At its second meeting the Group received a virtual briefing from the Cabinet Office in which an unnamed Government official *"outlined the significant challenges and difficult decisions that lie ahead"*.[338] Four days later, on 20 March 2020, the Group met again and this time agreed to hold weekly meetings until further notice, one assumes in anticipation of a pressing need for the Group's input on moral and ethical issues.[339]

At that meeting Cabinet Office officials gave a presentation on the provisions of the Coronavirus Bill which was being prepared for Parliament. The Co-chair of MEAG, Jonathan Montgomery, noted in response that the Group's role would be *"to offer advice and support on how the powers in the new Act could be implemented"*. The official record of the meeting records that MEAG members at this point *"expressed some reservations about the proportionality of the powers in the Bill, and the fact that it is in place for two years"*. Reportedly *"Cabinet Office colleagues said that they would return with evidence of further work on this subject"*, though there is no record of that having happened, and the Coronavirus Bill became law five days later.[340]

For its meeting on 25 March 2020, some of the members of MEAG had produced a draft guidance document intended *"to aid health workers in making decisions regarding care for patients during the Covid-19 outbreak"*, which appears to have been focussed on the prioritisation of critical care – by definition, a topic of life and death ethical significance.[341]

At its next meeting, on 1 April 2020, the Group considered the possibility of developing a set of ethical principles. It is not clear from the meeting summary specifically to what those principles related, though it is apparent from an addendum note added at a later stage that the principles were left unfinished because *"the group moved on to practical advice on particular issues"*.[342]

After an extended discussion on adjustments that could be made to existing Government guidance on end of life care and funerals, which took place across meetings on 8 and 9 April, MEAG next met on 22 April, with the members seemingly optimistic about their early achievements and about the prospects for the Group's future contributions.

"Members welcomed the news that the funerals guidance which the Group had discussed on April 8 and April 9 had now been published, and noted that it had been well-received. Members then discussed the operation and composition of the Group. Members felt that differing views and the wide range of areas of expertise were a

> *positive element for the Group, which enables fruitful discussions, and thus constructive advice provided on issues posed. [...]*
>
> *Members then talked about how MEAG could provide advice and input on issues it had concerns about. Members were positive about being able to raise matters. Jonathan [Montgomery] confirmed that he would write a submission for the England CMO, to invite him, in consultation with the other CMOs to consider commissioning MEAG to produce a framework to assist policy-makers take moral and ethical issues into account when developing policy. Such a framework would aim to include a statement of ethical principles that MEAG will develop, to be consistent with the national ethical framework. The MEAG would continue to be available as a forum for advice and discussion. Members agreed with this as a way forward".*[343]

This chimes with what one of our sources recalled: that in early 2020 MEAG members felt the group was valued and *"in demand"*.

A first knock-back

The Group's optimism appears to have been undercut when, a week later, the co-chair reported that *"he had spoken to CMO England [Professor Chris Whitty] about the Group's work, and that CMO was content with the Group's role in advising on specific issues as they arise. He had <u>advised against MEAG working to produce a document of principles</u> beyond what was already in place in the ethical framework for pandemic planning as this might <u>crowd out the capacity of MEAG</u> to consider detailed issues on which advice was being sought"*, (emphasis added).[344]

The summary of the meeting gives no further explanation as to why Whitty believed MEAG might be unable to advise on other issues while working to document a framework of ethical principles. MEAG was a committee of approximately twenty experts which had managed to meet almost weekly up until that point, which had not itself raised capacity concerns and which had volunteered to produce the framework only the week before. Nor is it evident from the official record whether any MEAG members objected to the CMO's advice. Nevertheless, it is apparent that this discussion brought a premature end to that idea.

A few days later, Jasvir Singh, co-chair of MEAG, spoke to a meeting of the UK's Joint Committee on Vaccination and Immunisation (JCVI) on the ethical considerations of vaccine prioritisation. The minutes of that JCVI meeting record that committee's understanding as follows:

> "89. MEAG had a diverse membership and range of views and was currently meeting on a weekly basis. MEAG was not at this stage in a position to give ethical advice on vaccine prioritisation but was expecting to start discussions on this shortly and could provide feedback on the outcome of this to the Committee.
>
> 90. The Committee noted that items likely to be discussed by MEAG included the difference between a transmission and mortality approach, and if a risk group strategy were employed, how these might be prioritised and also the issues of geography and ethnicity. The Committee noted that it would be useful if the ethics committee could give a steer on the questions being developed as part of the attitudinal survey on COVID-19 vaccination.
>
> 91. The Committee agreed that JCVI advice would be based on scientific principles from the available scientific evidence and this would not include detailed ethical considerations which were for DHSC to consider, informed by MEAG", (emphasis added).[345]

In other words, the JCVI would not contemplate ethical considerations because it had understood that MEAG's advice to

DHSC would be overlaid on the JCVI's scientific advice. The JCVI appears to consider this to be such a settled point that it was restated in the conclusion section of the minutes *"noting that DHSC would consider the ethical dimensions of [JCVI's] advice"*.[346] This was later to become highly significant when proposals for the mass vaccination of children and teenagers were assessed in the summer of 2021.

The appearance of progress

Two weeks later, on 13 May 2020, MEAG met again to discuss: *"... some of the moral and ethical aspects of how any future COVID-19 vaccination programme may be delivered"*. The Group also discussed how it could proactively provide advice on the Government's Covid-19 recovery strategy, agreeing *"that they would identify moral and ethical themes within the strategy, and at future meetings discuss how these themes could be addressed"*.[347] The notes of the meeting which took place the following week reveal that the discussion had, as planned, focussed on some of those themes.

By 8 July, discussions had moved on to identify learnings and missed opportunities from the course of the pandemic response up to that point, which led to a proposal for the Group to curate a series of stories from the pandemic that would illustrate *"the moral and ethical issues arising"* in a range of practical situations, to assist Government officials in their future policy-making.[348]

That discussion continued into the following week[349], when it was agreed that the stories should seek to illustrate the key principles set out in an existing Cabinet Office and DHSC ethical framework document[350] which referenced, among other objectives:

- Minimising the disruption to society caused by a pandemic.

- Proportionality, including:

- o *"those responsible for providing information will neither exaggerate or minimise the situation and will give people the most accurate information that they can";*

- o *"decisions on actions that may affect people's daily lives, which are taken to protect the public from harm, will be proportionate to the relevant risk and to the benefits that can be gained from the proposed action";* and

- o *"The media and other people responsible for communications will have an important role to play in ensuring that people know what the real situation is and what they need to do, without exaggerating or minimising the situation".*

- Reasonableness, including that decisions should be *"rational", "not arbitrary", "based on appropriate evidence"* and *"the result of an appropriate process, taking into account how quickly a decision has to be made and the circumstances in which a decision is made".*

The official summary of the meeting which followed on 12 August 2020 records that after a final review of these illustrative stories, MEAG members were hopeful that they would be used *"to influence and enrich policy making in the future"* and that among other outcomes officials would recognise that *"the measure of damage caused by Covid should not be limited to illness and death"*, and that *"more attention needs to be given to ensure some groups are not unintentionally overlooked by policy makers, for example young people".*[351]

Frustration builds

By 9 September 2020, possibly in a sign that MEAG was becoming disillusioned by a lack of engagement from the Government, the members noted the *"fast pace of change, such as the recently announced Rule of 6"*, and resolved to *"revisit the draft principles explored by the* *group at the start of the pandemic, whilst also remaining responsive at future meetings to requests for MEAG to provide advice".*³⁵²

The official summary relays that the Group then *"explored a range of options to increase the visibility of MEAG and identify opportunities to add value by improving links with policy makers and securing greater influence over decision-making".* To achieve this, it was proposed that MEAG *"reach out proactively to senior civil servants in key policy areas"*, identified as *"the Covid-19 vaccination programme, ethical questions around mass testing and the impact of Covid-19 on other areas of healthcare, such as cancer screening".*³⁵³

This was significant, both because it reveals that MEAG still aspired to engage proactively with decision-makers to bring ethical considerations to the fore; and because it affirms that each of the policy areas identified were clearly felt by MEAG to be within its moral and ethical remit.

The meeting ends with the Group recording a need to *"engage more closely with the four Chief Medical Officers"* and to *"seek feedback from civil servants as to the efficacy of the advice given by MEAG for their respective papers and presentations over the last 6 months".*³⁵⁴

Soon after, the Group met with senior DHSC officials, including Emma Reed, the senior DHSC official under whose sponsorship the Group had been formed, and Claire Vittery who was then Head of COVID 19 Vaccine Deployment in the Government.

Claire Vittery is reported to have *"sought consideration of how best to clearly communicate about potential COVID-19 vaccine candidates to explain the facts with clarity, and to encourage uptake of a COVID-19 vaccine; …"*. All that was recorded of the remainder of that meeting is that *"There was wide ranging discussion among the Group with many different views put forward"*; the notes of the meeting also record that two of the key recommendations provided to the DHSC officials were that *"Honest and clear information should be provided to allow the public to make an informed choice on vaccination.To be realistic about alternatives"* and that officials should *"Listen carefully to the actual concerns of individuals and give them the consideration they deserve"*.[355]

A second knock-back

At the next meeting, which took place on 4 November 2020, just two weeks later, the meeting summary records that following *"a recent meeting with the senior sponsor for the group, Emma Reed"* the two co-chairs of the Group *"had agreed to refresh the terms of reference to reflect MEAG's shift in focus on to response work, acting as a constructive sounding board and advisory group to officials in the earlier stages of policy development"*.[356]

One reading of this record is that Emma Reed, a senior DHSC official, directed MEAG to focus more narrowly on addressing only specific questions that were put to it, and possibly to be more constructive when doing so.

A moment of critical significance

Then, on 2 December 2020, in what appears to have been the most significant meeting of its existence, MEAG considered a paper which had been authored by Jonathan Montgomery and several other MEAG members, which appears to have been addressing the ethical considerations of Covid vaccine status certification.[357]

> *"Jonathan Montgomery introduced the topic by explaining that the CMO for England [Professor Whitty] had indicated that he was content for MEAG to discuss and provide an ethical steer on this issue and provide a report to him. It was also proposed that a paper be prepared for consideration by NERVTAG, SPi-B and*

> *SAGE to inform their discussion of the proposal. It was noted that many members considered that MEAG had been invited to advise at a very late stage of the process.*
>
> *A wide-ranging discussion identified the main points the committee wanted to draw attention to. It was agreed that there were some fundamental scientific questions outstanding, regarding both immunity to reinfection, conferred by a past infection and its duration, as well as the effectiveness of the vaccine to not only reduce the seriousness of disease in the recipient but also transmission of the virus to others. Answers to these questions would influence and inform the discussion [about] the value of certification".*[358]

A number of serious ethical concerns were then expressed about status certification, around human rights, public engagement and the risk that coercion would damage trust. The official record of that meeting is notably more extensive than almost all other MEAG meeting records:

"There were three key areas raising concerns:

1. Human Rights

There was considerable concern expressed that there were several human rights considerations that had not been given adequate attention to date. The question was asked "is certification necessary to control the pandemic and was it a proportionate response". This was considered doubtful and the risk of a range of different people being excluded due to inequity of access to the vaccine/certification system was also a concern. [...]

Although it was acknowledged that these issues were not insurmountable, they were areas of serious concern that would need to be carefully considered if this course of action was taken and be successfully implemented. [...] It was agreed by some members that there could be an argument for introducing certification in some circumstances e.g. healthcare workers – akin to the system for Hepatitis B vaccination. However, the outstanding question regarding the vaccine's ability to interrupt transmission would need to be answered before this could be recommended for further consideration.

2. Public Engagement

A lack of understanding by the public of the science behind the vaccination, its speed of development and what it would deliver in terms of protection was also a concern that needed to be addressed as well as greater public engagement in the process.

3. Trust

Another question that was raised regarded the motivation for the introduction of a policy of certification. There was a concern that it could be used as a way by Government and possibly employers to semi-coerce people into having the vaccine and this would not resonate well with the public and may, as an unintended consequence, further fuel public mistrust and suspicion. The timing of this proposal was discussed as members considered that in the initial stages of the roll-out, demand would likely outstrip the capacity in the system to supply the vaccine to all who wanted it. Therefore, it was considered that coercion was not needed to drive uptake. In addition, positive data generated from this initial period would also provide further confidence to those people who were currently reluctant to have the vaccine. [...]

It was agreed that a further version of the paper would be produced drawing on the main points and principles raised by members during the discussion to ensure the ethical issues were given proper consideration in further discussion of certification by other groups".[359]

We might assume that the 'other groups' referred to here must have included SAGE.

A third knock-back

Having expressed its ethical concerns about the Government's plan for a system of Covid status certification and then broken off for the Christmas break, the Group reconvened on 20 January 2021. Jasvir Singh, who appears to have spoken with Professor Whitty in the intervening period, provided an update:

> "... the CMO valued the presence of the MEAG and the ability to understand complexities, however <u>counselled against producing documentation that offered recommendations, given the political aspect of decision making</u>. The Group reflected on the role of MEAG and the relationship with the CMO/the Department, initially in relation to immunity certification, but also in relation to their wider remit and influence. The Chair highlighted that the terms of reference were being re-designed to more accurately reflect the role and influence MEAG played within government. These terms of reference were sat with DHSC officials to agree", (emphasis added).[360]

Read straightforwardly, the summary appears to evidence that Professor Whitty directed MEAG not to put its recommendations into writing – presumably including any of the concerns or advice expressed in December on the controversial topic of Covid vaccine status certification, which it seems Professor Whitty considered to be a political matter.

Why Professor Whitty felt that it would be inappropriate for expert ethical advice and recommendations on an ethically controversial topic to be put in writing, and thus capable of being shared with SAGE, Ministers, with Select Committees or with Parliament, is again a matter on which we can only speculate. It is also not clear to whom the paper produced by Jonathan Montgomery and colleagues was distributed, or what happened to it after it was presented to the MEAG meeting of early December.

Shortly after MEAG's December meeting, SAGE had specifically requested that input be sought from MEAG into a paper to be produced for SAGE on the topic of Covid status certification:

"Given the limited evidence around the outcomes if certification is to be introduced, pilot studies should be conducted including consideration of ethical concerns. ... ACTION: SAGE Secretariat to coordinate a single updated paper addressing science questions on certification, with input from NERVTAG, SPi-B and MEAG".[361] It is not clear what if any input MEAG was able to provide, but there is no further mention of that paper or of MEAG's input in SAGE's meeting records for December and January.

The Public Administration and Constitutional Affairs Committee of the House of Commons was the Select Committee which sought to evaluate moral, ethical and legal concerns with the Covid status certification proposals across a number of hearings commencing in March 2021.[362] It is notable, in light of Professor Whitty's apparent direction to MEAG, that the PACAC heard from many witnesses across those hearings, including experts, civil rights organisations and business leaders, but did not hear from any member of MEAG. In fact, the existence of MEAG was not mentioned in any of the oral evidence transcripts or in the report on this topic ultimately issued by the PACAC in June 2021.[363]

In what might be construed as barely-disguised outrage among its members, the official record of MEAG's 20 January meeting goes on to note that:

"The Group explored options to increase the effective influence of MEAG when not specifically consulted on decisions, and to highlight the role that ethics should play in decision-making while acknowledging and accepting political difficulties. ...

The Group discussed the relationship between legal obligations and ethical decision making and the role MEAG had to explain complexities".[364]

From this point, MEAG meetings became notably less frequent than had been the case in 2020.

Our sources confirmed they had found this disappointing, and that whereas *"initially the Government had seemed very accepting of our advice as things went on they seemed to want to do what they wanted to do for other reasons"*. *"It was a little bit frustrating"*, added another.

Beginning of the end

The next meeting, in February, considered a relatively uncontroversial topic, the NHS' screening backlog, particularly for cancer care appointments.[365]

At the following meeting, on 3 March 2021, MEAG was asked to address the narrow topic of age-based prioritisation in the phase 2 programme for distributing Covid vaccines. As an aside, and presumably having already recognised the direction of travel for the Government's vaccination strategy, *"It was also observed that the ethics of vaccinating children would be an appropriate topic for MEAG to consider in the future"*, adding that *"The Group agreed that where possible they would like to consider future items early on to maximise MEAG's ability to aid decision making".*[366]

On 31 March 2021, the Group met to discuss what, judging by the meeting notes, became another highly controversial and ethically challenging policy: the proposal for a vaccination requirement for care home workers. The 90 minute discussion seems to have been wide-ranging and balanced, though definitive conclusions are not drawn.[367]

A month later, on 28 April 2021, Cabinet Office and DHSC officials attended MEAG's meeting to revisit the controversial topic of Covid status certification. Notably on this occasion, however, MEAG was not asked to advise on the ethics of the proposal itself, but only on the narrow question of *"the conditions under which exemptions to COVID-status certification should be considered"*.[368] The official summary records a thoughtful discussion of that question.

A missed meeting

MEAG was scheduled to meet on 16 June 2021 to provide feedback and advice on a paper prepared by the DHSC on the vaccination of children and young people, and to discuss a memo prepared by some members of MEAG which was shared with all members of MEAG and with the DHSC.

We understand that the memo referenced the rapid rate at which adults had been vaccinated, recognised that vaccination could save lives but also cautioned that children needed to be thought about separately, not least because the Covid vaccines are invasive, irreversible and may have long-term side effects which have yet to be identified. The memo reportedly challenged the purpose of vaccinating children, questioned the known benefits and harms for individual children, and called for urgent consideration of the issues.

On the day, however, the DHSC cancelled the MEAG meeting, ostensibly because it had been revealed in the press late in the day on 15 June that the JCVI was preparing to advise Ministers against the mass rollout of Covid vaccines to children.[369] Though the roll out subsequently proceeded, the meeting was never reconvened.

An extended hiatus

MEAG was not then asked to meet again until September 2021. Objectively this seems a surprising moment for MEAG to have been given an extended break by the DHSC if one considers that, during that time, the Government was grappling with Covid status certification; a chaotic programme of testing and repeated self-isolations of children which politicians[370], experts[371] and parents[372] were by then decrying as unfair and unethical; and the JCVI was considering whether to recommend the mass vaccination of children – all of which engaged material moral and ethical considerations. MEAG consequently never had a chance to discuss the moral and ethical considerations of vaccinating children against Covid, despite the JCVI having confirmed that ethical considerations would form no part of its advice on vaccination strategy.[373]

The ending

On 8 September 2021, in the critical window when the four CMOs were being asked to reconsider the JCVI's decision to decline to recommend a mass vaccination of 12 to 15 year olds[374] – arguably one of the most contentious moral and ethical decisions of the pandemic, and possibly the decision that inflicted more damage to parental trust in public health than any other – MEAG was asked to advise on virginity testing.[375]

The CMOs decision in relation to 12 year olds appears expressly not to have considered ethical aspects: *"… this UK CMOs advice is purely clinical and public health derived and has not taken issues outside their clinical and public health remit into account".*[376]

On 27 October 2021, as the Covid passport debate was crescendoing, MEAG was asked to advise on an extension to the statutory storage limits for eggs, sperm, and embryos.[377]

On 15 December 2021, as attention moved to the difficult question of whether the Covid vaccination programme should be extended to 5 year olds, MEAG was asked to advise on the use of AI (artificial intelligence) in medical imaging.[378]

MEAG was not established to focus exclusively on Covid topics, so it was not per se unorthodox for the Group to be asked to consider non-pandemic topics; but it seems surprising that the Group's attention was diverted during this key period in pandemic policy-making. In any case, these were the last three meetings of MEAG; *"they [DHSC] just didn't send any further business"*, explained one of our sources.

"I think in the end they realised that you can't have a moral and ethical committee without trespassing on things that Ministers think are political judgments... and that's why it was shut down", said another.

The disbanding of the Group does not appear to have been announced by the DHSC and no public explanation has been given for its premature demise. We are left with questions:

1. Why in March 2020 did Prof Chris Whitty not want MEAG to draw up a set of ethical principles to guide the Government's pandemic decision-making? And why in January 2021 did Prof Whitty again discourage MEAG from putting its advice in writing?

2. Did Emma Reed direct MEAG to change its terms of reference at the end of October 2020, and if so why did she want MEAG to focus only on specific questions asked of it?

3. Why was MEAG not consulted on child vaccinations after it had specifically identified it as an ethical issue worthy of early consideration, and after the June meeting of MEAG to consider

precisely that topic had been postponed? And consequently what if any ethical advice did the CMOs receive before they overruled the JCVI's decision not to recommend the vaccine for teenagers in September 2021?

4. Why did MEAG not meet between June 2021 and September 2021 during which time the Government was grappling with at least three profoundly ethical issues?

5. Why did MEAG not meet after December 2021, and who ultimately approved the decision to allow MEAG's mandate to expire in October 2022?

6. Other than through discussions with and advice from MEAG, how were moral and ethical considerations identified and taken into account in the Government's pandemic decision-making?

Coda: MEAG in the Covid Inquiry

In initial hearings of the official Covid Inquiry, such brief mention of moral and ethical aspects, and of MEAG, as has been made have, as of the time of writing, assumed a greater or more central role for the Group than the official records reveal to have been the case, an assumption which has not as yet been corrected by any Minister or official, including:

- Oliver Dowden MP, responding to Hugo Keith KC (Counsel to the Inquiry) on 21 June 2023: *"So [MEAG] arose from a consideration that government would have to make difficult decisions and we would have to -- it would -- as, again, the title suggests, it would give rise to moral and ethical questions, and we felt it was appropriate to have a body to help us with that. Indeed, I signed off the creation of the Moral and Ethical Advisory Group as a minister...".*[379]

- During Hugo Keith KC's questioning of Emma Reed of the DHSC on 27 June 2023 Keith recalls: *"MEAG ... was put in place, the Moral and Ethical Advisory Group, and that gave valuable assistance, of course, during the pandemic on the moral and ethical issues"*.[380]

A 2022 paper authored by a group of academics has concluded that *"as a national government ethics advisory committee, MEAG was underutilised as a forum for coordinating ethical expertise"*, and that *"ethical considerations have been simultaneously widespread in public debate, yet marginalised in policy responses"*.[381] A final question might therefore be asked as to why Ministers and senior officials appear to have been content to allow the Covid Inquiry to proceed on the understanding that MEAG's advice played a significant role in decision-making when the evidence appears to show the contrary.

A GRIEVOUS POLICY CHOICE: SCHOOL CLOSURES

"In all actions concerning children, whether undertaken by public or private social welfare institutions, courts of law, administrative authorities or legislative bodies, the best interests of the child shall be a primary consideration."

UN Convention on the Rights of the Child, Art. 3(1)

A CATALOGUE OF FAILURES

We end our case studies where UsForThem started as a campaign group: with school closures. Although perhaps less sensational than some of the other topics we have covered, for us it is the most shocking: featuring not only a total failure by Ministers to weigh risks against perceived benefits, exposing a generation of children to harm, but also a failure to heed the warnings of experts, including the Government's own experts, time and time again. The full extent of those missed opportunities is sobering; we have summarised them at the end of this chapter.

Closures were not favoured by the planners

Prior to the Covid pandemic, the UK's pandemic plan, which had been updated most recently in 2011, assumed that mass school closures should be avoided: *"Once the virus is more established in* the country, the general policy would be that schools should not close – unless there are specific local business continuity reasons (staff shortages or particularly vulnerable children). ... Such a step would therefore only be taken in an influenza pandemic with a very high impact and so, although school closures cannot be ruled out, it should not be the primary focus of schools' planning".[382]

During the 2009/10 Swine Flu epidemic, which disproportionately affected children, 70 of whom died in the UK, schools had remained open throughout.[383]

More harm than good

On 10 February 2020, as the Covid pandemic was breaking, the SPI-M-O sub-group (Scientific Pandemic Influenza Group on Modelling, Operational) of SAGE published its first consensus view on the impact of mass school closures. At this very early stage it was already recognised that school closures could be counter-productive to reducing transmission and infection rates, not least because infections appeared to be more severe in the older generations (a fact subsequently born out globally by the morbidity and mortality data) who would inevitably be called upon for childcare support by working parents in the event of school closures: *"putting children in the care of their grandparents may result in a higher number of severe cases".*[384]

On 19 February, SPI-M-O's updated consensus view noted that the magnitude of the impact that school closures would have would be very uncertain, and highly sensitive to the role that children play in transmission. Any impact from school closures was expected to be *"highly limited"* and therefore that longer closures would have greater effect than shorter closures.[385] The modelling that had been done at that stage assumed that children would have a role in transmission similar to that for influenza (by the following month SPI-M-O had acknowledged that children had a lesser role in transmission of Covid than for influenza).

On 26 February, Matt Hancock, the Health Secretary, relayed to Parliament that the UK would act proportionately, with no policy for blanket school closures: *"schools should stay open, with no blanket ban, unless there are specific reasons for them not to"*.[386] And this was for good reason: it had been well-known to the Government's contingency planners that, beyond education, schools play an important broader role in child development and, crucially, in safeguarding.[387]

Despite this, we have identified just one advisory paper produced in the six weeks before the Government's decision to close schools which alluded to safeguarding concerns. That paper, produced by the SPi-B sub-group of SAGE (the behavioural science sub-group) in March 2020, reported that *"SPi-B have a consensus view that school closures will be highly disruptive and likely to present an unequal burden to different sections of society"*; and then *"… almost all strategies will result in reduced, or changed, adult oversight of children. This presents a risk of unintended consequences"*.[388]

On 17 March, the day before the first mass school closures in the UK, the SPI-M-O group recorded in its third 'consensus view' document[389] that *"The impact of school closures, as a stand-alone policy, on COVID-19 would be expected to be smaller than for influenza"* and consequently *"schools would have to be closed for longer to have the same [mitigating] effect"*. The paper then further acknowledged that there was *"still a great deal of uncertainty around the extent to which children have a role in the transmission of [Covid]"*, and suggested that children could be only 25% to 75% as likely to transmit the virus as an adult. In other words, children were thought to be materially less likely to transmit the virus than most adults.

A GRIEVOUS POLICY CHOICE: SCHOOL CLOSURES

The group's statement concluded that *"Our best assessment is that [school closures] would reduce the reproduction number [of Covid] by between 10% and 20%. We do not know how likely it is that this will change the reproduction number from being above one to below one"*; and school closures *"would need to last several months"* to achieve even this result.

A major academic study led by UCL and published three weeks later affirmed that conclusion: *"We know from previous studies that school closures are likely to have the greatest effect if the virus has low transmissibility and attack rates are higher in children. This is the opposite of COVID-19. Data on the benefit of school closures in the COVID-19 outbreak is limited but what we know shows that their impact is likely to be only small compared to other infection control measures such as case isolation. ... Additionally, the costs of national school closures are high – children's education is damaged and their mental health may suffer, family finances are affected, keyworkers may need to stay home to look after children and vulnerable children may suffer most".*[390]

The policy changed, but the risk of harms remained

On the morning of 18 March, SAGE had a meeting and then changed its advice to recommend implementing school closures nationally as soon as practicable, albeit it was still uncertain as to whether this would reduce the R rate. The minutes record discussion of the impact on adults – work, childcare, transmission – but never the effect on children.[391] Certainly it appears that SAGE did not contemplate the broader picture, as Lord O'Donnell, a peer and former Cabinet Secretary later suggested it should have done while giving evidence at the official Covid Inquiry:

> *"So, for example, closing schools would have an effect on transmission, which experts in epidemiology could tell you something about, but in order to understand the overall impact and put this to ministers, you needed to have someone saying, 'What's*

127

the impact of that on the children, on their education? What's the impact on teachers? What's the impact on the mental health of the parents and, in due course, on the economy as a whole?'".[392]

Indeed, as we discuss later, it is telling that it was not considered necessary to include an educational psychologist within the SPi-B sub-group of SAGE until a month after schools had closed.

On the afternoon of 18 March, Gavin Williamson, the Education Secretary, delivered a statement to Parliament: *"I said before that if the science and the advice changed, such that keeping schools open would no longer be in the best interests of children and teachers, we would act. We are now at that stage"*.[393]

He went on to say: *"The public health benefits of schools remaining open as normal are shifting. It is also clear that schools are finding it increasingly difficult to continue as normal, as illness and self-isolation impact on staffing levels and pupil attendance"*. (By mid-March, it was reported that 20% of teachers were self-isolating and that school attendance was between 70 and 80%.)

Consequently: *"After schools shut their gates on Friday afternoon, they will remain closed until further notice"*.[394] Children of key workers and those who were known to be vulnerable were excluded, but otherwise this amounted to a blanket withdrawal of schooling for all school-aged children. At the same time, Williamson confirmed that all school exams would be cancelled.

Almost immediately, and continuing into April, a series of safeguarding flags were then raised:

1. Childline, on 27 March 2020, reported that even in the very first week of school closures, calls to the children's helpline rose by 10%.[395]

2. The NSPCC warned on 2 April that *"The impact of the coronavirus lockdown has increased online risks and brewed a perfect storm for offenders to abuse children"*.[396]

3. A cross-party group of MPs wrote to the Home Secretary on 16 April to highlight that *"A terrible and disturbing aspect of this pandemic is that illegal activity online, including child abuse, appears to be escalating"*.[397]

4. A BMJ editorial titled *'A shift in focus is needed to avoid an irreversible scarring of a generation'*,[398] pointed out that a perfect storm of locking of children in 'pressure cooker' environments, the absence of external oversight, and a 22% increase in alcohol sales since the start of the lockdown, risked a *"secondary pandemic"* of child neglect and abuse.

Within the first month of the first lockdown alone, Great Ormond Street Children's Hospital had reported a 1,493% rise in incidents of suspected abusive head trauma involving children at that hospital: *"Ten children (six boys, four girls; mean age 192 days, range 17 to 401 days) with suspected AHT were seen during this time in comparison with a mean of 0.67 cases per month in the same period over the previous 3 years"*.[399]

Promises were made

When schools first closed in March 2020, the Government promised that remote learning would be both logistically achievable and a suitable substitute for the learning time that would be lost. Yet in early 2020, just before that first lockdown, Ofcom's Technology Tracker had estimated that *"between 1.14 million and 1.78 million children under the age of 18 lived in households without access to a laptop, desktop or tablet in the UK"*, and that between 227,000 and 559,000 children lived in homes with no access to the internet.[400] By 13 July

2020 (the end of the academic year), the Government had delivered just 212,900 laptops and tablets, and 49,700 internet routers.[401]

Indeed, there was no legal obligation for schools to provide remote learning facilities until 22 October 2020.[402] Consequently, until then many pupils, and particularly those in the least privileged areas of the country, received (at best) paper handouts of topics that parents could teach their own children at home with little offered by way of active education.

Vulnerable children dropped off the radar

On 22 April 2020, the first of twenty hearings of the Education Select Committee (ESC) under the collective inquiry title of *'The impact of COVID-19 on education and children's services'* was held, in which Vicky Ford MP, at that time the Children's Minister, answered questions about the closure of schools:[403] *"We have put vulnerable children at the forefront of our thinking, right from day one. That is why we took the very difficult decision to close schools—it was a difficult decision—but then the important decision to make sure that they would remain open for key workers' children and vulnerable children".*

A week earlier, however, advice produced by the SAGE modelling sub-group, SPI-M, drawing on school attendance figures provided by the Department for Education, had confirmed (albeit out of view in an annex) that *"94% of vulnerable children are not in school".*[404]

The same SPI-M paper commented that: *"It is critical to consider the wider social and developmental impacts of interventions on children – looking at the whole child and their experience, rather than solely on direct epidemiological impacts or issues in isolation"*; and, in relation to those apparently not in school, asked *"where are these children? What are they doing? How are they being supported, and importantly, safeguarded?".*[405]

That paper went on to detail the many harms that would be inflicted on children by school closures, including impacts on mental health, physical health, inequalities, and social and emotional development; it also warned that *"These will likely worsen the longer that schools remain closed, and the country is subjected to lockdown"*.[406]

Parliamentarians were alarmed

The fact that only around 5% of the most vulnerable children were in school was picked up by the BBC on the morning of that first ESC hearing of 22 April, in a report headed *'Tiny fraction of 'at risk' children attending schools'*.[407] In the hearing, Tom Hunt MP, a member of the ESC, expressed his concern: *"Did the Government ever consider going further than keeping the option open for vulnerable children to go to school and making it a requirement that they must go to school? It greatly concerns me that the number of vulnerable children who had been expected to go to school so far is below what was anticipated"*.[408]

Vicky Ford MP responded: *"Tom, first there is a really important Government message—stay home, protect the NHS, save lives. ... Just because the attendance at school may be low does not mean that those children are not being safeguarded in other ways"*.

The Minister's statement appears to have overlooked that by this time most social work protections for vulnerable children had been either suspended or moved to a remote footing. Three days later, the Children's Commissioner, Anne Longfield, pointed out that, in addition, many potentially vulnerable children would not yet be known to child protection services. In a paper titled *'We're all in this together?'*, she had also cautioned that *"the loss of support networks, alongside the anxiety and financial pressures caused by Covid-19"*, was likely to push certain families to crisis point and identified categories of children that were likely to be at most risk.[409]

Comments from the Department for Education's Chief Scientific Adviser, Osama Rahman, to a Science and Technology Select Committee hearing a few weeks later on 13 May 2020 indicated that SAGE had not regarded children's health and welfare as being a scientific matter to be weighed against the objective of reducing the rate of transmission:

> *Chair: In terms of the impact on the welfare, wellbeing and, quite possibly, the health of children, is there anyone in the Department for Education making that assessment and contributing to the discussions in SAGE?*
>
> *Osama Rahman: The meetings of SAGE I have attended have focused on the science around things like the transmission of the disease and susceptibility to catching it. … I think that what you are asking is a broader question about the sort of evidence, evaluation and assessment you would want to have in any policy. It seems to me that is not necessarily a science or SAGE question. I understand why you say that is a departmental question.* [410]

As we now know from evidence submitted to the official Covid Inquiry, and from other sources, SAGE had become focussed narrowly on measures for reducing transmission, and 'protecting the NHS', while the Ministers and officials whose role was to protect and advocate for schooling and for the safeguarding of children believed that decisions affecting children and their schooling would be – indeed should be – determined by the best scientific minds; in other words, by SAGE.

Vicky Ford MP, the Children's Minister, made clear her narrow reliance on scientific advice when appearing before the Education Select Committee on 22 April 2020: *"The re-opening will only happen when we have the scientific advice that it is safe to do so"*.[411]

A GRIEVOUS POLICY CHOICE: SCHOOL CLOSURES

The following month Nick Gibb MP, the Schools Minister, explained to the same committee: *"We are very much led by the science … so we will wait to see how the transmission rate falls further, and whether it falls further, and the advice of SAGE. We are totally led by the science. … Unless the science indicates that it is safe and wise to [reopen schools], it will not happen".*[412]

Tragic consequences soon followed

Not long after those Select Committee hearings, on 17 June 2020, Arthur Labinjo-Hughes, a vulnerable child aged six, was murdered by his parents who had kept him out of school and had evaded the interest of the local child protection service. In the aftermath of the Labinjo-Hughes case, Anne Longfield told *The Guardian* newspaper that Arthur's vulnerability had been exacerbated by lockdown, saying that *"a lot of the services went on to the screens for children, and this child in particular, Arthur, wasn't in school. And it's much easier for families who want to evade view to do that when they haven't got someone in the room".*[413]

Although the Labinjo-Hughes case was the most prominently reported, between April and September 2020 there were 285 reports of child deaths and incidents of serious harm in England alone, representing a year-on-year rise of more than 25%.[414]

Special needs were neglected

The families of children with special educational needs and disabilities (SEND) became the subject of the Education Select Committee's focus at a hearing held on 1 July 2020.[415] By means of the Coronavirus Act 2020, the Government had temporarily amended[416] the local authority statutory duties owed to SEND children from an absolute duty to deliver against special educational and healthcare plans to a duty to use 'reasonable endeavours':

Chair: Thank you. May I open the session by asking: have children with special educational needs been forgotten or left behind more than other children during the coronavirus pandemic that we have had to endure?

Amanda Batten (Chair, Disabled Children's Partnership): At the Disabled Children's Partnership we surveyed over 4,000 families with disabled children during May to get their experiences of lockdown, and, Chair, you are absolutely right. That was the predominant finding, that families feel very much forgotten. Overall, the picture from the survey was one of exhaustion and stress, so a lot of families are not only home schooling, they are also home-nursing, administering therapies, some doing 24/7 care, generally with very little support. We are seeing the impact of that on children with SEND. Some 45% of parents said that their child's physical health had deteriorated, and just over 70% said their child's emotional or mental health was worse. [...]

Chair: What I want to crucially know is: have they been forgotten in terms of support? Everyone seems to be talking about children in general but there has not been a lot of talk about children with special educational needs during the coronavirus.

Philippa Stobbs (Vice-Chair, Special Education Consortium): I do not think they have been forgotten. The problem is the waiving of the main duty, the section 42 duty to make the provision in a plan. The waiving of that duty and the reasonable endeavours duty has been interpreted so variably locally. There is some stunning provision that has been made for some children and families in some areas. The difficulty is that in other areas parents have had no contact with either their child's school or their local authority about what is going to be provided for them through that reasonable endeavours duty. The impact of that, as families testify, is absolutely devastating. The pre-existing inequalities in the system have been exacerbated because so little has been done in some places for children who are already experiencing difficulties in their education.[417]

Some six weeks later, Olga Freeman murdered her disabled son Dylan while at her *"wits' end"* during the prolonged lockdown.[418] Dylan had required round-the-clock care and had attended a special school five days a week until schools were closed. The trial judge remarked: *"I have no doubt at all that you were a remarkably loving and dedicated mother to a vulnerable child until multiple pressures overwhelmed you and your mind was swamped by a destructive illness with florid psychotic elements"*. Generously attributing school closures to the virus rather than to policy decisions, the judge added: *"To some unknowable extent, it should be recognised that Dylan was an indirect victim of interruption to normal life caused by the Covid-19 pandemic"*.

A summer of political chaos

On 1 June 2020, schools across England began to reopen, initially just for two of the primary school year groups, but it was not until the start of the next full term in September 2020 that schools fully reopened.

During the intervening summer period, there were chaotic scenes as the Department for Education tried and failed to grip the red-hot topic of cancelled exams and substitute grading systems, a fiasco which led to the eventual resignation of both the Chief Executive of the exam regulator, Ofqual, and the Permanent Secretary at the Department for Education.

An Institute for Government report published the following year heavily criticised the missed opportunity for Ministers to use that summer period to make better preparations for likely winter disruption: *"The government's failure – indeed refusal – to make contingency plans for schools and exams in the summer of 2020 is the most unforgivable aspect of its handling of education during the coronavirus pandemic"*. An unnamed Downing Street official was quoted as having said there had been a *"clear steer"* from the Prime Minister not to make contingency plans that summer because *"if you prepare for these things not happening, then the outcome is that they are far more likely not to happen… people will look for the easy way out and take it"*.[419]

School reopenings were hobbled by the testing regime

The eventual reopening of schools in September, announced in July, was made conditional on a Covid testing regime that was not yet in place, and a system of bubbles, in which children would be confined to learn and play in small groups. When it came to implementation the plan proved complicated.[420]

"It will be immediately apparent to anyone reading this guidance that it is enormously challenging to implement," said Geoff Barton, the general secretary of the ASCL, the headteachers union, adding that the logistics were *"mind-boggling"*. Kevin Courtney, the joint general secretary of the NEU, a teachers' union, said the guidance amounted to *"rushed-through ideas"* based *"more on hope than on science"*.[421]

When children then returned to school in September, the testing system quickly came under strain and just one week into the new term the idea of part-time schooling was being considered.[422] Disruption was then further escalated as bubbles of children, in some cases whole year groups, were being sent home from school when just one pupil tested positive for Covid.[423] This is despite COBRA being briefed in October that primary schools appeared to have less of an impact on transmission.[424] As the chaos proliferated, school attendance plummeted.

Standards collapsed, harms proliferated

At the end of October 2020 a report by The London School of Economics Centre for Economic Performance had revealed that only 6 out of 10 school children were receiving a full education,[425] and a major report in November from Ofsted, the Government's schools and social care inspectorate, lamented that many children had regressed in their basic skills during lockdown and school closures.

Amanda Spielman, Ofsted's chief inspector of schools commented shortly after that *"The big picture for me here is ... quite how much children lose when they don't have school. Obviously first and foremost it is around the education they are missing but so much also around personal developments and the physical fitness which of course flows through into mental health but physical health matters as well".*[426]

Ofsted's conclusions echoed comments in a joint briefing paper from the SPi-B sub-group of SAGE and the Department for Education, dated 4 November. That paper recorded a litany of harms flowing from the closure of schools including negative impacts on educational outcomes, inequalities and attainment; loss of opportunity to identify emerging learning problems; impairments to mental health, and for adolescents in particular; cognitive, social, and emotional developmental outcomes at risk; physical health at risk; psychological inequalities; increased exposure to the internet, including harmful online content; missing of routine childhood vaccinations; increased isolation and loneliness exacerbating mental health issues; reduced access to essential services for vulnerable children, with the most vulnerable being the most negatively affected; missed opportunities for detecting early signs of abuse and neglect; and loss of access to free school meals and knock-on nutritional effects. *"[M]any more young people will die from suicide than Covid-19 this year"*, the paper noted.[427]

It also advised that such limited international evidence as had been collected was suggesting that remote learning for anything more than a very short period of time was *"likely to result in poorer educational outcomes"*.[428]

Senior officials knew the risks, and limited benefits, of closing schools

That briefing paper was distributed to SAGE members for a meeting on 4 November at which at least six of the Government's most senior scientific advisers are recorded as having been present, and at least ten senior officials from the Department for Education, the Cabinet Office, the Home Office and other government departments.[429] The National Statistician was tasked at that meeting with leading a working group to assess data on transmission in children and schools so that SAGE could consider that new evidence within 3 to 4 weeks.

In Parliament, on 2 November 2020, the Prime Minister had told MPs *"We have … a moral duty to keep schools open now that it is safe to do so, because we must not let this virus damage our children's futures … and I am pleased that that will command support across the House"*.[430] Keir Starmer MP, Leader of the Opposition, had responded that *"We all agree that schools should be kept open"*.[431]

Soon after, as schools were forced to lean heavily on remote learning to maintain even basic levels of educational provision, a second Ofsted report published in December 2020 laid bare what almost every parent already knew: remote learning had proven to be no substitute for learning in school, and repeat exclusions from school, often as a result of a single child testing positive for Covid in a bubble or year group, had already wrought a huge attainment cost on their children. Amanda Spielman estimated that in educational terms by that point most children were six months behind where they needed to be.[432]

A heavily disrupted winter term ended soon after with Sadiq Khan, the Mayor of London, and head teachers calling for schools with high infection rates to go fully online for the final two weeks of term. Gavin Williamson resorted to threatening legal action to prevent London boroughs and schools from turning their pupils away.[433]

A fraught Christmas break followed, during which Wiliamson repeatedly insisted there was *"no plan to close schools"*,[434] while battling growing resistance to the opening of schools from school leaders who were warning that the mass testing-edifice, around which the possibility of keeping schools open had been constructed, was *"undeliverable"*.[435]

During this period, SAGE was refining its understanding of the role that children and schools had played in transmission, having commissioned further work on that topic at its meeting on 4 November 2020. By 10 December 2020, that further work had confirmed that:

> *"Emerging SIS [School Infection Survey] data and further ONS analysis continue to support the statement from SAGE 65 [the meeting of 4 November] that 'ONS data from 2 September to 16 October show no difference in the positivity rates of pre-school, primary and secondary school teachers and staff, relative to other workers of a similar age (medium confidence)'"*.[436]

In other words, transmission taking place in educational settings appeared to be no greater than transmission taking place in other settings. As Professor Mark Woolhouse subsequently told the Covid Inquiry, the November lockdown proved that schools were not a driver of transmission as schools remained open and cases fell in society and in classrooms.[437]

Schools were anyway closed again

On 1 January 2021, Gavin Williamson announced that primary schools in London would need to close until at least 18 January. According to the transcript of an Education Select Committee hearing held two weeks later, the Department for Education had sent a letter to the Chair of that committee (among others) on 2 January 2021 which referenced a London School of Hygiene and Tropical Medicine report which had said: *"School closure would have only a minor and temporary effect on transmission rates, and the wider impact of this on children's social, physical, educational and emotional development would be significant"*.[438]

On 4 January 2021, just hours after he had told parents across the country that it was safe to send children back to the classroom and with Gavin Williamson apparently facing *"a battle against the teaching unions"* and local councils to keep schools open, the Prime Minister announced the closure of all schools until at least 22 February:[439]

> *"Parents whose children were in school today may reasonably ask why we did not take this decision sooner. The answer is simply that we have been doing everything in our power to keep schools open, because we know how important each day in education is to children's life chances. And I want to stress that the problem is not that schools are unsafe for children – children are still very unlikely to be severely affected by even the new variant of Covid. The problem is that schools may nonetheless act as vectors for transmission, causing the virus to spread between households"*.[440]

At the same time, the Prime Minister announced that exams would be cancelled for a second year in a row. The general secretary of the ASCL headteachers union, Geoff Barton, was quoted on the same day as saying that headteachers were *"relieved the government has finally bowed to the inevitable and agreed to move schools and colleges* to remote education in response to alarming Covid infection rates"; and Patrick Roach, the leader of another teachers union, was quoted as saying that it was right for the PM to respond to unions' calls for nationwide remote learning.[441]

A fortnight later, on 13 January 2021, as Parliament resumed and Gavin Williamson appeared before the Education Select Committee,[442] Robert Halfon MP, referring to the DfE's 2 January letter noted, *"That was sent out to us on 2 January, based on, as I understand it, looking at the new variant of Covid. What changed in a few days that school closures would suddenly have a dramatic effect on transmission, whereas on 2 January the PHE advice was that it had a marginal effect?"*

Williamson's reply – *"it became clear as a result of that further data that was coming in that it ... would play a role in suppressing movement within the communities where schools are…"* – appeared not to cut it. *"It was only two days later that this evidence changed"*, replied Halfon incredulously.

Reporting by *The Telegraph* has subsequently revealed a broader context to that change in position, and possibly a reason why Gavin Williamson had found it hard to articulate a clear reason for the abrupt u-turn of 4 January: *"Despite ministers including Matt Hancock saying that they were doing all they could to keep schools open, behind the scenes the then health secretary [Hancock] was running a "rearguard action" to keep pupils at home. WhatsApp messages reveal that while he was offering to help Sir Gavin [Williamson] to his face, behind his back Mr Hancock and his advisers were mocking him ...".*[443]

Evidence of serious harms continued to accumulate

On 19 January 2021 the Education Select Committee met again, with witnesses including Dr Jenny Harries (Deputy Chief Medical Officer for England at the Department for Health and Social Care), Professor Russell Viner (President at the Royal College of

Paediatrics and Child Health), Osama Rahman (Chief Scientific Adviser at the Department for Education), and Dr Dougal Hargreaves (Deputy Chief Scientific Adviser at the Department for Education).[444]

With evidence accumulating about the harmful effects of school closures on children, the Chair of the Committee had asked the Department for Education, *"when you are making decisions about school closures, what risk assessment do you do in the Department for Education as to whether or not the closure to deal with the virus makes the risk even worse for children and young people in mental health, education attainment and so on?"*. Dr Hargreaves explained that while the educational and mental health impacts on children were *"absolutely on the agenda at the Department for Education ... our team is small and a lot of our focus has been on ... transmission questions. We have heavily relied on working in partnership with outside bodies—RCPCH is a very important partner and there is a number of other important partners— understanding what is going on with children and young people's mental health and how we can best tackle that"*.[445]

He sought to reassure the Select Committee that *"it is very much on the agenda that over the next six months we are looking up to build up a more comprehensive database"*; the Chair did not appear to be reassured: *"shouldn't this be done when the decision is made to close schools?"*, Halfon replied.

Professor Viner, the President of the DfE's *"very important partner"* on whose advice the Department had *"heavily relied"* – the Royal College of Paediatrics and Child Health – then left the Select Committee with little room for doubt about the extent of accruing harm: *"I am aware of about 75 reasonable quality international publications on the harms to children and young people from the first wave of the pandemic. We have around 25 academic publications from the UK and there is 50 from elsewhere and they tell a very consistent story. It is*

A GRIEVOUS POLICY CHOICE: SCHOOL CLOSURES

a story of considerable mental health harms". Professor Viner added: *"When we close schools we close [children's] lives, not to benefit them but to benefit the rest of society. They reap harm when we close schools".*[446]

Eight days later, on 27 January 2021, the Prime Minister extended the period of school closures for a further two and a half weeks, until 8th March 2023.[447]

A meeting of SAGE took place on the following day – 28 January – at which there was a discussion of the role of school closures in reducing transmission, the minutes for which record that *"The extent of the impact on transmission and the role played by transmission within schools versus transmission in the wider community associated with schools being opened remains uncertain and difficult to quantify".* That discussion concluded with a strong and unambiguous warning of harms for children:

> *"<u>There is still clear evidence of the negative educational impact</u> of missing school as well as evidence that school closures cause impairment to the physical and mental health of children. One systematic review concluded that school closures as part of broader social distancing measures are associated <u>with considerable harms</u> to children and young people's health and wellbeing including emotional, behavioural and restlessness / inattention problems and overall psychological wellbeing. Certain studies included in the review reported suggestions <u>of greater impact in the poorest children and widening of inequalities</u>",* (emphasis added).[448]

Chaotic scenes for the remainder of the school year

In the period following that second lengthy blanket closure of schools, children's education was subject to further sustained disruption as a result of the Covid testing strategy to which school

143

access had been tied. At one point near the end of the summer term in 2021 some one million children in state school education alone – over 14% of the country's school age population – were stranded at home after being forced to self-isolate.[449] Just 5% of those children were confirmed as having the virus.

That immediate crisis came to a head when 48 MPs expressed objections to the Prime Minister in a letter on 30 June 2021,[450] though it was only from 16 August 2021 (at least three weeks after the school year had finished for most children) that children under 18 years of age would cease to be required to self-isolate if they were identified as a close contact of a positive Covid-19 case.[451]

When the Hancock WhatsApp messages were later revealed, it became apparent that Matt Hancock had known from as early as November 2020 that self-isolation could safely have been reduced from 10 days to 5 days, but chose not to allow that policy change because he believed it could have given the impression that Ministers had made a mistake.[452]

ANALYSIS

Policy decisions not Covid closed schools

The repeated exclusion of healthy children from schooling and extensive school closures between March 2020 and the end of 2021 was a consequence of policy choices made in the face of clear advice and evidence of the disproportionate and long-lasting harms that would follow. It was well known and documented from the early stages of the pandemic that excluding healthy children from educational settings would be especially damaging for those children who were already deprived, and for the most vulnerable children.

That early advice and evidence has been born out, and we know that in particular the safeguarding harms suffered by some children as an indirect consequence of school closures were great, up to and including death. Decisions were made which knowingly compromised the health of children, almost all of whom are exposed to minimal risk of serious harm from the virus itself,[453] in order to protect the health of those most at risk: the elderly and vulnerable people with comorbidities.

It has been said that the Government faced a difficult task in balancing the life expectancy of 80 year olds with the life chances of 8 year olds;[454] put simply, it made a series of policy choices that prioritised the former and under-recognised the ethical and safeguarding duties owed to the latter. Indeed this has now been confirmed by a study led by academics at University College London: *"As young people weren't considered to be at high risk from Covid-19 directly, pandemic policy decisions largely ignored their needs and resulted in their long-term detriment"*.[455]

The chimaera of reducing transmission

From the outset mass school closures were not meant to be on the agenda. As early as February 2020, SAGE recognised that even leaving aside the direct harmful impacts on children of exclusion from school settings, the practical consequences of closing schools – particularly for working families – could even exacerbate transmission rates. SAGE consistently recognised, right up until the moment that schools were in fact closed, that the mass closure of schools would have, at best, an uncertain and limited impact on transmission.

Despite data evidencing that transmission rates in school on the whole reflected transmission rates in the community,[456] the reduction of those rates within school settings appears to have remained a key performance indicator for some Ministers and officials throughout the pandemic period.

Consequently key decisions around schools and access to education too often appear to have failed to have taken into account, or at least to have weighed insufficiently, the already-known harms (not to mention the possibility of yet-to-be-discovered harms) for children.

Decisions made in full knowledge of harm

The extensive harms accruing to children from prolonged absences from school, including deprivation of social interaction, physical activity and pastoral care, and increased screen time, have been overwhelmingly established and documented. As we show in this chapter, they were warned to policy-makers on numerous separate occasions. Sadly, they have been proved right. Across the cohort of school-age children, physical well-being has deteriorated,[457] mental health illness has soared,[458] educational attainment has regressed.[459]

Vulnerable and disadvantaged children have fallen even further behind, and an array of negative social impacts continues to emerge. At the extremes, some of the vulnerable children who fell out of the education system are known to have been recruited into criminal organisations including county lines drug-dealing gangs;[460] school attendance has been socially devalued such that one in five children are persistently absent from school;[461] and according to a Centre for Social Justice report published in January 2022, nationwide close to 800 schools had an entire class-worth of children permanently absent.[462] Perhaps most tragically, serious incident notifications from local authorities – reporting serious harm or death involving a child – rose by 20% during the pandemic.[463]

The many examples of the advice and warnings provided to the Government which we have documented in this chapter are just a portion of the substantial body of advice and evidence that was produced, primarily for consumption by Ministers and officials. It is almost indisputable at this stage, therefore, that key decision-makers had unambiguous notice of the serious near-term and longer-lasting harms that they were inflicting on children.

For a period of close to two years, flags were raised repeatedly before, during and between the periods of school closures, including by the Education Select Committee, by the Royal College of Paediatrics and Child Health, by MPs, by medical experts, by campaigning organisations (including UsForThem), and by the Children's Commissioner – the individual appointed by the Government to advocate for and advise on the safeguarding of England's 9.1million[464] school-aged children. But these flags were ignored.

Promises left blowing in the wind

When these key decisions were taken, they were often justified on the basis that mitigating strategies that would significantly reduce harmful impacts either already existed or would promptly be devised. Yet all too often those strategies were ineffectual, incapable of delivery or simply never materialised:

- As we recorded earlier in this chapter, when schools were first closed in March 2020, the Government promised that remote learning would be both logistically achievable and a suitable substitute for the lost learning time in school. Yet there was no obligation for schools to provide remote learning facilities until 22 October 2020,[465] and consequently many parents received only simple paper handouts explaining topics that could be taught at home.

- From the earliest days of mass school closures, Ministers gave assurances that the damage knowingly inflicted on children's education would be substantially mitigated by a comprehensive support package for educational catch-up. Gavin Williamson, announcing the catch-up programme in June 2020, had said *"We cannot afford for any of our children to lose out as a result of Covid-19. The scale of our response must match the scale of the challenge"*,[466] followed by the Prime Minister who spoke about a *"massive catch-up operation"*.[467]

The plan that was eventually adopted[468] fell so far short of the support deemed necessary by Sir Kevan Collins, the 'catch up Tsar' appointed to devise the package, that it prompted his immediate resignation:[469] *"It is too narrow, too small and will be delivered too slowly,"* he said, adding that the average primary school would receive additional direct support of just £6,000 a year, equivalent to £22 per child. *"The support announced by government so far does not come close to meeting the scale of the challenge and is why I have no option but to resign from my post"*.[470]

The inadequacy of that catch-up package has since been affirmed by a long line of school leaders and by the Education Select Committee.[471]

- And school openings in January 2021 were made conditional on a testing regime which, even leaving aside the ethical concerns of mandatory mass testing of children,[472] had been branded impossible to deliver by all of the people and organisations that would be tasked with delivering it.[473]

An August 2021 Institute for Government report gave a withering assessment of the readiness of Ministers to make promises that were not then kept:

"Throughout 2020, not just the prime minister but education ministers and in particular Gavin Williamson, the education

secretary, seemed determined to appear to be in control of events that they could not in fact control. There were repeated assertions that this or that would happen – that test kits would be available in schools in September, for example, or that schools absolutely would reopen in January 2021, or that exams would definitely be held in 2021 – up to the point where they did not happen, forcing last-minute U-turns".[474]

A prolonged experiment

Covid discriminates against the elderly and the clinically vulnerable, and almost continuously through the pandemic the Government and its experts could not help from being aware that almost all children were at negligible risk of suffering serious harm from the virus – official Covid mortality and morbidity statistics both nationally and globally have consistently evidenced that understanding.[475] Consequently, almost by definition, any virus control measures directed at children have thus been measures for the benefit and protection of others; children's health and well-being were sacrificed for the sake primarily of older adults and the clinically vulnerable.

As Dr Alberto Giubilini of the Oxford University Uehiro Centre for Practical Ethics has explained: *"So the idea is that you could put some burden on children to protect older people and this was not necessarily wrong in itself, but there is an issue around proportionality. Is it proportionate to put a burden onto young people in the form of school closure for the sake of older people? There was not enough consideration about the burdens we were imposing on children at this time, in terms of harms and risks for their present and future interests. The priority was to focus on COVID 19, to focus on protecting people from COVID 19, even those who didn't need that kind of protection like children, because we have made this the condition for reopening society. But it was a political decision, not a scientific one, and political decisions require a level of public scrutiny and societal negotiation that never happened.*[476]

In the early part of the pandemic, when there was greatest uncertainty about the severity and transmissibility of the virus among the population, and while safe and effective vaccines remained an aspiration, an argument might have been made that a short term sacrifice of children's social and educational needs could be ethically justified.

When it became apparent that school closures would continue beyond the initial three week period that had been announced, school closures became a prolonged experiment which socially and educationally isolated all, and especially discriminated against those children in socio-economic cohorts that were already disadvantaged.

As harms accrued, growing numbers of experts, including groups of paediatricians,[477] raised moral and ethical concerns about the alarming trajectory of that social intervention, especially given the uncertain public health benefit[478] and the fact that for periods in the UK non-essential amenities for adults – including shops, restaurants and even theme parks – were prioritised for openings ahead of schools.[479]

As the pandemic progressed, the legally-protected rights of children to receive an education,[480] became conditional on compliance with clinical measures of disputed efficacy and known harm[481] to children: no test, no school; and then no mask, no school.

While some Ministers and officials expressed a determination to mitigate the harms inflicted on children by the Government's policy decisions, as we have seen those aspirations too often fell short with even the most vulnerable children, including those with special educational needs, becoming simply items on a long governmental 'to do' list:

Vicky Ford MP speaking to the Education Select Committee: *"It was a pleasure to appear before your committee last week to discuss the Government's response to the Covid-19 crisis. I particularly welcomed the focus on vulnerable children. As I noted in the hearing, they have been identified by the Cabinet Office as one of the Government's top 15 priorities during this crisis".*[482]

The persistent failure to stand up for the most vulnerable in society by those in whose hands the protection of the rights and interests of those most vulnerable resides was nothing if not a moral and ethical failure.

A COMPASSIONATE COMMON SENSE PERSPECTIVE

In the course of researching this chapter we spoke to Dr Gavin Morgan, educational psychologist at University College London, and member of Sage sub-group SPi-B.

His recollections helped to shed light on how children came to have been so dreadfully overlooked. With his permission, we have included an extended excerpt of that interview here.

* * *

When Dr Morgan was asked to become involved with SPi-B, the decision to close schools had already been taken. He was approached, he believes, almost as an afterthought: *"Somebody somewhere had the good idea that if we're closing schools, perhaps we ought to speak with an educational psychologist"*, he told us.

Many of his comments confirmed what we had understood to have been common criticisms of SAGE and its sub-groups: taking a narrow scientific focus, with determination to present a consensus view. As the only child and educational psychologist in SPi-B, Dr Morgan recognised that he had a different approach to others: *"it wasn't necessarily how I would have done things and how I would have constructed things…there was a lot of groupthink, this idea that we need a consensus…"*.

One of the things Dr Morgan told us he had focused on was the need to identify an 'exit' from school closures. This was something that had troubled us during the period of our campaigning to get all children full time back into school: *"Where is the off-ramp?"*, one of our briefing papers to MPs had asked during the dark days of January 2021.

To Dr Morgan, the lack of any planning for how to get children back into schools at the outset was a serious error: *"If we're making a decision to close schools, before we'd even have done that we needed a strategy, a plan about how to reopen them. And that never happened"*, he said, before recounting that he had made his concerns clear at the outset of his involvement in the sub-group. At the very first meeting he had attended he had said that it was easy to close schools but *"It's gonna be far harder to reopen them. But there was no plan. No strategy. I kept saying 'where's the road map?'"*.

In Dr Morgan's view, a key issue was *"the fear campaign had been 'so successful' (in inverted commas), that parents were then too scared to think about sending their kids back"*. He was at pains to add, though, that despite the bad press that SPi-B have since had, *"at no point did SPi-B ever sit around and say 'how can we scare people?'"*.

Some months later Dr Morgan's advocacy within SPi-B contributed to keeping masks off primary school children (and delaying their introduction for secondary pupils), of which he was proud. We can only reflect on how different the outcomes for children might have been had his compassionate common sense child-centred perspective been in the room before the decision to recommend school closures was taken.

WARNINGS GIVEN. WARNINGS IGNORED.

At the start of this chapter we referenced the many occasions on which harms or the risk of harms were identified to decision-makers. Over the course of the pandemic many individual experts and organisations (UsForThem included) sounded repeated and escalating alarms about the scale of harms impacting children flowing, predominantly, from school closures. The following are all examples of warnings having been delivered by governmental bodies, Government-appointed experts and advisory groups, and Parliamentary committees. All were ignored.

1. **Pre-pandemic:** Previous pandemic plans had been predicated on the basis that mass school closures were to be avoided. Learning 14 from Operation Cygnus in 2016 had provided *"DfE should study the impact of school closures and also examine the possibility of keeping schools open by getting retired teaching staff to return to support the profession and by the temporary upskilling of students"*; but it appears this had never been followed up on. DfE did not have a plan for continuity of education, either by way of keeping schools open, or via remote learning. Indeed, in a fieldwork exercise that ended on 7 March 2020, just before the first lockdown, Ofcom had estimated that between 1.14 million and 1.78 million children under the age of 18 lived in households without access to a laptop, desktop or tablet in the UK, and that between 227,000 and 559,000 children lived in homes with no access to the internet.

2. **February to March 2020:** It was **clearly documented in SAGE papers** during these months that the impact that school closures would have on stemming transmission was likely to be highly limited, and was uncertain. This view was reconfirmed as late as 17 March 2020, **the day before the first school closures**, in a

paper in which SAGE also made clear that if schools closed, they would need to be closed for a lengthy period of time to have any impact. **This was never communicated to the public.** The same paper also noted that **the impact of closing universities was expected to be relatively small**, because university students are a relatively small proportion of the UK population.

3. **Spring 2020:** Following the first school closures, a series of safeguarding flags were raised by the Education Select Committee, SPI-M, the Children's Commissioner and children's charities, but they were not addressed.

    Vicky Ford told the ESC in April 2020 that *"We have put vulnerable children at the forefront of our thinking, right from day one. That is why we took the…important decision to make sure that [schools] would remain open for key workers' children and vulnerable children"*. The week earlier, however, an SPI-M paper, drawing on school attendance figures provided by the DfE, had revealed that *"94% of vulnerable children are not in school"*. *"This does not mean that those children are not being safeguarded in other ways"*, said Ford, apparently overlooking that by this time social work protections for vulnerable children had either been suspended outright or moved to a remote footing.

4. **Summer 2020:** Failure to contingency plan for Autumn term 2020. There was no plan for schools returning when it was inevitable there would be a winter uplift in illness. This meant that, when the new term started in September, children and staff had to navigate frequently changing guidance and rules. Schools had to focus on adapting their premises and practices to accommodate the new guidance and rules rather than on teaching and helping their pupils to catch up. Children had to spend time at home rather than in school, and had sport, music, drama and other non-academic activities repeatedly cancelled.

5. **Summer 2020 and ongoing:** The educational damage to children was obvious and evidenced from early on in the pandemic. Boris Johnson and Gavin Williamson made many promises about their commitment to providing catch-up opportunities for children, including over the Summer. Those plans were so under-resourced that the catch-up Tsar, Sir Kevan Collins, resigned. The effective failure of the catch-up programme was subsequently the subject of an Education Select Committee report.

6. **November 2020:** A major report from Ofsted lamented the harm already caused by school closures. Ofsted's conclusions echoed comments in a joint briefing paper from the SPi-B sub-group of SAGE and the Department for Education, dated 4 November, which had recorded a catalogue of harms flowing from the closure of schools (including negative impacts on educational outcomes, inequalities and attainment; loss of opportunity to identify emerging learning problems; impairments to mental health, and for adolescents in particular; cognitive, social, and emotional developmental outcomes at risk; physical health at risk; psychological inequalities; increased exposure to the internet, including harmful online content; missing of routine childhood vaccinations; increased isolation and loneliness exacerbating mental health issues; reduced access to essential services for vulnerable children, with the most vulnerable being the most negatively affected; missed opportunities for detecting early signs of abuse and neglect; and loss of access to free school meals and knock-on nutritional effects).

That briefing paper stated that *"many more children would die from suicide than Covid-19 this year"*. It also made clear that transmission in schools was likely to mimic community transmission, and the evidence that schools were drivers was very mixed. Teachers were considered to be at no more risk than any other professionals. That SAGE meeting was attended by **at least six of the Government's most senior scientific advisers**, and at least ten senior officials from the Department for Education, the Cabinet Office, the Home Office and other government departments.

7. **December 2020:** SAGE refined its understanding of the role that children and schools had played in transmission, having commissioned further work on that topic at its meeting of 4 November. By 10 December, that further work had confirmed that: *"Emerging SIS [School Infection Survey] data and further ONS analysis continue to support the statement from SAGE 65 [the meeting of 4 November] that 'ONS data from 2 September to 16 October show no difference in the positivity rates of pre-school, primary and secondary school teachers and staff, relative to other workers of a similar age (medium confidence)'"*. In other words, **transmission taking place in educational settings appeared to be no greater than transmission taking place in other settings**.

8. **January 2021:** according to Education Select Committee records, the DfE sent a letter to the Chair of that committee (among others) on 2 January 2021 referencing a London School of Hygiene and Tropical Medicine report which had stated: *"School closure would have only a minor and temporary effect on transmission rates, and the wider impact of this on children's social, physical, educational and emotional development would be significant"*. On 4 January 2021, hours after he had told parents across the country that it was safe to send children back to the classroom, the Prime Minister announced the second period of prolonged school closures.

9. **January 2021:** with evidence of mounting harms flowing from school closures, Dr Hargreaves, the Deputy Chief Scientific Adviser at DfE, reported to the Education Select Committee

that *"it is very much on the agenda that over the next six months we are looking up to build up a more comprehensive database"* [of harms]. The Chair replied *"shouldn't this be done when the decision is made to close the Schools?"*. At the same hearing Professor Viner, the President of the Royal College of Paediatrics and Child Health left the Select Committee in no doubt about the extent of accruing harm: *"I am aware of about 75 reasonable quality international publications on the harms to children and young people from the first wave of the pandemic. We have around 25 academic publications from the UK and there is 50 from elsewhere and they tell a very consistent story. It is a story of considerable mental health harms"*. Professor Viner added: *"When we close schools we close [children's] lives, not to benefit them but to benefit the rest of society. They reap harm when we close schools"*.

PART 3

TAKING STOCK

Across the previous chapters we have sought to bring to life some of the most acute governmental failures of the pandemic period. At their best, these have involved errors in decision-making processes that will resonate far beyond the pandemic. At worst, they may have involved the evasion or subversion of good governance, government for the public good, and ethical safeguards.

At least some of the most severe aspects of the catastrophe of our pandemic response might have been avoided had it not been for the failure, or circumvention, of a series of checks and balances designed to ensure balanced and ethical public decision-making, free from improper bias and influence.

That is the focus of our next few chapters.

AN UNFETTERED EXECUTIVE

"Of all tyrannies, a tyranny sincerely exercised for the good of its victims may be the most oppressive. It would be better to live under robber barons than under omnipotent moral busybodies. The robber baron's cruelty may sometimes sleep, his cupidity may at some point be satiated; but those who torment us for our own good will torment us without end for they do so with the approval of their own conscience."

C. S. Lewis, Essays on Theology

GOVERNANCE ABANDONED

How the Government should operate

Ministers are empowered individually to make decisions within their areas of competence, taking advice from subject matter experts within their departments and, where relevant, external experts. Senior civil servants report to their departmental Ministers. Junior Ministers report into their senior departmental Ministers; and those senior Ministers report into the Prime Minister.

Ministerial activity – indeed all of the activity of the Government – is conducted under the oversight of the most senior governance body in Government: the Cabinet. In this sense, the Cabinet is to the Government what the parent company board of directors is to a corporate group. On matters of greater significance decisions may be made by the Cabinet rather than by individual Ministers. By long-standing constitutional convention, members of the Cabinet take collective responsibility for decisions made by the Cabinet.

Ultimately all Ministers, including the Prime Minister, are held accountable by Parliament for the decisions and actions of their departments and of the Government as a whole. This system of governance and Parliamentary accountability forms the bedrock of our representative form of democracy.

Governance is a broad umbrella under which an array of checks and balances are designed to provide structure and rigour to decision-making, and provide clear lines of reporting and accountability. Good governance is a safeguard against capricious, misguided, biassed and, simply, poor decision-making. Alongside decision-making processes and procedures, there are high level standards of conduct which decision-makers are expected to observe in their management activities. In the public sector, the unifying principles to which all public servants are subject are known as the Seven Principles of Public Life, or sometimes by their original name – the Nolan Principles. The seven principles are: Selflessness, Integrity, Objectivity, Accountability, Openness, Honesty and Leadership.

The Cabinet Office and HM Treasury have issued a Code of Good Practice for good governance in central government, the introduction to which recognises the role of governance in the business of government: *"Good corporate governance is fundamental to any effective and well-managed organisation – be it private or public sector – and is the hallmark of any corporate entity that is run accountably and with the long-term interest clearly in mind. Ensuring that central government departments are run as efficiently and effectively as possible is central to this goal"*.[483]

How our Government operated during the pandemic

Matt Hancock: What are we trying to achieve in this meeting?

Michael Gove: Letting people express concerns in a therapeutic environment before you and I decide the policy

Matt Hancock: You are glorious [484]

Those three short lines are indicative of so much that went wrong with our pandemic response, revealing contempt for the role of governance and process; an arrogance that the expertise and perspectives of others are inconsequential; a streak of deception in the charade of listening; and a complacency in the casual acceptance of these plainly unacceptable traits among fellow ministers.

Our earlier chapters host many other comparable instances of Ministers and officials falling short of the standards of public life to which they were subscribed. Examples include:

- when Matt Hancock announced the outcome of the Government's June 2021 consultation on the care home workers vaccination requirement, the responses to which had substantially rejected the proposal, saying *"Through our consultation we have listened to the experiences and concerns of providers and people living and working in care homes to help shape our approach"* before apparently ignoring what he had heard and pushing ahead as originally planned;

- when a month later, the Government gave MPs just 90 minutes to debate the legal measure to effect the care home workers mandate, which *"fundamentally change[d] the balance of human rights in this country"*, and was decried by the Chair of the Public Administration and Constitutional Affairs Committee as *"nothing short of a disgrace"*;[485]

- when in December 2021, following the CMOs controversially recommending the vaccine for school-aged children, officials at the Department for Education published an advertisement and accompanying tweet which said *"Vaccines give your children the best possible protection against the virus, and helps keep them in school"*, making no reference to natural immunity, to risk or to possible side effects,[486] and after Chris Whitty had specifically emphasised the necessity of informed consent, including the need for clear explanation of *"potential benefits, potential side effects and the balance between them"*.[487]

- when, in August 2020, the Education Secretary announced that his department was changing its advice on masks in schools, relying on the WHO having changed its advice as the justification.[488] However, Matt Hancock's subsequent revelations that the decision was driven by reaction to Nicola Sturgeon's decision to introduce them in Scotland (*"cue much-tortured debate between myself, education secretary Gavin Williamson and No 10 about how to respond. Much as Sturgeon would relish it, nobody here wants a big spat with the Scots"*)[489] show this to have been a political decision;

- when, in December 2020, Matt Hancock asked an aide *"When do we deploy the new variant"* to *"frighten the pants off everyone with the new strain"*.[490] This marked such a grossly unethical deviation from established principles of public communication that it prompted MPs to launch an investigation into the use of scare tactics.[491]

Policy-making hijacked by extraneous factors

It is evident from the rich insights of the Matt Hancock WhatsApp disclosures that some of the most controversial and damaging pandemic decisions were made not on the basis of objective, data-driven considerations but for reasons of political expediency, rivalry, personal favour or ambition, and to attract media and public credit.

Spontaneous decision-making taking place outside of formalised governance processes lacked the discipline, rigour and integrity of fully reasoned and tested decisions, particularly as regards the weighing of costs and benefits, and the evaluation of core assumptions and evidential justifications.

From what we have been able to see from even the limited window to which we have had access, the extent and frequency of departures from the core values of public life enshrined in the Nolan Principles has astonished us.

Consequential decisions were taken outside formal governance, and with no paper trail

An important report produced in March 2021 by the Public Administration and Constitutional Affairs Committee (PACAC) of the House of Commons[492] found that the governance arrangements for decision-making during the pandemic were, from the very earliest stages, far from clear.

The Government had initially established four pandemic decision-making groups in April 2020 (covering healthcare; general public sector; economic and business; and international issues) only then to replace them by September with two Cabinet Committees (the Covid 19 Strategy Committee; and the Covid 19 Operations (Covid-O) Committee).

Operating alongside these Cabinet Committees was an unofficial sub-group, or 'quad', of influential Ministers (the Prime Minister, the Chancellor, the Health Secretary and the most senior non-departmental Cabinet Minister (Michael Gove)) aided by a small number of senior advisers (including the Prime Minister's adviser, Dominic Cummings). That Quad had made many of the most significant decisions among themselves apparently outside of, or at least as the quoted exchange above demonstrates, with pre-emptive disregard for, the formality of Cabinet governance structures. The role of that Quad of Ministers was described in the Constitutional Affairs Committee report, generously, as *"unclear"*.

No records of the meetings or deliberations of the Quad of Ministers have been published, presumably because it was not in fact a formal decision-making body. Similarly any minutes taken of the meetings of the key Cabinet Committees have not been made publicly available either. Consequently it is remarkably difficult for anyone not involved in those discussions to understand how decisions – many of era-defining significance – were made.

That same PACAC report commented that:

> *"Press reports of a 'quad' of Ministers making decisions in April raise questions of a parallel governance structure in addition to the formal Cabinet Committee structure. Such parallel systems risk creating silos where decisions are made without the full and proper discussion, advice or consultation that would be expected in Cabinet Committees".*[493]

In a March 2023 interview with *The Telegraph*, Jacob Rees-Mogg, a Cabinet Minister during the pandemic, has described how data and other information pertinent to critical decisions made by the Government were not shared with the Cabinet, and instead Cabinet Ministers were given pre-Cabinet briefings in which they were, in effect, told what had been decided by the Quad of Ministers.[494]

Yet it appears that even the integrity of the Quad as a ministerial decision-making body was undercut by a proliferation of informal chat groups in which opinions, concerns, questions and relevant information were exchanged among inconsistent but overlapping memberships. Notably, and surprisingly given the immense public spending implications of so many of the Government's pandemic policy choices, the Chancellor at the time, Rishi Sunak, and his senior Treasury officials appear not to have been included in the three most active WhatsApp groups.[495]

Indeed the use of WhatsApp groups was one of the key early controversies of the Covid Inquiry, and representative of the flawed governance around pandemic policy-making. That the Cabinet Office felt it necessary to take legal proceedings to resist disclosure to a public inquiry led by an Appeal Court judge of informal ministerial communications on the basis that they could also contain irrelevant or personal information is a matter of constitutional concern. At the time of writing other key Ministers are still refusing to hand over caches of their WhatsApp messages.[496]

For our representative democratic model of government to remain democratic, other than in name only, the business and decisions of the Government, however recorded, must always remain amenable to scrutiny – and thus accountability. Instant messaging by Whatsapp may have supported an immediacy in decision-making that formal memoranda, presentations and minuted meetings could not match, but it equally meant that substantive decisions and the evidence base for them could not easily be tracked, tested, or audited after the fact, nor (as noted above in relation to the Chancellor's apparent exclusion from key chat groups) that all relevant people could be assured of being involved at key moments.[497]

By way of comparison, juxtaposing the apparently informal and undocumented decision-making processes of senior Ministers against decision-making in private sector organisations, every UK company is legally obliged to create records of all matters discussed at meetings of its directors and to maintain those records for at least 10 years; failure to do so is an offence for which each director of the company is liable.[498]

Poor governance and opacity limited the ability to challenge the basis of decisions...

Decisions taken in closed WhatsApp groups eroded the possibility of scrutiny and timely challenge – both at the time from Cabinet colleagues and MPs and later by Select Committees.

The guiding principle, as set out by the Public Administration and Constitutional Affairs Committee (PACAC), should have been that, *"Clear accountability for decision making is absolutely integral to our democracy and the system should be quite simple: Departments and their Permanent Secretaries are responsible for advising the Government, and Ministers are accountable to Parliament for decisions based on that advice"*.[499]

A vivid account of the reality of scrutinising decisions taken within the opaque framework of Covid sub-committees and WhatsApp side-chats is found in a series of excoriating exchanges recorded in reports of PACAC hearings:

> *"... this Committee has struggled to establish who the Government sees as accountable for the data underpinning decisions on Covid 19... [An earlier] report concluded that governance arrangements have not been clear and this remains so"*.[500]

Explaining the role of Michael Gove, Chancellor of the Duchy of Lancaster, as Chair of the key operational committee, Covid-O, the PACAC records continued:

> "Michael Gove is accountable to Parliament for cross-government coordination of the response to Covid 19 and for ensuring these decisions are informed by data... Establishing accountability for decision making on Covid-19 was not an aim of this inquiry but the Committee had expected that a Minister would be able to account for the data underpinning decisions. Based on publicly available information, the Committee had expected to hold the Chancellor of the Duchy of Lancaster to account, as the responsible Minister.
>
> [...] It is not acceptable to pass responsibility for decisions between the Cabinet Office and the Department of Health and Social Care when so much is at stake. Lines of accountability must be clear and decision-making must be transparent".[501]

These comments were made in relation to the PACAC's inquiry into the data underpinning key Government decisions. Given the assumed centrality of rigorous scientific data to any government response so frequently presented as 'Following the Science', these were revealing comments and had far-reaching implications, and the particular issue identified by the Committee in this case was not an isolated occurrence.

Minutes of the meetings of SAGE, for example, the key scientific body informing the Government's policy decisions, were kept from public view at the outset of the pandemic, and were only later forced into the public domain when a judicial review of the scientific basis for the first lockdown decision was brought to the High Court.[502]

A further legal action in the High Court also then forced the Government to reveal previously withheld information about the awarding of Covid-related public procurement contracts worth £248 million which were meant to have been published within 30 days of the award of the contracts.[503]

... which allowed decision-making discipline to deteriorate further

In the absence of transparency and scrutiny, personal prejudices and competitive grievances proliferated. *The Telegraph* exposed Simon Case, who as Cabinet Secretary is the country's most senior Civil Servant, as having written that it was *"hilarious"* that in February 2021 travellers had to isolate on their return to the UK, with Matt Hancock gleefully responding that *"We are giving big families all the suites and putting pop stars in the box rooms"*.[504]

The same newspaper article reported that Case had said, this time in relation to key workers and school closures, *"the thing I want to avoid is conscientious public servants struggling to do their jobs with kids at home ... whilst commercial lawyers will just take the piss"*.[505]

We know also that, at times, personal ambition overrode sensible policy-making. Matt Hancock is revealed to have written in a WhatsApp exchange that expanding testing in care homes could *"get in the way"* of his self-declared target of processing 100,000 Covid tests per day.[506]

At times, Ministers even resorted to outright blackmail – notoriously Matt Hancock discussed a plan to block funding for a new centre for disabled children and adults as a way of pressuring a rebel Tory MP to back new lockdown restrictions, with Hancock threatening to take the plan *"off the table"* if James Daly, the Bury North MP, sided against the Government in a key vote on the introduction of tougher new local lockdown tiers for England.[507]

We are not able to explain how this behaviour could ever have complied with the Nolan Principles of selflessness, objectivity, openness, honesty and leadership.

The output of rushed informal decisions was confusing or ambiguous rules

Ministers were soon making the rules so fast, and frequently without having had to justify their decisions to colleagues let alone adversaries, that it became almost impossible for them to articulate the rules, let alone for others to follow them. Confusion proliferated as to what was guidance and was law. The Police and the Courts struggled with rushed and unspecific legislation, and as a consequence even seemingly frivolous questions had occasionally serious consequences for a few unlucky members of the public: Was a scotch egg a meal?[508] Was a stroll with a takeaway coffee a lawful walk or an unlawful picnic?[509] Was buying a book in a supermarket prohibited as an unnecessary purchase?[510]

When the Crown Prosecution Service conducted a review in May 2020 it concluded that at least 28% of charges brought in connection with alleged breaches of lockdown rules had been charged incorrectly, including 18 which had been prosecuted to the point of a conviction. Marie Dinou, who was arrested, charged, detained in cells for two nights, prosecuted, convicted and sentenced to a substantial fine for being on the platform at Newcastle railway station was a miscarriage for which the British Transport Police apologised. She was convicted under the Coronavirus Act for not providing reasons to travel – there had in fact been no such offence, nor did the police have the power to detain her unless they suspected she was potentially infectious.[511]

In further aggravation, as was later revealed and extensively dissected, Ministers and officials serially ignored or broke the rules they were imposing on the rest of the country: Matt Hancock's socialising with his aide, Gina Colangelo; Dominic Cummings' trip to Barnard Castle; and the entire Partygate affair.

SCIENCE AS A SWORD AND A SHIELD

The Science

As we've shown in earlier chapters, Ministers frequently deferred in their decision-making to scientific expertise and simultaneously used 'The Science' as a shield to justify and defend their decisions and inactions.

If the vaccination of children is arguably the most ethically contentious example of Ministers relying on, or seeking out, scientific evidence to support controversial policy choices, then lockdowns and school closures were the most indiscriminate.

The extent to which Ministers, including in particular the Quad of Ministers, were ostensibly in thrall to the Government's scientific advisers, led by Sir Patrick Vallance (Chief Scientific Adviser) and Chris Whitty (Chief Medical Officer) and their deputies, buttressed by SAGE, was well-documented even before the Covid Inquiry began.[512] *"[E]verything we do is based scrupulously on the best scientific advice... Last week we asked everyone to stay at home if you had one of two key symptoms: a high temperature or a new and continuous cough. Today, we need to go further, because according to SAGE it looks as though we're now approaching the fast growth part of the upward curve"* [513], had said the PM in March 2020 in a statement setting the tone for much of the two years that followed.

Also well known is the disastrous impact of their ostensibly unwavering allegiance to The Science in promoting epidemiological considerations to the exclusion of a more holistic balancing of risks, harms and benefits.

Greg Clark MP, Chair of the Science and Technology Select Committee: "On 23 April you wrote, 'I do think scientific advice is driven far too much by epidemiology—and I'm an epidemiologist.' Can you explain what you meant by that?"

Professor Mark Woolhouse, epidemiologist and member of SAGE: "Yes, I can. I was particularly concerned that we were looking at only one side of the equation when assessing the costs and benefits of lockdown. There has been a lot of emphasis on the public health burden of Covid-19. In the early stages of the epidemic, before we had large amounts of data, that was largely on the basis of modelling, and that is all right and proper and as it should be, but we are looking literally at only one side of the equation when we do that.*

*The other side is the harms done by lockdown. By those, I mean the harms in reduced access to healthcare provision, which has been very marked during this epidemic, the harms to our mental health and social wellbeing, the education of our children and our economy. It seems to me that a balanced assessment of the merits of lockdown requires both sides of the equation to be modelled. We were looking only at the public health side".[514]

Blinded by science: inadequate weighing of harms against benefit

From early on, while evidence of the scientific efficacy and benefits of key interventions had been either fragile or completely absent, the range of likely harms often seemed predictable, even to non-scientists such as us. Indeed as we've already commented, it has since transpired that senior officials and, we can presume, Ministers sometimes knew of those risks and harms because the Government's own expert advice – on the occasions when broader advice was sought – was predicting them; yet they were not acknowledged or at least were kept from view.

Freedom of Information Act requests submitted by UsForThem have established that there were times when no assessment of harms or risks of harm was made before effecting an intervention. For example, we discovered that the decision to require children to wear masks in classrooms was made without any formal harm assessment; indeed that assessment was not completed until 17 months after the decision was taken. Even then, the assessment fell far short of what one might have expected of a rigorous objective and evidence-based process, instead relying on surveys of teachers, among other sources.[515]

Worse, it became clear from those forced disclosures that the masks in class policy had not been properly assessed for risk or benefit, efficacy or safety, but instead was based on a crude political desire not to be seen to be undercut by the First Minister in Scotland, Nicola Sturgeon MSP:

> *"Nicola Sturgeon blindsided us by suddenly announcing that when schools in Scotland reopen, all secondary school pupils will have to wear masks in classrooms. In one of her most egregious attempts at one-upmanship to date, she didn't consult us. The problem is that our original guidance on face coverings specifically excluded schools. Cue much tortured debate between myself, education secretary Gavin Williamson and No 10 about how to respond. Much as Sturgeon would relish it, nobody here wants a big spat with the Scots. So, U-turn it is".*[516]

Worse still, even in October 2023, with the benefit of two years of reflection on the harms not only of masking schoolchildren but of asking them to be surrounded and taught by masked adults, with the benefit of studies showing the deleterious effects of masking on both child health and educational attainment[517] and with some 5 million children in the UK now falling short of their speech and language milestones, there are still those in positions of relevant authority who appear unable to comprehend the necessity of balancing harms and risks against actual and perceived benefits. In an evidence session in the official Covid Inquiry during which Sir Peter Horby, a member of SAGE and the chair of NERVTAG, was questioned on the topic of mandating facemasks for the public, on which he had said *"...that data was fairly clear that there may be some small benefits, but it wasn't clear and the evidence was weak"*; shortly after Baroness Hallett, the inquiry chair, made this astonishing intervention: *"I'm sorry, I'm not following, Sir Peter. If there's a possible benefit, what's the downside?".*[518]

The Government's failure to balance harms and risks of harm against actual and perceived benefits can be seen to have infected almost every single intervention. In large part for this reason a group of dozens of Conservative Party MPs – known as the Covid Recovery Group (CRG) – formed to advocate for costs to be considered alongside benefits. At one point the CRG furiously demanded, *"We cannot support this approach further unless the Government demonstrates the restrictions proposed ... will have an impact on slowing the transmission of Covid, and will save more lives than they cost... To this end, Government must publish a full cost-benefit analysis of the proposed restrictions on a regional basis so that MPs can assess responsibly the non-Covid health impact of restrictions, as well as the undoubted impact on livelihoods".*[519]

This myopic focus on perceived scientific or medical benefits (and typically on benefits to the older adult portion of the population) to the exclusion of common sense, predictable and predicted risks and harms was – and unfortunately, it seems, remains – in our view unforgivable.

It was mostly a mirage anyway...

We now know that, from beginning to end, much of 'The Science' turned out to have been unreliable or plain wrong, including, it appears, the scientific modelling forcefully invoked to trigger the March 2020 national lockdown.

The controversy surrounding the modelling data[520] produced by a team led by Professor Neil Ferguson of Imperial College London is worth pausing on as a key early example of potentially flawed science, if only because of the severity of the impacts it triggered for our children, our society, our national health and our economy.

Among the challenges laid by independent experts and commentators[521] [522] is that although Ferguson's team went on to claim credit for saving millions of lives,[523] their modelling was unstable from the outset and is alleged to have been validated using its own hypothetical projections as a counterfactual for what would have happened had lockdowns not been used.[524] Even at the time, experts cast doubt on its reliability, pointing out a historical pattern of over-estimation of viral impact by Imperial College's modelling team.[525]

Regardless of the many criticisms of the Imperial College paper, though, the real outrage is the Government's use of that data. This was a lone modelling study, which according to Anders Tegnell, at the time Sweden's state epidemiologist, was *"... not a peer-reviewed paper... It might be right, but it might also be terribly wrong. In Sweden, we are a bit surprised that it's had such an impact"*.[526]

Yet it was being used to justify the most severe societal restraints imposed by the State in a generation. It is mind-boggling that nobody in the Government is reported to have sought a second opinion. Again, we cannot explain how this approach to decision-making for one of the most seismic moments in the pandemic could ever have been considered consistent with the Nolan Principle of Objectivity: acting and taking decisions using the best evidence.

A second pertinent example comes from information first identified by Fraser Nelson in December 2021 following a conversation he had on social media with Graham Medley, the chair of the SAGE modelling committee and a professor at the London School of Hygiene & Tropical Medicine (LSHTM). The LSHTM had the week before that conversation published a study on Omicron. That study had assumed that the Omicron variant, which had recently begun to circulate, was as deadly as the Delta variant.

In the conversation it became apparent from Mr Medley's comments that only 'bad case' situations had been modelled by SAGE. *"Decision-makers don't have to decide if nothing happens"* [in other words, doing nothing requires no decision], Medley had explained to an incredulous Nelson, who replied *"so you exclusively model bad outcomes that require restrictions and omit just-as-likely outcomes that would not require restrictions"*. *"We generally model what we are asked to model"*, Medley replied. *"Okay, so you were asked to model bad Omicron outcomes and make no comment as to the probability [of those outcomes occurring]"*, continued Nelson. *"We model the scenarios that are useful to decisions"*, explained Medley.[527]

As Nelson commented at the time: *"In my view, this raises serious questions not just about Sage but about the nature and quality of the advice used to make UK lockdown decisions. And the lack of transparency and scrutiny of that advice"*.[528] This was mission-critical modelling being used to justify material decisions on interventions impacting millions of people.

Other significant policy decisions which we now know were not made on the basis of well-tested, or in some cases even any, evidence include:

- The 'rule of six' intervention, which was introduced in September 2020 and extended to cover under-12s in England despite Scotland and Wales having exempted children and Helen Whately, then the Minister for Adult Social Care, telling Matt Hancock on 11 Oct 2020, that she wanted to *"loosen on children under 12"* in Tier 1 as *"it would make such a difference to families and there isn't a robust rationale for it. Now is a really good chance to show we have listened. (Lots of MPs were pushing on this during last weeks' debates)"*; Hancock replied simply *"[Number 10] don't want to go there on this"*.[529]

- The decision to put the UK into a second lockdown, where academics Raghib Ali and Carl Heneghan, who had been asked to advise the Government, spotted that the graphs used to sell to the public were based on out-of-date data.[530]

- The requirement to wear facemasks, the efficacy evidence base for which had been hotly contested,[531] and in relation to which Jeremy Farrar (SAGE member at the time and now Chief Scientist at the WHO) has since admitted to the Covid Inquiry (on 29 June 2023) that there was no UK scientific consensus.[532]

In his controversially candid evidence given to Parliament in May 2021, Dominic Cummings, one of the few senior officials to have been privy to the decisions of the Prime Minister and the Quad of Ministers in the first phase of the pandemic, alleged that science was used as a shield by Ministers so that if things went wrong blame could be deflected.[533] A similarly revealing comment appeared in witness testimony given to the Covid Inquiry by Sir Patrick Vallance, who purportedly kept a diary during the pandemic. *"Ministers try to make the science give the answers rather than them making decisions"*, Vallance had written on 7 May 2020.[534]

Vallance's testimony also reveals that, behind closed doors, Ministers readily dropped their attachment to The Science: *"There was no opportunity for SAGE or the subgroup members to understand, moreover, how politicians were interpreting their advice or translating it into policy, and therefore there was never any meaningful engagement at which the politicians, the civil servants and the scientists could engage in discussions about the appropriateness of policies or areas where policies might be needed".[535]

Conversations we have had with former members of MEAG have only served to reinforce our impression that when the cameras were not rolling, inconvenient scientific advice – and ultimately in the case of MEAG an entire inconvenient advisory body – could be quietly dropped. *"We were giving advice which wasn't taken"*, one former MEAG member told us, while – for balance – pointing out that in many groups a natural divergence of opinion would mean some advice would, likely, always not be taken.

Dr Gavin Morgan, an educational psychologist at University College London and member of SAGE Sub-group SPi-B, told us that *"By the turn of the year [2020], we [SPi-B] had become sidelined and were meeting very, very infrequently. We'd lost any impact or influence"*. He has pointed out elsewhere that *"there was no consultation [with SPi-B] about face masks in schools"*, before saying that he had *"raised questions a few times with other SPi-B members and with people who also sit on SAGE. We don't know why we weren't consulted"*.[536]

In Dr Morgan's view, *"I think SPi-B were a useful kind of whipping boy at times because the Government always said, 'oh, we're listening to the science… Well, they certainly cherry picked what they listened to. As I said, I was a voice, a lone voice at times, but I was certainly a voice that was ringing alarm bells, so I wasn't being listened to. They cherry picked the advice to suit their agenda, which isn't open, honest, transparent Government".*

DISRESPECT AND DISREGARD

It is not always possible to impute a generous reading to ministerial dealings with Parliament. Across the period of the pandemic Ministers have frequently treated Parliament with a lack of respect and disregard for its constitutional role that at times has strayed into – and been called out as – contempt. There are many contenders, though perhaps the most vivid example of Government dealing with Parliament and its committees in a manner which some MPs described as contemptuous is found in the exchanges on vaccine status certification discussed in some length in our chapter on Covid Passes.

Other examples include:

- the Department for Health and Social Care's abject failure to produce an impact assessment for Parliament when the care homes staff vaccine requirement legislation was presented for a vote.[537] The Deputy Speaker called the situation *"totally unsatisfactory"*,[538] and another MP complained in the House of Commons: *"How can we hold the Government to account if they will not even answer our questions?"*.[539]

- An incident, occurring the fortnight before this, in which the Speaker had rebuked the Health Secretary, Matt Hancock, for similarly showing a *"total disregard for this Chamber"* by briefing the media on new lockdown measures before he had given a statement to Parliament.[540]

- The fact that when on 13 March 2020 the Advisory Committee on Dangerous Pathogens (ACDP) advised Jonathan Van Tam, Deputy Chief Medical Officer for England at the DHSC that it had downgraded Covid from its initial categorisation as a

High Consequence Infectious Disease, no announcement to Parliament appears to have been made. That was a Friday. On the following Monday (16 March 2020), Matt Hancock described the pandemic to Parliament as *"the most serious public health emergency that our nation has faced for a generation"*, but still made no mention of that most recent and pertinent advice about the virulence of the virus.[541] We do not know whether the recommendation of ACDP the Advisory Committee on Dangerous Pathogens (ACDP) was communicated to the Health Secretary, but it seems inconceivable that it would not have been.

More than once Parliament rebuked Ministers for their disrespectful treatment of Parliament. In a debate in the House of Commons shortly before the first six-monthly vote for the continuation of the Coronavirus Act, in September 2020, the Speaker of the House issued a stinging rebuke to the Prime Minister whose Government, he said, had shown a total disregard for Parliament: *"The way in which the Government has exercised its power to make secondary legislation during this crisis has been totally unsatisfactory"*, he fumed.[542] In June 2021, a further rebuke was delivered – for briefing journalists ahead of Parliament.[543]

On numerous occasions, Ministers have also appeared to deflect or disregard inconvenient questions from parliamentarians. In a debate on childhood vaccination tabled by Miriam Cates MP in September 2021, a number of MPs had raised urgent, detailed concerns relating to child welfare and safety stemming from the highly unorthodox CMO 'workaround' process by which the vaccination programme had been extended to children.

Those concerns included detailed questions about the sufficiency of clinical benefit, and about the detection of any longer-term, unknown harms. The MPs involved had clearly researched the topic so that they could ask well-informed questions.[544] The response given by Maggie Throup, Parliamentary Under Secretary of State at the Department of Health and Social Care, is a masterclass in deflection, recycling information already in the public domain and, one presumes, well-known to the MPs:

> "The MHRA authorisation decision confirmed that vaccines are safe and effective for this age group...In August, the committee advised an initial dose of the vaccine for all healthy remaining 16 and 17-year-olds...We received advice from the four chief medical officers, and it was made publicly available and deposited in the Library for Members to read in full".

Seemingly forgetting that her appearance in the House of Commons was to account to her peers rather than to cheerlead for the Government, she continued:

> "I am very grateful to everyone who has played a crucial role in the success of the vaccine roll-out ... I pay tribute to my predecessor, my right hon. Friend the Member for Stratford-on-Avon (Nadhim Zahawi) ... for his efforts in successfully delivering the vaccine programme, with more than 93 million doses administered in the UK and more than four fifths of adults receiving the protection of two jabs ... The MHRA is the best medical regulator in the world ... We are now moving forward with the same sense of urgency that we have had at every point in our vaccination programme".[545]

A more recent example, in the House of Commons in January 2023, is Esther McVey MP asking Maria Caufiled MP, Parliamentary Under Secretary of State at the Department of Health and Social Care, about the causes of excess deaths:[546]

> "The Chief Medical Officer recently warned that non-covid excess deaths are being driven in part by patients not getting statins or blood pressure medicines during the pandemic. However, when

looking at the data on statins on OpenPrescribing.net, which is based on monthly NHS prescribing, there appears not to be a drop, so where is the evidence? If there is none, what is causing these excess deaths? Will the Minister commit to an urgent and thorough investigation on the matter?"

In a reply that briefly sparked public outrage, Caulfield conspicuously declined to engage properly with the question, and instead recited a generic non-answer:

"We are seeing an increase in excess deaths in this country, but we are also seeing that in Wales, in Scotland, in Northern Ireland and across Europe. There is a range of factors. As we saw, there was an increase in December in the number of people being admitted with flu, covid and other healthcare conditions. That was seen not just in this country, but across Europe".

The evasion of accountability

On some occasions even Select Committees have struggled to persuade Ministers and senior civil servants to engage meaningfully on important topics. While Ministers are by convention expected to attend before Parliament if called by Select Committees, whose role is to scrutinise Government activities and to hold Ministers to account, a Minister cannot typically be compelled to attend.

As the most senior Minister in the Cabinet after the Prime Minister, Michael Gove's refusal in February 2021 to appear before the Public Administration and Constitutional Affairs Committee to answer questions about accountability for the data underpinning Government decisions on Covid drew extreme ire from that Committee:

"The Committee was very disappointed that when the Chancellor of the Duchy of Lancaster declined to appear before the Committee on 4th February, Ministers sent in his place were poorly briefed and unable to answer the Committee's questions. The ability of Select Committees to hold Ministers to account for decisions is a vital part of the democratic process. This is particularly true at a time when the country is facing the toughest possible restrictions on our freedoms, and when (as we have previously reported on) detailed scrutiny of the Government's decisions has not always been possible in the timeframes required. The Chancellor of the Duchy of Lancaster's refusal to attend this Committee and account for decisions made by the taskforce he chairs is <u>contemptuous of Parliament</u>", (emphasis added).[547]

This egregious example of a Minister evading Parliamentary accountability during the pandemic is illustrative, we suggest, of a broader disrespect and disregard displayed by senior Government Ministers,[548] and on occasion also officials,[549] during that period and since.[550]

RUPTURED ETHICS

There are many areas of policy-making where ethical considerations must be weighed, and where there is consequently space for debate about the best, or most ethical, decision in light of those considerations. It can also be recognised that ethics may evolve over time to reflect societal changes. That said, most could acknowledge that there are some core ethical principles which have become close to absolute in their modern expression: the right to life enshrined in the UN Universal Declaration, for example.

Significant ethical issues inevitably arose in policy decisions made across the pandemic period. Some of those issues arguably invoked ethical principles that would have been considered close to absolute by pre-pandemic standards of public health and medical ethics.[551]

Other issues were at the very least deserving of meaningful debate within and outside of Parliament.

Yet at critical decision points in the pandemic, conversations about ethics appear to have been almost entirely absent from government, and nor did Parliament debate those topics. To the extent that such commentary occurred outside Parliament it appears to have gone unnoticed, been ignored or, in some cases, to have been actively suppressed by the Government.[552]

Lockdowns

Decisions to impose regional and national lockdowns appear to have been driven by a narrow focus on containing and controlling transmission of the virus and on reducing the potential for exceptional demands on the NHS. Those decisions, however, appear largely to have ignored the effect on healthy populations and the poorer sections of society.

As ethicist Alberto Giubilini warned writing in *The Spectator* in November 2020, *"When it comes to public health, the ethical balance is simply expressed: how do you achieve a certain public health goal with the fewest restrictions on individual rights? … There are issues to weigh up carefully on both sides — it is about finding the right balance. This is more acute in pandemic handling because it is not simply the case of lives vs liberty. Lockdown kills, too, so the right balance is even harder to strike"*; he went on to say, in relation to the UK's second lockdown, *"there are alternatives that better strike a balance between individual rights and collective interest. They have been ruled out, however, without adequate, rational ethical scrutiny"*.[553]

Visitor bans imposed by NHS trusts for much of a two year period leaving left the terminally ill to die without a chance to see loved ones, deprived often vulnerable patients of important advocacy support and left mothers alone to give birth. The withdrawal of social service support for vulnerable and disabled children commonly involved those in the most desperate need being left without essential care.

Vaccination program

A vaccines program which relied on coercive and overtly emotionally manipulative marketing to the public,[554] which was rolled-out on a universal basis (disregarding the benefits of cultivating natural immunity among low risk cohorts) and which was often justified by over-stated benefits for both individuals and communities[555] falls far short of, or negates entirely, the foundational medical ethical standard of informed consent.

The extension of that intervention, utilising novel vaccine technology, to low risk children absent a clear Covid health risk impacting those children and prior to any long-term safety data on the extent of the risks to children, and to pregnant women absent any data on the impact of the vaccine on unborn children, to many seemed to cross further foundational ethical lines.

Indeed, more generally the status of children as a cohort needing protection and safeguarding by adults engaged an array of ethical issues.

Safeguarding of children severely neglected

School closures prioritised adults' needs over the needs of children: *"The policy and ethical implications of ongoing mandatory school closures, in order to protect others, need urgent reassessment in light of the very limited data of public health benefit"*, wrote one set of experts in August 2020.[556]

Ethical considerations are exacerbated when one considers the 2.3 million children in the UK who were plunged into a state of food insecurity as a result of that policy; the many vulnerable children left exposed to the risk of serious abuse and even death; and the disproportionate impact on already disadvantaged families: *"[School closures are] the single biggest generator of inequality that I've ever seen in my lifetime from one single policy"*,[557] commented Jay Bhattacharya, Professor of Medicine, Economics, and Health Research at Stanford University.

The prolonged mass testing of children despite the invasive nature of the tests and the significant psychological harm of repeated isolations of children as a result of the policy generated sufficient concern in the UK among experts, politicians and parents eventually to trigger a session of an All-Party Parliamentary Group.[558] Giving evidence, Dr Angela Raffle, a public health consultant and a member of the UK Government's National Screening Committee, commented:

> *"SARS-CoV-2 testing of healthy school children needs to stop. The World Health Organisation cautions against mass symptomless testing because of high costs, lack of evidence on impact, and risk of diverting resources from more important activities. There is no sound evidence that testing children leads to reduction in serious cases of COVID-19.*
>
> *The policy decision in England to introduce school testing appears to have been a political decision, to create the impression of safety, rather than investing in staffing and ventilation which would have made an impact. The tests being used have not been properly evaluated as self-tests or for use in children. Children are low transmitters compared with adults. The net effect of the school testing is harmful because of the trauma of repeated testing and the disruption to children's lives through repeated exclusion and isolation".*[559]

Mandatory masking of school pupils as a de facto condition of education was imposed and then continued despite strident resistance from groups of experts, teachers, parents[560] and politicians.[561]

As highlighted in our chapter on the children's vaccination programme, the extension of the universal vaccination program to children under 16 years of age was unorthodox and unethical, not least in its procedural aspects and in its subsequent marketing strategy.

Many, if not all, of the policy decisions highlighted above would have registered somewhere between dubious and unconscionable for many ethicists and public health experts under pre-pandemic norms and well-recognised public health ethical principles of beneficence, bodily autonomy and 'do no harm'. Indeed a myriad of expert commentators expressed serious concerns about those and other ethically-significant pandemic policy choices, both contemporaneously and since.

As is often quoted, the true measure of any society can be found in how it treats its most vulnerable members.

What we've sought to evidence in this chapter is that ethical infringements were not isolated, nor were they even a series of discrete exceptional incidents; rather, the evidence is that across this period the Government normalised and leveraged a process of governance which ignored, and at times excluded, ethics.[562] This became a response without ethical guardrails. While ethical standards may evolve or flex over time, a crisis is arguably the most important moment for ethical standards to remain intact; if our Government cannot remain faithful to ethical principles at the peak of an ethical dilemma, can it claim to be ethical at all?

In our conversation with him, Dr Gavin Morgan expressed a view that we believe he shares with many others; certainly we share it: *"I think the Government were making things up on the hoof a lot of the time, but they certainly weren't being open, honest and truthful; and that is the cornerstone of any modern democracy. We lost that during the pandemic and we gladly gave it up. And that was very concerning for me".*

INDUSTRY INFLUENCE AND A REGULATORY DEFICIT

If public health was not already a multi-billion dollar industry, it has become so as a result of the pandemic.

For 2022, Pfizer reported global revenue of US$100 billion. More than half related to sales of its Covid vaccine and its Paxlovid antiviral treatment.[563] This followed an already record-breaking year in 2021 in which Pfizer's revenue had reached US$81 billion, again fuelled in large part by super-sized sales of its Covid vaccine.[564] By way of comparison, the GDP of Luxembourg for 2022 was approximately US$83 billion.[565]

Prior to the pandemic, Moderna had been a loss-making company. Yet in 2022 it reported sales of US$19.3 billion following a record-breaking year in 2021 which its sales increased more than 12-fold to US$7.2 billion, 96% of which had been attributable to its Covid vaccine. Moderna's profit on those sales was US$4.9 billion in 2021 and US$8.4 billion in 2022 — the former equating to a profit margin of 68%.[566] For Moderna and its directors and investors, the pandemic was to be a life-changingly positive event.

Plainly, the major pharmaceutical groups active in the public health system have enormous resources at their disposal. The directors and senior managers of those groups have legal duties (alongside personal financial incentives) to use those resources to advance the success and profitability of the companies they command. As a 2005 Parliamentary report observed: *"The pharmaceutical industry* is a business, with obligations to its shareholders. The regulator should expect it to use any legal means to provide a return on investment".[567]

For all of the good words spoken about pharma groups being driven by ethical and medical callings, companies such as Pfizer which professes to have *"always had a noble purpose rooted in our commitment to patients",*[568] at the same time have had to acknowledge that *"As a science-driven global biopharmaceutical company, we remain focused on advancing our pipeline, supporting our marketed brands and deploying capital responsibly, with a focus on initiatives that can help contribute to our long-term revenue and future growth",*[569] (underlining added).

We contend that vast resources beget vast influence. That the pharma industry has nurtured and leveraged its resources to acquire influence is not a new revelation. Mainstream media organisations and investigative journalists have on countless occasions exposed the corrupting effects of pharma industry conflicts and influence. Even as we write, conflicts and improper influence continue to be exposed by reporters in relation to drug approval processes[570] and 'miracle' weight-loss treatments.[571]

Whistleblowers too have provided insights into the behaviour and mindsets of pharmaceutical marketing departments and their beneficiaries: *"Everybody is begging for money; nobody has any money. The government doesn't have any money, universities don't have money, nobody has money. The only ones that have money are these big multinational corporations. And they have lots of money, and they use that money to basically buy influence".*[572]

This does not mean that the entirety of that industry has engaged in dubious practices at all times; but the assertion that at least some in the industry have sometimes engaged in distasteful, unscrupulous or amoral practices, and that this has been an issue which has persisted for decades is, we suggest, beyond dispute.[573]

The pandemic

There are different interpretations of the pandemic's storyline. The conventional or official interpretation is that in the face of a global health emergency, the pharmaceutical giants mobilised, took considerable risks, and delivered a miraculous panacea the benefits of which have definitively outweighed any risk of harms; this can be heralded as a triumph of innovation and collaboration and is thus deserving of appropriately rich reward.

We offer that there is at least one other interpretation: that pharma groups made record-breaking profits by capitalising on a deficit of governance and ethical decision-making to secure lucrative de-risked contracts which underwrote the development of products that were State-marketed to entire populations, including cohorts of millions who arguably did not need and should never have been offered, let alone pressured into accepting, a novel medical product.

A history of bad behaviour

The global pharma industry has a track record of prioritising its commercial ambitions ahead of the public good. For those who wish to acclimatise themselves to this subject, *Bad Pharma: how medicine is broken, and how we can fix it*, by Ben Goldacre,[574] is a good place to start. It is a 400 page exposé of industry-wide maladies spanning poor safety and trial practices, inadequate data transparency, regulatory capture and unprincipled marketing practices.

Many of these issues had previously been surfaced by a Parliamentary Select Committee, which considered the pharmaceutical sector's influence in public health almost twenty years ago. That review culminated in the publication of an excoriating report which identified extensive examples of conflicts and damaging corporate practices; cited countless failures of the pharma regulatory regime; and made many recommendations for reform and action:

"Our overriding concerns are about the volume, extent and intensity of the industry's influence, not only on clinical medicine and research but also on patients, regulators, the media, civil servants and politicians"[575] and *"There is evidence that in certain areas, company influence is excessive and contrary to the public good".*[576]

The Select Committee was also concerned by what it appears to have regarded as the industry's capture of the main medicines regulator, the MHRA.

"The relationship between the industry and the MHRA is naturally close. There are regular interchanges of staff, common policy objectives, agreed processes, shared perspectives and routine contact and consultation. ... Such closeness provides the basis of the trust that the MHRA said it relied on as an integral part of the regulatory process. Trust is critical in the relationship between regulators and industry. ... However, at the heart of this inquiry are the concerns of those who believe that the MHRA is too trusting".[577]

Other criticisms included evidence of the use of dubious PR tactics and the suppression of bad safety data: *"Efforts to undermine critical voices in particular were identified, under terms of 'issues management'"*; poor quality medical trials: *"the current system of clinical testing provides ample opportunities for bias"*; compromised research articles: *"... there is a bias towards submission of articles that show new drugs in a positive light".*[578]

Conflicts and dependencies

The pharma industry is huge, and in the UK at least pharma groups provide only limited disclosure of their financial arrangements with third parties. Consequently it is not feasible to attempt a complete exposition of the conflicts and dependencies that may presently exist. What follows therefore is simply a sample of some of the evidence which suggests that the serious concerns which the Health Select Committee identified in 2005 remain as relevant today – and crucially were present throughout the pandemic response period – as they were almost twenty years ago.

A disclaimer: in the sections which follow, by contemplating the possibility for conflicts to have arisen or for influence to have been acquired, we are not suggesting any causal connection between particular decisions or outcomes and actual or potential conflicts or financial relationships, less still that any specific policy decisions or individuals were subject to improper influence. We are merely noting the fact that certain relationships have existed. We also recognise that in areas of specialist expertise it is inevitable, and indeed desirable, that the public sector should benefit from private sector knowledge and experience provided the attendant risks of conflicts and exploitation can be appropriately managed and controlled. Nevertheless, in view of the track record of the pharma industry globally and long-standing concerns raised in the UK, and the centrality of the industry to the global pandemic response, it cannot be the case that the risk of conflicts or influence affecting key decisions is off limits. With that in mind…

Some key individuals

Alongside the Chief Medical Officer for England, Professor Chris Whitty, two of the most high profile public health officials during the pandemic were his Deputy Chief Medical Officer, Professor Jonathan Van-Tam, and the Chief Scientific Advisor, Sir Partrick Vallance. Between them, as custodians of 'the science' to which Ministers had committed their fidelity, for a period these three officials together held perhaps the greatest level of influence over UK public health policy as has ever been held by unelected officials.

Among the decisions of seismic consequence with which we know or might reasonably ask whether one or more of these senior officials were involved – either directly as a decision-maker or by contributing materially to the pre-conditions for the decisions of others – were:

1. the decisions to order the UK into repeated national lockdowns;

2. the decisions to pre-order millions of vaccine doses prior to licensing approvals being granted (indeed we believe this was a core element of Van-Tam's role, as we explain below); and

3. the sequence of decisions to extend the vaccine roll-out to teenagers and children (discussed in our chapter addressing those decisions).

Each of those decisions had the potential to impact and, we suggest, did positively impact the financial interests of all of the major pharmaceutical groups active in public health and in particular those involved in the development of Covid vaccines.

Until he took up his government post in 2017, Sir Patrick was President of R&D at pharma group GSK, having been employed there for twelve years, and as a result he held deferred bonus awards (shares or share options) in GSK reportedly worth £600,000 in 2020.[579] As well as being Chief Scientific Adviser when the pandemic broke, Vallance went on to chair the International Pandemic Preparedness Partnership (PPP) initiative announced in April 2021 with a mission to cut the time to develop vaccines for new diseases to 100 days. Vallance was quoted as saying *"...the first 100 days in a pandemic are crucial to changing the course of a disease. In those 3 months, diagnostics, therapeutics and vaccines are key weapons"*.[580]

The Government confirmed in September 2020 that Vallance had *"no input into contractual and commercial decisions on vaccine procurement"*,[581] i.e. he was not in the room when those deals were negotiated. We would contend, however, that a precondition to the UK's £6 billion 'on risk' pre-ordering of vaccine doses and the subsequent presentation of those vaccines as the only means of exiting the pandemic was the acclimatisation of the public to the propositions that everyone was at risk, that natural immunity would not offer sufficient protection and that vaccines would be the only means of remaining safe.

Though not the sole contributor, Vallance was undoubtedly one of the key architects of the information campaign which duly propagated those messages, including as a regular presenter of data and opinion to the public which in some cases – such as his infamous 'charts of doom' presentation on 21 September 2020 in which he asserted that *"the vast majority of us are not protected in any way"*[582] – were criticised for being alarmist.[583]

As Deputy Chief Medical Officer throughout the pandemic Jonathan Van Tam was a key face of the Government's response. According to his official government biography he is stated to have led on health protection – a central pillar of which, we might reasonably assume given the thrust of the Government's pandemic response, was the vaccine roll-out. He was also a member of the UK Vaccines Task Force which, according to the Government, made decisions on *"all vaccine supply contracts and major investments in manufacturing and clinical opportunities"*.[584]

In June 2022, the Government announced a strategic mRNA vaccines research and manufacturing partnership with Moderna, following negotiations led by the Vaccines Task Force of which Van-Tam had, until his retirement a few months earlier, been a senior official.[585] In December 2022 that partnership was cemented into a 10-year deal on undisclosed *"commercially sensitive"* financial terms.[586]

Following his retirement from the Government in March 2022, Van-Tam took some time out before it was announced that he had joined Moderna in May 2023 as a senior medical consultant.[587]

We do not suggest any favour was given. However, it is in fact immaterial. It suffices to observe that the optics of Van-Tam's move from public procurement to private producer are terrible.

Situations such as this raise a question. When an individual in a position of significant authority and influence within the Government, a regulator or our public health infrastructure knows, or simply suspects, that they may seek employment in the private sector in the near term, could this at some level be capable of influencing the manner or the vigour of their dealings with the private sector while still in that public role? If so, surely that possibility will be apparent to, and therefore in principle *capable* of exploitation by, the industry.

As documented in press reports in November 2020,[588] a hedge fund co-founded by the then-Chancellor Rishi Sunak before he entered politics held a stake in Moderna which had been valued at approximately US$500 million. Though it appears that Sunak ceased to have any active role in relation to his private investments when he became a Minister, including any residual interest in the hedge-fund that he co-founded,[589] he declined to confirm whether he or his family would benefit from the performance of that investment after Moderna's share price surged on news of its successful vaccine trial.

In March 2023, Sunak was pressured into publishing his personal tax details, at which point it was reported[590] that the disclosures revealed that Sunak had earned £4.8m over the previous three tax years of which approximately £410,000 was derived from his MP and ministerial salaries. This does not tell us whether Sunak

INDUSTRY INFLUENCE AND A REGULATORY DEFICIT

benefited financially as a result of Moderna's success; it does though suggest – unsurprisingly – that Sunak (or his family) has continued to benefit from the performance of at least some of the investments he made before he entered office, and that the returns on those investments could have been of an order of magnitude, to the ordinary taxpayer, gives rise to the perception of a risk of conflict or bias.[591]

To reiterate, we are not suggesting any individual wrongdoing. We cannot know whether the prospect of future returns or career advancements influenced any person's advice, opinions or decisions. We have no reason to doubt the express disclaimers made in relation to the circumstances above.

That said, we have some observations. First, we challenge the notion that it was acceptable for so many senior decision-makers to be even *potentially* personally implicated by the significant policy decisions within their control or influence, and particularly when those decisions had societal and generational-defining impacts. This is the case notwithstanding that individual conflicts or financial arrangements may have been disclosed.

Unlike in business where the personal interests of senior executives and the corporate interests of the companies they control typically are aligned in seeking lawful and sustainable profits, in the administration of public health there is no certainty that the personal financial interests of senior decision-makers benefitting from the performance of pharmaceutical companies will always be aligned with the health interests of the public.

Second, if potential conflicts or risk of bias resulting from financial arrangements are not fully transparent to the public, the absence of transparency is problematic, and not only aggravates the existence of the potential conflict or risk of bias but also itself damages public trust in the decision-making process. Certainly Sunak's political opponents seized on his reluctance to discuss his financial interest, if any, in Moderna: *"The truth with this trust is that the only people that are blind to it are the public. The chancellor only set up the trust 18 months ago but the public has no idea where the money is or whether there is a conflict of interest".*[592]

Third, it is also not the case that this is an issue limited to only isolated instances among the most senior echelons of decision-makers. In September 2020, it was reported that Sir John Bell, a member of the Vaccine Taskforce and as head of the National Covid Testing Scientific Advisory Panel the country's so-called "Test Tsar", held £773,000 worth of shares in pharma company Roche where he had been a non-executive director until March 2020.[593] In May 2020, Roche had sold the government £13.5m of antibody tests, a decision in which Sir John has stated that he played no part. Though he confirmed to the Mail on Sunday that his interests in Roche had been fully disclosed to the Department for Health and Social Care, it was reported that following the deal with Roche, Sir John had appeared on Channel 4 News and Radio 4's Today programme to describe the tests as a *"major step forward"* – but failing to mention his links to the firm.[594]

Issues can equally arise in the reverse situation, where pharma sector executives hold roles outside the industry which could potentially be leveraged to benefit their employers. In April 2022, Stuart Carroll, a former member of the UK Vaccines Task Force, took on the role of Director of Market Access and Policy Affairs for Moderna.[595] In January 2023 he also then accepted a senior fellowship position at the Policy Exchange think tank.

Soon after, in 2023, Mr Carroll authored two joint articles for print media with former UK Vaccines Minister Nadhim Zahawi,[596] referencing the success of the UK's vaccine procurement process but also including comments such as *"[The Vaccines Task Force] eschewed the idea of the pharmaceutical industry as a 'black sheep', but rather, a critical partner to the NHS"*, *"Covid-19 vaccines have saved over 100,000 lives in this country alone"*, and *"There's a strong case to refocus on vaccines policy itself. With the 'triple threat' (of COVID, flu and RSV) likely to loom large again this winter"*. Mr Carroll used his personal Twitter/X account to promote each of the two articles, and to repost supportive third party comments for them.[597]

For both articles Carroll was bylined only as 'a Senior Fellow at Policy Exchange and a former member of the Vaccines Taskforce', and similarly at that time the profile for his personal Twitter/X account highlighted his former membership of the VTF but did not disclose his role at Moderna. Objectively, Moderna's commercial interests could be advanced by remaining a 'critical partner' of the NHS, and equally by any refocusing of vaccines policy which results in more mRNA vaccines being purchased and deployed.

Again, we reiterate that we have not selected any of the examples described above to suggest that any wrongdoing has taken place. Nor do we suggest that these examples are the only examples of their kind – they are simply examples. What they exemplify, however, is an apparent absence of transparency.

A BMJ investigation in December 2020 suggested a more generalised normality in this lack of transparency, with the Government refusing to release details of any financial conflicts of members of key advisory panels.[598]

The broader healthcare ecosystem

Personal and financial relationships and incentives of these kinds appear in fact to pervade the political, regulatory, healthcare and patient ecosystem surrounding the pharma industry. We know for certain that we cannot see it all, because at present only a portion is required to be disclosed, under a voluntary scheme operated by the industry's trade association, the ABPI.[599] Crucially that scheme does not currently cover payments made to organisations and individuals outside of the healthcare and medical sciences sector, so if a pharmaceutical company were to make a grant or donation to, for example, a social media organisation or influencer, that payment may not surface in the UK unless the recipient entity was itself required, or chose, to disclose the payment.

The King's Fund is a health sector think tank which describes itself as an independent charity, and has the following to say about its independence: *"We pride ourselves on being trusted for the objectivity of our work and independence from vested interests, with the freedom to speak up and determine our own work programme"*.[600] Yet in 2021, according to the ABPI database, it received event sponsorship funding of £64,000 from Pfizer alongside a donation or grant of £26,000 from UCB, a Belgian pharma group; in 2022 it received event sponsorship funding of £70,000 from Pfizer, alongside another £26,000 from UCB, £20,000 from Merck, £26,000 from Boehringer and £40,000 from AbbVie in addition to a further £27,200 from AbbVie for undisclosed services provided.

In January 2022, the Kings Fund published a report on the Covid-19 vaccination programme reflecting that *"The Covid-19 vaccination programme has been one of the few almost unqualified successes of the UK's response to the pandemic"* (and for good measure added: *"Just as a full examination of vaccine hesitancy is beyond the reach of this report, so is a proper analysis of the impact of the anti-vaccine movement. It was clearly poisonous"*).[601]

According to the ABPI database, **The Royal College of GPs** had received £48,974 in disclosed donations or sponsorships from Pfizer in 2020, £102,820 in 2021, and £283,056 in 2022 – objectively substantial sums. A cursory search of the RCGP's social media channels surfaces, for example, a post enthusiastically celebrating its GP members having hit a target of delivering 10 million jabs a few weeks into the UK's vaccine roll-out in February 2021, not unlike how a private company might celebrate hitting a sales target,[602] and then later calling for measures to increase vaccine uptake among certain groups.[603]

Myocarditis – or inflammation of the heart tissue – is an acknowledged risk associated with Covid-19 mRNA vaccination,[604] so one might have expected organisations concerned with heart health publically to have addressed the possibility of that risk crystallising for some people. The **British Cardiovascular Society** seemed alive to the possibility of myocarditis in relation to the virus itself, and had included a detailed briefing on its website in 2020: *"COVID-19 has been associated with myocarditis and there have been reported cases of severe myocarditis with reduced left ventricular systolic function"*.[605] As far as we have been able to determine, however, no commentary in relation to the risk of myocarditis following vaccination appears on the society's website. According to the ABPI's data, The British Cardiovascular Society accepted £31,000 in sponsorship and a £10,000 donation or grant from Pfizer in 2020, and a further £10,000 donation or grant from Pfizer in 2022.

According to the ABPI's data the **British Society for Heart Failure** received sponsorship payments from Pfizer of £67,500 in 2020, £12,500 in 2021 and £7,500 in 2022. Whilst we were able to find a clear and prominent position statement on their website to the effect that *"people with heart failure are at increased risk of severe COVID-19. The BSH strongly recommends that all those eligible accept vaccination, if offered"* [606] (a position statement also containing, incidentally, the claim that the vaccine prevents disease – a claim manifestly shown to be inaccurate in the case of the Covid vaccines), we were not able to find any commentary on the society's site acknowledging a risk of heart injury following vaccination. Indeed, the society's position statement expressly explains that it had *"been produced to reassure health care professionals and patients of the safety and benefits of the new vaccines"*.[607]

These are just four examples among thousands. Included among the recipients of pharma industry benevolence disclosed in the ABPI database are many NHS trusts, hospitals, and research organisations; many of the Royal Colleges,[608] many of the leading medically-focussed academic institutions in the UK, patient groups, private healthcare providers, GP surgeries, and individual medical practitioners.

Our analysis of the ABPI's data[609] indicates that in the case of Pfizer, one of the most prominent pharma groups in the UK during the core pandemic period of 2020 and 2021, thousands of healthcare organisations and individual professionals received sponsorship, grants, donations and other payments across those two years, including:

- The British Cardiovascular Society (£41,000 in 2020)

- The British Society for Heart Failure (£67,500 in 2020, £12,500 in 2021)

- The Royal College of GPs (£48,974 in 2020, £102,819 in 2021)

- The Royal College of Physicians (£87,376 in 2020. £290,850 in 2021)

- The British Pain Society (£240,997 in 2020, £6,000.00 in 2021)

- AMEE, the health professions education association (£370,800 in 2020)

- World Federation of Neurology (£82,406 in 2020, £7,240 in 2021)

- WebMD UK Limited (£184,478.07 in 2020, £178.065.84 in 2021)

- Economist Group Limited (£119,975 in 2020, £22,151 in 2021)

- International Longevity Centre UK (£208,593 in 2020, £39,382 in 2021)

...as well as the tantalisingly opaque organisation 'London Investigators Research Network' (£40,911 in 2020, £26,284 in 2021).

Also in the database were payments to a scattering of governmental agencies including:

- The National Institute for Healthcare and Clinical Excellence, NICE (£82,032 in 2020, £193,354 in 2021)

- The UK Health Security Agency (£186,480.00 in 2020, £53,227 in 2021)

- Public Health Wales (£12,320.00 in 2020)

Of the academic organisations which have received significant funding from the pharma ecosystem, Imperial College London stands out. Imperial's infamous March 2020 modelling paper – subsequently the subject of significant controversy – had included predictions of mass deaths in the UK and concluded that *"...epidemic suppression is the only viable strategy at the current time"*;[610] in a sense that paper set the tone for the entire UK pandemic response.

Also included in that paper was a statement that: *"The major challenge of suppression is that this type of intensive intervention package – or something equivalently effective at reducing transmission – will need to be maintained <u>until a vaccine becomes available</u> (potentially 18 months or more) – given that we predict that transmission will quickly rebound if interventions are relaxed"*, (emphasis added).[611]

Just over one month after this pivotal paper was published, it was reported that Imperial College had received £22.5 million in funding from the UK Government for vaccine research and development,[612] and subsequent public disclosures in the US suggest that Imperial also received in that year (2020) at least US$108 million in funding from the Bill and Melinda Gates Foundation. BMGF is a private philanthropic organisation which has been open about its ideological commitment to vaccine-based solutions for global health issues and which has significant financial ties to the pharmaceutical industry. When Professor Neil Ferguson, head of the Imperial modelling team, was called to give evidence to the official Covid Inquiry, surprisingly not a single question was posed about the presence of what appears to be a material actual or potential conflict of interest.

Not all of the payments we have highlighted above appear as individually significant as the sums received by Imperial College, but on any measure the overall amounts involved *are* significant. From what we can see in the ABPI's database, between 2019 and 2022, disclosable 'transfers of value' to healthcare organisations from the pharma industry aggregated to £500 million, and transfers of value to healthcare professionals (i.e. individuals) over the same period amounted to a further £110 million. This is only the *disclosable* transfers of value.

That said, even modest donations or sponsorships – carrying in some cases the implicit carrot of potential further more valuable donations or sponsorships in the future – have the *potential* to create unconscious favour or bias, incentives to feel inclined to promote or support, or at least disincentives for any comment or question which might be perceived as critical or unsupportive.

To give just one relevant example, the **Royal College of Midwives** is an organisation that one might expect to assess critically the possibility of near- or long-term side effects from the use of any new medical product with pregnant women. Indeed, evidencing a thoughtfully cautious predisposition in October 2020, the RCM published a paper titled *'Caffeine in Pregnancy'*, in which the college's concern about the risks and benefits of consuming caffeine during pregnancy were considered.[613] That paper included a detailed review of evidence from studies of caffeine use in pregnancy, fully referencing relevant scientific papers and journals and indicating how many of these papers were peer reviewed, as well as examining documented links between caffeine intake, fertility and miscarriage, birthweight, stillbirth and longer term impacts on newborn children.

That scientific approach contrasted starkly with the apparent paucity of information made available about the Covid-19 vaccine in a leaflet published in early 2021 on the RCM's website. That leaflet made a number of bold, unqualified and unreferenced statements about the vaccine:[614]

"Although the vaccine itself is new, it's based on science that's been used safely for pregnant women for many, many years – like the whooping cough or flu vaccines".

"The vaccine doesn't contain any live virus, so it can't be passed to your baby through the placenta".

"In the UK and USA alone, over 200,000 pregnant women have now been vaccinated, with no adverse effects on the woman, pregnancy or baby".

That leaflet contained no reference to documented side effects or the possibility of as yet unknown longer-term risks of a product utilising for the first time novel mRNA technology in a vaccine (it is uncontroversial to note that the medical technology used in these novel vaccines is not comparable to that used in traditional vaccines such as whooping cough or flu vaccines[615]). Moreover, no medicine is ever judged completely safe so it is hard to understand on what basis the RCM felt it was possible at such an early stage to assert definitively that there would be *"no adverse effects on the woman, pregnancy or baby"*.

According to the ABPI data, the Royal College of Midwives had received £7,500[616] in event sponsorship from Pfizer in 2020. One might judge this amount to be too low conceivably to have made any difference to the RCM's assessment of the safety and appropriateness of the Pfizer and Moderna mRNA vaccines for pregnant women. That is hard to second guess, but we suggest that this would be to miss two points. First, it is not only an amount received today that is capable of affecting one's inclination to support, advocate or resist from criticism; the implication and anticipation of further amounts that might then follow tomorrow could equally be impactful. Second, if the amount received had indeed been so immaterial as to have been meaningless to the recipient, could it not have declined sponsorship from a pharma group so as to avoid even the perception of a risk of conflict in the future?

Why does this matter?

Whether small or large in value, financial relationships of this kind pervade the healthcare industry: from individual doctors, to GP surgeries and private clinics, to NHS trusts and research facilities, and to supposedly independent organisations each of which in their many different ways had a role to play in supporting the pandemic response – whether by providing data used to guide policy-making, by advising on policy options, by echoing and reinforcing official messaging or otherwise.

This matters because there is more than a theoretical possibility that the pervasive nature of financial relationships of these kinds gave rise to bias which has impacted pandemic policy-making, in some cases affecting millions of people.

It also matters because it goes to the ethical question of whether consent based on information which might have been subject to undisclosed risks of bias or conflict can form a basis for informed consent. Taking the example of the Royal College of Midwives leaflet, objectively it would surely have been relevant for any pregnant woman planning to accept a medical intervention informed by information published by an ostensibly objective royal college, to know whether that information was subject to *any* risk of bias.

Despite a portion of the industry's financial dealings having been disclosed in the ABPI's database, we suspect it is not widely known by readers outside of the pharma industry that apparently independent societies, royal colleges, charities, universities and even government agencies benefit from grants, donations, sponsorships and service fees from the pharma industry. Certainly, we would not have been aware of this ourselves prior to 2020.

Were this better known, it might at the very least affect the public's understanding and acceptance of any pro-pharma industry or product-promotional public health commentary produced by those organisations. It may also help the public to assess whether the absence of commentary from those organisations which either is critical of or raises questions about particular products or treatment strategies, is surprising.

The regulatory system is also compromised

We might question why the pharma industry seems repetitively over many years to have been able to exploit its influence to further its commercial objectives. One of the most compelling explanations is perhaps: because it can. By this we mean that there is, and has been, no effective brake to restrain the industry from pursuing its commercial interests to the fullest, using all of the means and resources at its disposal. In other industries, that brake is applied in the form of an effective regulatory system.

At the core of the pharma regulatory system in the UK is the MHRA, a governmental agency operating within the Department for Health and Social Care, and a system of legislation which requires approvals for clinical trials and licensing for medicinal products, and which limits the ways in which those products are then marketed, distributed and used within the UK.

As of 2022 the MHRA was reported to be funded between 75% and 86%[617] by fees and levies from the pharma industry it regulates.[618] Is it not reasonable to ask whether this financially-based symbiosis, along with senior personnel recruited back and forth between the industry and regulatory bodies including the MHRA, have contributed to a situation in which the regulatory culture and the mechanisms available to enforce the UK's system of pharma industry oversight have been blunted by conflicts and financial dependencies.

In fact it is no secret that the regulator has been shaped to the industry's needs. In a speech in March 2022 the head of the MHRA, Dame June Raine, famously hailed the transformation of the MHRA *"from a watchdog to enabler"*.[619] This was quite an astonishing transformation for an authority whose core function had until then been *"to protect and promote public health and patient safety, by ensuring that healthcare products meet appropriate standards of safety, quality and efficacy"*.[620]

Concerns about funding conflicts extend also to advisory panels providing regulators with 'independent' expert advice. A 2021 investigation published by the BMJ[621] found that several expert advisers on the JCVI (as well as on the Covid-19 vaccine advisory committees in the US) had financial ties with vaccine manufacturers; previous investigations had found, in relation to the US medicines regulator the FDA, that committee members with financial interests in a sponsoring pharma firm were more likely to vote in favour of approving the sponsor's product.[622]

The 2021 BMJ investigation was highly critical of the level of disclosure around potential conflicts required from those on advisory panels, noting that *"the UK government requires panellists to disclose conflicts only from the previous 12 months, which can miss significant financial payments that occurred in recent years. We also found examples where panellists disclosed to committees their grants, patents, and other industry relationships in their publications, but it seems that the committees did not find these matters worth making public, and they remained undisclosed until now"*.[623]

The extent of potential conflicts and regulatory capture in the pharma regulatory system is not new. Indeed it was remarked on by the Health Select Committee report of 2005 that *"The relationship between the industry and the MHRA is naturally close. ... However, at the heart of this inquiry are the concerns of those who believe that the MHRA is too trusting"*.[624] The potential for conflicts and capture also arises by virtue of:

- The fact that current and former senior government and regulatory officials either have been or may aspire to become senior pharma industry employees, or otherwise benefit from industry funding or sponsorship (a topic dealt with earlier in this chapter).

- The fact that the DHSC, its regulatory agencies and elements of the NHS enjoy grants, donations, sponsorships and service fees paid by the pharmaceutical industry.[625] In addition to direct financial relationships, those agencies, and the NHS, also work with pharma industry organisations on collaborative ventures where funding of special projects and research is provided by pharma groups. That is not to say that any of those arrangements are necessarily improper, simply that they give rise to sponsor/beneficiary, provider/client or partnership relationships which are inconsistent with the arms length relationship that should subsist between a supervisory authority and the businesses it supervises.

- The fact that the pharma industry's self-regulatory authorities (the PMCPA[626] and PAGB[627]) are funded entirely by the industry, staffed in large part by seconded or former senior industry officers, and (in the case of the PMCPA) remains operationally part of the industry's main trade body, the Association of the British Pharmaceutical Industry.

Regulatory capture should be a serious concern for us all. Sociologist Donald Light of Rowan University in New Jersey is one of numerous commentators worldwide who has pointed out the potential for regulatory capture by industry funding to impact patient safety: *"It's the opposite of having a trustworthy organisation independently and rigorously assessing medicines. They're not rigorous, they're not independent, they are selective, and they withhold data. Doctors and patients must appreciate how deeply and extensively drug regulators can't be trusted so long as they are captured by industry funding".*[628]

BMJ figures indicate that in 2022 the proportion of positive MHRA approval decisions for new medicine licensing applications stood at 98.5%.[629]

The regulators are under-resourced

In contrast to the vast financial and human resources available to the UK pharmaceutical industry, the bodies responsible for monitoring and enforcing the regulatory rules governing the research, development, manufacture and sales practices of the pharma industry have been under-resourced and remain inadequate, exacerbating their financial reliance on industry fees and levies.

Indeed in February 2021, just as the MHRA should have been most focussed on monitoring the roll-out of the largest and fastest vaccine programme in UK history, it was announcing to its staff a redundancy process affecting one fifth of its entire workforce including some from key areas including product licensing and safety monitoring.[630] We can only speculate as to the effect this had on the culture and morale of the organisation, as well as its ability to perform critical safety functions.

The MHRA's regulatory role of monitoring the promotional marketing of prescription-based medical products by pharmaceutical companies has for many years been substantially delegated to the pharma industry trade body, the ABPI, and specifically to the ABPI's own self-regulatory agency the PMCPA. The PMCPA has just 10 members of its staff, two of whom are administrative support staff.[631] The industry has in that respect largely been left to regulate itself, and it appears that the human and financial resources with which this self-regulatory authority has been endowed have been inadequate.

In December 2021, UsForThem raised a complaint with the PMCPA concerning what we alleged to have been misleading and unsubstantiated claims concerning the safety and risk profile of Covid vaccines for young children which had been made by Pfizer's CEO, Dr Albert Bourla, in an interview broadcast by the BBC.[632] That complaint took a full year to be determined, with some of the most serious elements of our complaint ultimately upheld in our favour by an Appeal Board, during which period the offending article and interview remained unaltered. We have published a detailed account of that experience.[633]

Determining complaints of this nature is one of the core functions of the PMCPA. We might question why, with one of the most well-resourced industries sitting behind it, this industry-created regulatory authority has not been funded sufficiently to hire the staff necessary to enable it to perform its core functions in a timely manner.

The regulatory framework is also incomplete

Though clinical trials, the licensing of medicines and devices, and the promotion of those products are regulated, there is at present no regulatory or governmental body in the UK which oversees the manner in which pharmaceutical groups organise and manage their business affairs or control their business operations in the UK.

Consequently, though pharma groups like all corporations are subject to general laws applicable to conducting business in the UK, such as corporate governance rules, bribery and corruption offences, transparency rules for government lobbying, and civil liabilities for defective products, they are not presently subject to a single system of oversight which requires them, for example, to:

- avoid and/or manage conflicts of interest;

- act responsibly, with integrity and fully transparently when exercising their financial influence;

- pay regard to, or indeed prioritise, the safety or personal health interests of the users of their products, or of public health more generally, recognising that those interests may not always align with their own commercial interests.

There is, therefore, no regulatory authority with the resources and powers to be able to investigate or sanction pharma groups which misuse their very significant financial influence; or which fail to meet high standards of corporate probity in their business dealings; or which act inconsistently with internationally-accepted standards of medical ethics or 'good clinical practice'; or which subordinate honesty, integrity and transparency in their dealings with consumers, regulators or government to their own business interests and the financial interests of their shareholders.

For an industry of such size, influence and — most importantly — with the potential to cause serious harm to individual and national health, we find this surprising. High street financial advisers and mortgage brokers are currently subject to a greater level of such supervision than pharmaceutical companies.[634]

Consequently, in the UK, the pharma industry enjoys a largely unrestrained legal freedom to leverage its significant resources and relationships with the Government and aspiring senior officials, the NHS and the broader healthcare ecosystem, healthcare professionals, its under-resourced regulators, academia and the media.

Moral hazard in relation to vaccines

As regards Covid vaccine manufacturers, layered over these industry-wide issues of oversized influence and a regulatory deficit is the matter of moral hazard.

Ordinarily when developing and selling medical products, manufacturers are subject to external controls (medicine licensing regimes) and internal controls (reputational, legal and financial risk management processes) which in principle should maintain an element of balance between the commercial interests of the manufacturer in recovering its development costs and maximising its sales, and the safety and health interests of the consumers of its products.

Vaccines are, however, different from most other medical products and devices developed and sold by pharmaceutical companies insofar as, typically, the potentially costly element of legal liability for harms caused by the products is transferred to the governments which acquire the vaccines and fund the vaccination programmes. For the UK this was, and remains, the case for any risk of harms caused by the Covid vaccines, which were underwritten by the Government by what are believed to be full-coverage indemnity arrangements.[635]

In the case of Covid vaccines, the justification for these indemnity arrangements is, broadly, that because the products used novel medical technology, needed to be developed at speed, and were prepared for public use without the opportunity to analyse long-term safety data, the risk of being sued by thousands or millions of consumers for harms caused by those products would have outweighed the financial incentives to develop and sell their products, and consequently the manufacturer would not have been able to make them available for public use.

In Moderna's case, this implies that the company would have quantified the downside risk of being sued as having potentially outweighed the benefit of this formerly loss-making company generating profits of more than US$13 billion in just two years; and for Pfizer, it implies that the scale of the latent legal risk associated with its Covid products was valued at more than the profit derived from sales of more than US$100 billion over the same two year period.

Unfortunately for the public, indemnity arrangements such as these by their nature create unhelpful incentives for both the manufacturers and for the governments giving the indemnities. Manufacturers are, in effect, absolved from the financial risk of their products causing serious adverse effects which otherwise might have had a moderating effect on safety decisions and on sales practices; with a full-coverage indemnity in place, once a product has been approved for use there will only ever be a financial upside in selling more vaccine doses. Governments, on the other hand, have assumed potentially significant financial exposures, and therefore at the same time in principle have an incentive to discourage, disparage or suppress the reporting of incidents of adverse effects which might trigger liability arising under those indemnities.

Conclusions

When in 2016 Transparency International investigated corruption in the industry, its report described *"[a] weak legislative and regulatory framework because of poor investment, a lack of oversight and national regulatory frameworks that are often decentralised and reliant on self-regulation for key decision-point[s]"* and *"[t]he potential for undue influence from companies, due to a high degree of autonomy over key decision points and unparalleled resources, on policy and regulation so profit maximisation goes beyond ethical norms and negatively impacts health outcomes and public health objectives".*[636]

Though the public does not yet have access to complete and comprehensive information to validate it, the thesis we have sought to outline in this chapter is that with its enormous financial resources and weak regulatory oversight, the pharma industry may have colonised almost the entirety of the public health world to the extent that one might question whether public health serves the interests of the pharmaceutical industry more than vice versa.

For as long as the senior executives of pharmaceutical groups remain compelled by their legal duties as directors to generate the greatest sustainable and lawful return on investment for their shareholders; for as long as they also remain free from countervailing regulatory duties to prioritise the interests of the consumers of their products, and to minimise conflicts of interest and the exercise of soft influence; for as long as government indemnities skew the relationship between risk and reward; is it not inevitable that the industry will continue to fund the research and education; leverage influence over governments, regulators and health institutions; and pursue sales and marketing strategies that in each case are most likely to maximise investment returns, whether or not those sales and strategies produce positive health outcomes?

Our comments here are not a judgement on the people involved in researching, developing or distributing vaccines; our criticism is of the perverse conditions which jeopardise public health on such a grand scale. As the author Ben Goldacre neatly put it: *"[i]t's possible for good people, in perversely designed systems, to casually perpetrate acts of great harm on strangers, sometimes without ever realising it".*[637]

At the start of this chapter we suggested that an alternative interpretation of the pandemic storyline is that pharma groups capitalised on governmental chaos to secure valuable contracts to deliver products to entire populations en masse, and co-opting the mechanisms of the State and its public health apparatus to become a sales force on steroids.

To address the question of 'why would they do this?', we suggest the answer, in light of our comments above, is simple: because they could.

WHERE IS THE PARLIAMENTARY BACKBONE?

"Limited Parliamentary scrutiny is not simply a mild inconvenience but often affects the quality of legislation."

**House of Commons Public Administration and Constitutional Affairs Committee
8 September 2020**

On 19 March, the Coronavirus Bill appeared in draft form in the House of Commons. It was 329 pages long and among many complicated provisions intended to enable Ministers to raise public spending and marshall health resources, it sought powers for Ministers and the police to quarantine infectious people, ban gatherings and delay elections.[638]

This landmark piece of new and essentially emergency legislation was debated for just six hours in the House of Commons and seven and a half hours in the House of Lords. For comparison, the EU Withdrawal Bill, which was approximately one third the length of the Coronavirus Bill, was debated in Parliament for more than 272 hours before it passed into the statute book.[639]

That the Government set out to utilise, and indeed magnify, public fear of the virus and of its potentially devastating effects on the nation's health infrastructure, as a means of influencing and controlling the public's behaviour has by now been well-documented.⁶⁴⁰ A lesser-discussed aspect of that fear-based behavioural strategy is the extent to which it was deployed within Parliament to cultivate an exaggerated sense of emergency.

When Matt Hancock appeared in Parliament on 23 March to shepherd the Coronavirus Bill through the House of Commons, his oratory rose to the occasion: *"Coronavirus is the most serious public health emergency that has faced the world in a century. We are all targets, but the disease reserves its full cruelty for the weakest and the most vulnerable. To defeat it, we are proposing extraordinary measures of a kind never seen before in peacetime. Our goal is to protect life and to protect every part of the NHS. This Bill, jointly agreed with all four UK Governments, gives us the power to fight the virus with everything that we have"*. The Bill passed its final stages of the House of Commons later that day.

That evening the Prime Minister appeared on national television to tell the nation in unambiguous terms: *"you must stay at home"*⁶⁴¹ and for those who did not follow the rules, he added, the police will have the power to enforce them. This was not in fact true because the legislation under which that lockdown was formalised was put in place only three days later.

The following day, Parliament passed within the space of one day a piece of legislation called the Contingencies Fund Act 2020, the effect of which was to allow the Government to spend, beyond its existing budgets for the year, an *additional* £266 billion of public funds with no advance parliamentary scrutiny.⁶⁴² According to former Supreme Court Judge Jonathan Sumption this departed from a 150 year-old constitutional principle that Parliament should control how public funds are spent.⁶⁴³

The Coronavirus Act finally became law on the 25th March, but it was ultimately not this Act which the Government then used to enforce the first nationwide lockdown – the Coronavirus Act did not contain powers that would have enabled Ministers to order the lockdown. Instead, that most serious intervention was given legal force by a measure made under the Public Health (Control of Disease) Act 1984 called The Health Protection (Coronavirus, Restrictions) (England) Regulations 2020. The Public Health Act ostensibly was not intended to be used for such wide-reaching and draconian public health purposes (it was primarily concerned with quarantining infectious individuals or isolating contaminated premises), but the Government concluded – presumably on the basis of advice from the Attorney General – that it could nevertheless use that legislation to order a lockdown of the entire population.[644]

On 26 March, three days *after* the Prime Minister had ordered the public not to leave their houses, Matt Hancock finally signed The Health Protection Regulations into law under an emergency legislative procedure which in exceptional circumstances enables a Minister to make a law before Parliament has had any opportunity to debate it. Those Regulations came into effect when Matt Hancock signed them at 1pm. Parliament first had sight of the Regulations some ninety minutes later, and they were published for public viewing a further 30 minutes later. Parliamentarians were however unable to debate this significant legislative measure until 6 weeks later because Parliament had entered its Easter recess at the end of the previous day.

In the first House of Commons debate on the Regulations, on 4 May 2020, Justin Madders MP speaking for the Official Opposition remarked pointedly that *"a couple of hours' debate weeks after the regulations were introduced cannot in future be sufficient to provide the level of examination and scrutiny that such sweeping laws require"*. Nevertheless, the regulations (which had already been in force for 6 weeks) were approved by the House of Commons after less than two hours of discussion.

Jonathan Sumption's lucid analysis of this short period of emergency law-making questioned the timing of the legislative process:

> "Why did the government, once they had announced the lockdown on 23 March, wait for three days until 26th before making their regulations, and then resort to the emergency procedure on the ground that it was so urgent that Parliament could not be consulted in advance? The obvious answer, I am afraid, is that Parliament adjourned for the Easter recess on 25th. They deliberately delayed their urgent regulations so that there would be no opportunity to debate them before the recess".[645]

At the very point the entire population of the UK was being subjected to the greatest confiscation of rights and personal liberties this country has known in modern peacetime, Parliament was in recess.

Kept at arm's length

Parliamentarians, like the rest of the working population, were sent home on 25 March 2020 for the Easter recess and Parliament did not then sit again until 21 April. While in theory parliamentarians were permitted to attend the Houses of Parliament in person after that date, most could not do so without breaking Covid restrictions, especially in relation to travel, and the Speakers' offices had imposed limits on the number of people permitted to sit in each Chamber.[646]

While the formal mechanisms of Parliamentary scrutiny including Select Committees, Parliamentary debates, and the system of oral, urgent and written questions from MPs calling Ministers to account continued, in practice those mechanisms were severely disrupted for the remainder of 2020 with the rules flip-flopping between parliamentarians not being allowed to sit in the chamber, to only being able to vote in the chamber, and was thus mostly operating on a hybrid model.

Like the rest of the public, all parliamentarians, including the peers in the House of Lords, found themselves quickly contending with what appeared to become an impregnable wall of official consensus across the Government and the media, combined with the public condemnation, smearing and outright censorship, of those perceived to doubt or question any official or media-adopted narrative. Some of that smearing, and attempts at silencing, came from other parliamentarians. Neil O'Brien, a Conservative Party MP, was so prolific in his criticism of lockdown sceptics[647] that he became known as the Covid Attack dog[648] and was hailed in the UK media as an inquisitor of lockdown deniers.[649] O'Brien frequently called for the censorship and disciplining of MPs who questioned any of the Government's interventions, including many among his own party.[650]

It was against this background that Parliament sought to discharge its constitutional functions.

An explosion of law-making

582 Covid-related legislative measures were presented to Parliament in the two years to 3 March 2022. This was a third of all the legal measures presented to Parliament during this period.[651] 100 of those measures were signed into law by a Minister *before* having been presented to Parliament under an emergency legislative procedure; and an astonishing 417 measures were 'made negative' during the same period, which means they automatically became law after being presented to Parliament (without debate), unless within 40 days the House of Commons passed a resolution to annul them, which it rarely does;[652] in fact, the last time a legislative measure was annulled in this way was in 1979.[653]

The Coronavirus Act 2020 included provisions which required the Government to seek Parliament's approval for its continuance every six months. This 'sunset' arrangement had been structured so that Parliament's choice was either to continue the legislation in full or to reject it in full – there was no opportunity for amendments, and just 90 minutes of debate was allowed for each renewal. A Parliamentary committee which reviewed the Coronavirus Act shortly before it expired in March 2022 noted that this had had *"a deleterious effect on Parliament's ability to scrutinise and amend emergency provisions"*.[654]

Parliament's vote on 14 December 2021 for a tightening of intervention measures, known as Plan B, is yet another excellent example of how the volume of legislation meant the quality of scrutiny suffered.[655] A single debate took place in the House of Commons for votes on four separate legislative instruments providing for: mandatory face coverings for retail premises and public transport, daily Covid testing, Covid passes for access to nightclubs and larger venues and an vaccination requirement for all NHS staff.

As we showed earlier, the latter two restrictions in particular had significant implications for the lives and livelihoods of the affected workers, the operation of the NHS and for the economy, yet the Parliamentary debate took place over less than five hours and with all four measures debated together.

That particularly congested debate also coincided with the Partygate revelations – so opposition MPs used the opportunity to make repeated reference to that scandal rather than using their time to scrutinise the new laws under consideration. The NHS staff vaccination proposal consequently received surprisingly little attention; yet this was a piece of legislation that 65% of the public did not support.[656]

All four measures were approved, albeit the Government had to rely on votes from opposition MPs to clear the Covid Pass vote after 99 of its own MPs rebelled.

While acknowledging that there were very many new laws on which MPs were asked to vote – arguably too many realistically to scrutinise – it is equally lamentable that there were some very impactful policy decisions taken by the Government over which Parliament had no say because their implementation did not require legislation, and the Government as not obliged to consult with Parliament. School closures were a prime example.

Pandemic pressures were compounded by pre-existing obstacles

Even before the complications of the early phase of the pandemic, parliamentarians were weighed down in ways which negatively affected Parliament's scrutineering capacity.

In fact it had been recognised for many years that MPs have suffered from having to combine limited capacity and limited supporting resources with a significant workload of local constituency commitments to manage alongside the business of Parliament.[657] More than ever before, many MPs also now need to juggle commitments to young families. As the Hansard Society explains in its guide for new MPs *"No other job can really prepare you for what it is like to transition from being an ordinary member of the public to a Member of Parliament"*.[658]

Thus it was suboptimal that the election of 140 new MPs in the General Election at the end of 2019 meant that, when the pandemic struck, over 1 in 5 MPs had barely even set foot in Parliament let alone acquired meaningful experience of how legislative processes are conducted in practice. This will inevitably have hampered not only the ability but the willingness and confidence of those MPs to stand out in an unexpectedly intense period of law-making and governmental policy-making.

Too much was waived through

One can start from a position of having some sympathy for the difficult job of an MP, and particularly for a new MP starting work in early 2020, but once the initial wave of panic and confusion had broken – probably from May or certainly June 2020 – and with the scale of harms from lockdowns and school closures already painfully apparent, we were entitled to expect more from our representatives.

Too often MPs simply got out of the Government's way. Even among the measures that were the most contentious and most challenged that we have documented, and where experienced MPs were calling out Ministers for their contemptuous treatment of Parliament, those measures still passed, and comfortably for the most part. As we explained in our chapter on the Covid Passes legislation, a rebellion of historical proportions failed to slow the measure from becoming law, and despite furious condemnations by MPs in the chamber of the Government's handling of that and other critical legislation, there was conspicuously no meaningful consequence for any Minister. When Ministers suffer no penalty for treating Parliament as a derided impediment rather than as the sole source of the democratic legitimacy for all of the Government's actions, what incentive is there to behave differently the next time?

It cannot have helped matters that, astonishingly, at the outset of the crisis MPs had been explicitly asked not to impede the Government. On the day the first lockdown was announced, the Speaker of the Commons had said to MPs: *"I understand the wish of Members— particularly those not able to attend the Chamber—to fulfil their duty to* hold the Government to account. However, I urge Members to think twice before tabling parliamentary questions. In particular, they may want to think about the impact of such questions on Government officials who are working incredibly hard to respond to the current crisis".[659] MPs were in effect being asked not to trouble the Government with distracting questions, while also being kept away from the chamber – a terrible precedent for any representative democracy.

Rather than see themselves as a safeguard to governmental overreach, we saw parliamentarians become cheerleaders for the Government's authoritarianism. This is no more strikingly illustrated than by Parliament's enthusiastic support of efforts to control pandemic-related false information by any means necessary. Unfortunately as shown in the official records of the Select Committee hearings which had called social media companies to appear in April 2020 and then again in December 2020, the thrust of Parliament's input was to press for a more aggressive approach to removing not only demonstrably false content from their platforms but also 'disputed' content:

> "Twitter's spokesperson, Katie Rosborough, has previously stated that the company 'will not take enforcement action on every Tweet that contains incomplete or disputed information about COVID-19'. What is the reason for this approach, given that it implies that Twitter will not take action against disputed information even where you are aware of it?".[660]

In fact, ensuring that the attack on harmful information was sufficiently severe became the main theme of at least two Select Committee hearings in 2020. The social media groups, initially reluctant to stray too far into moderating legitimate public square debate, were encouraged by Parliament to support and amplify 'trusted' news sources (being those that were already amplifying Government messages). This was captured in a letter from the DCMS Select Committee to Google: *"How have you been working with partners in the Trusted News Initiative to ensure that authoritative information is surfaced appropriately and misinformation is demoted on your platforms? Are you supporting or amplifying the output of traditional news organisations? If so, how, and if not, why not?"*.[661]

Even when Parliament was proactive and prodigious in its scrutiny of the Government's decision-making, it was often unable to hold back the tide of damaging policies. Take school closures: between April 2020 and July 2021 the ESC held twenty hearings under the heading of *'The impact of COVID-19 on education and children's services'*, in addition to a series of accountability hearings, sessions on school exams, and on educational recovery, and across all of these hearings Ministers and senior Covid policy officials were called multiple times to account for their actions.

Those Ministers and officials were repeatedly and often pointedly challenged both on their policy choices, and on the adequacy of the promises of governmental support for educational recovery by which those choices, impacting millions of children most of whom were at negligible risk of serious harm from the virus, had been justified.

But this did not prevent decisions being made which were demonstrably and disproportionately harmful to children; and, at best, ethically questionable. Nor did it prevent Ministers repeatedly deflecting the Committee's legitimate concerns. Nor did it act as a deterrent against chaotic decision-making with frequent u-turns. And ultimately nor could it protect children or their education.

We can only speculate as to why that was. To an extent, the Parliamentary transcripts reveal that those responsible for policy decisions were prone to self-affirm the accuracy and appropriateness of their decision-making come what may, and to reassure that the concerns of their inquisitors had already been or would in the near future be taken into account. Rarely does one find an admission that

– in the thick of a complicated pandemic – there might have been a mis-step, or that all relevant factors might not have been taken fully into account, or indeed that there might have been a better decision made. Over time such a consistent level of assuredness stretches credulity, and gives the impression that Parliamentary accountability was too often regarded as a gauntlet to be run rather than an opportunity for Parliament to exercise its constitutional functions. It seems there was, and remains, an issue about the extent to which Ministers and their officials remember that, constitutionally, their authority derives exclusively from Parliament.

From the Government's forcing through of controversial Covid Passes against the recommendations of the Public Administration and Constitutional Affairs Committee, to the repeated frustration of Parliament's demands for impact assessments and the countless examples of hollow promises and unsubstantiated claims presented in the chambers and in Select Committee hearings; our earlier chapters have evidenced Parliament and its Select Committees being treated less than respectfully, from a lack of candour through to outright contemptuous, and yet in almost also cases without consequence.

To try to understand how this was allowed to happen, and why Ministers and officials were not more forcefully held to account, we have read accounts authored by parliamentarians, and spoken to many ourselves. The impression we have is that the pressure to vote along party lines remained particularly strong during the pandemic period. Parliamentarians, and particularly MPs, who questioned the need for lockdowns and other liberty-infringing interventions were often forcefully challenged by their colleagues, and the press.

The procedures governing the operation and legislative business of Parliament are complex and couched in a somewhat specialist vernacular. Hundreds of pieces of technical legislation, some with voluminous details, pass through Parliament via a variety of differing procedures. It can be difficult for MPs to remain fully across all of this technical paperwork, let alone form and express opinions on them. For this reason MPs must commonly rely on their parties for guidance on how to vote.

That said, even when an MP takes an interest in the details and has views on a piece of legislation passing through Parliament, it is a long-standing convention and expectation in our system of representative democracy that, other than on votes of conscience, MPs should ordinarily vote with their party. The rationale for this convention is that voters elect MPs on party lines rather than as independent individuals, and they do so on the basis of the relevant political party's manifesto; it follows that an MP's constituents are entitled to expect their representative to vote in support of the policies of the party for which they voted.

There is also then a system of 'whipping' by which political parties seek to canvass the localised or personal concerns of their MPs in advance of policy decisions and legislative votes, with a view thereby to maintaining voting discipline throughout the party. The effect of all this is that, in the party system, MPs can find that they are obliged to support policy and legislation with which, personally and privately, they may not fully agree.

But there is another more significant – and, incidentally, remediable – factor which seems to have received surprisingly little attention. It is the fact that any one time, almost 20% of MPs hold a salaried governmental position and are therefore in practice unable to critique the Government's policy decisions or challenge Government-backed legislation.

As of 24 April 2023, there were 133 ministerial posts, held by 124 people, out of a total of 650 MPs. This is a high proportion compared to many other jurisdictions and concerns have been expressed by parliamentarians that it is too high.

"There is a strong case for re-examining the number of government ministers that the country needs, as well as the statutory limits on these numbers that currently exist", concluded a report of the Public Administration Select Committee in 2009 (at which point there were 'only' 119 Ministers).[662]

In addition, as of November 2022, there are some 41 Parliamentary Private Secretaries[663] who, while not members of the Government, are expected to vote in support of Government motions and to *"avoid associating themselves with recommendations critical of or embarrassing to the government"*.[664]

It should be obvious why this system diminishes Parliament's ability to discharge its constitutional role, and why our democratic system of government is weaker for it.

We deserved better

In a recent report which makes sensible and pragmatic recommendations for improving Parliament's scrutiny of legislation, the Hansard Society has warned that *"the price of poorly-conceived, poorly-drafted and poorly-scrutinised legislation is paid by citizens across the country who are subject to its detrimental effects. Unless the problems with the system are addressed, public acceptance of the democratic legitimacy of delegated legislation will come under increasing strain"*.[665] On the basis of what we have seen, and documented in this and other chapters, we can only agree.

Parliament was not outright denied opportunities to apply scrutiny and to hold Ministers and officials to account for the policy decisions that we have unpicked in earlier chapters. As we have seen, at a few critical moments when checks and balances were much needed, Parliament's opportunity was more limited than parliamentarians had rightly expected. We have also seen how Ministers and officials almost routinely evaded, deflected or disregarded Parliament's attention. Nevertheless, it is also the case that Parliament's oversight of the Government was at times woefully inadequate.

Whatever the causes, the uncomfortable truth is that our Parliament failed us: it failed to provide adequate challenge to an increasingly authoritarian Executive; it failed to curb that Executive's legislative overreaches; it failed to act in response to ministerial disrespect and disregard for the democratic processes and traditions of Parliament; it failed to protect the interests of the most vulnerable; it failed to protect the interests of children; it failed to protect care home workers. And even now, with experts warning of an unexplained excess deaths catastrophe of equal proportion to the pandemic itself, it is still so far failing to act.

This is not merely an historical intellectual problem. It is a current and continuing real world threat. As we draw all of the threads together, current threats are the focus of our penultimate chapter.

PART 4

CURRENT THREATS

The legacy of our pandemic past threatens our present. The threat manifests in different ways.

Firstly, through the fact that so many of the conditions which enabled the terrible pandemic decisions described in the previous chapters remain present today – in that sense these were not merely historical failures, but symptoms of persisting deficits of governance, transparency, ethics, truth even. In this status quo, we see a harbinger of future crises. Without correction we are setting ourselves up to relive a cycle of poor, unethical and damaging decision-making.

Secondly, through the trail of harmful consequences flowing from the pandemic response which in themselves risk our collective prosperity and wellbeing: astronomical public debt; a degradation of the sanctity of schooling and education; a generation of 'ghost children', individual tragedies which can be expected to create significant further burden on the welfare state; the health of the population deteriorating and a public health system which, ironically, has shed credibility, trust and resources. Rather than fulfilling the mantra of 'Build Back Better', the pandemic response has left the country poorer, angrier and more divided than ever.

Some of these factors deserve more explanation:

Hardwiring and turbo-charging a failed interventionist approach

We have campaigned against, and continue to reject – at least in the context of this virus – the heavily interventionist approach not, principally, because the methods were flawed (though credible experts have by now evidenced either the limited or negative effectiveness of key interventions such as school closures, masking of children, digital contact tracing and lockdowns), but because almost any mass societal intervention carries a risk of harms, and sometimes serious harms, the weighing of which is critical to determining whether intervening is net positive or net negative.

Our position has always been simple: that an intervention is not appropriate if it cannot be demonstrated that the benefits outweigh the harms and risks of harm. Having spent three years immersed in the evidence base, and having read thousands of personal accounts from supporters of UsForThem, we believe that it will be impossible ever to show that the benefits of lockdowns, school closures and the masking of children ever outweighed the predicted and now readily visible long-term harms which have flowed both directly and indirectly from each of them. We believe there is also a serious question to be addressed about the benefits of vaccinating those at very low risk, including in particular children in the case of Covid. It is unfortunately indisputable that most of these interventions had a disproportionate impact on children.[666]

Yet almost unbelievably given the trail of destruction left behind by these and other measures the first time around, not only are some of the most controversial restrictions being hailed as successes, but there seems to be a narrative building – most notably in the testimony given at the official Covid Inquiry – that the key learning from this pandemic is to intervene faster and harder.[667] [668]

Experts opine that the country is now primed not only to repeat but to accept future lockdown instructions and social restrictions. Professor David Halpern – head of the Government's behavioural science 'nudge' unit and a member of the behavioural sub-group of SAGE – told *The Telegraph* that now the public has practiced the lockdown drill we would likely do it again if asked: *"they might protest, 'do we really have to do it?' [Showing] good healthy scepticism. But once you've exercised those muscles, they're more likely to be reused again"*, describing this as the beginning of a *"habit loop"*.[669]

In June 2023, Stella Kyriakides, the European Commissioner for Health and Food Safety (whose Twitter bio, apparently without irony, reads *"Human rights advocate"*), tweeted to announce that vaccine passports were set to become a global standard:

"Today an [EU] success story becomes a [global] standard. Working with @WHO, the system will be scaled up at global level to deliver better digital health services for all".[670]

Quite aside from the significant moral, legal and ethical concerns with such a scheme, there is little evidence to suggest that it would actually work. Yet the EU and WHO tie-up would make this a global offering with the spectre of enabling, or perhaps mandating, the widespread use of de facto medical identity cards which in time could allow governments to decide to limit movement within or between countries, or to limit access to services or amenities, for those who cannot satisfy a government-approved medical status.

Similarly, while a degree of international cooperation and coordination in public health may well make sense, how many readers would feel comfortable about proposals, currently progressing behind closed doors in Geneva, and with only minimal visibility accorded to Parliament, for new powers and resources to be granted to the WHO – an organisation accountable only to itself and substantially funded by private money – not only to coordinate but to direct the management of pandemics?

The proposals under consideration envision a dramatic ceding of rule-making discretion, and of national autonomy over health spending, to the essentially unelected director-general of the WHO. We have analysed these gravely concerning proposals in commentary which also details the funding structures behind the WHO and explains why that organisation – 80% or more backed by private money, a significant portion of which is linked to the pharmaceuticals industry – can be expected to prefer an interventionist approach to managing future regional and global pandemics.[671]

For these purposes, it suffices to note that not only does this risk supercharging the failed Covid response, but also opens the door to mandatory and highly controversial measures including quarantining, lockdowns and mandatory vaccination being ceded to administrators beyond the reach of Parliamentary accountability.

The ramifications of these provisions which strive to rewire, potentially permanently, the relationship between the state and the individual and to give a supranational, unelected organisation autonomy over elements of national health, economic and social policy are matched by an astonishing inertia from elected politicians. Using a Freedom of Information Act request, UsForThem asked the Government to explain at what level of seniority within the Government the WHO negotiations have been coordinated. The Government has so far refused to disclose any information about the UK's negotiating team for those generationally significant new international accords.

Censorship

As we have shown earlier, investigative journalists in the UK, and to an extent disclosures to Select Committees and in the official Covid Inquiry, have revealed that government units have been intensively policing the public square throughout the pandemic, and through relationships with social media and other technology companies have sought to direct and in some cases close down lawful debate.

The UK has not been alone in this aspect. The extensive use of this apparatus of suppression has attracted free speech legal actions in the US under the 'First Amendment' right. This has forced disclosure of internal government communications and of communications between government and social media groups, which have revealed the scale and complexity of the operations involved, and has coined the phrase 'the censorship industrial complex'. News reports document that censorship by the US government included *"coercion and significant encouragement"* when it repeatedly — and often successfully — lobbied social-media companies *"to remove disfavored content and accounts from their sites"*.[672] Among the topics targeted for suppression were views and alleged 'misinformation' that did not accord with the US government's stance on the Covid lab-leak theory and the efficacy of pandemic lockdowns and vaccines.

We have little reason to believe that what has been forced into the open in the US was unique to that country. Indeed, having been on the receiving end of what seems to have been monitoring and – we believe – censorship ourselves, we have long suspected that what little has so far been exposed in the UK will prove to be part of a pervasive State-led effort to control discussion, reporting and commentary. Whether private sector platforms and influencers, and initiatives such as the Trusted News Initiative, have unwittingly or knowingly participated in this effort remains to be understood.

Regardless, that the suppression of dissenting views has involved non-state actors is now readily apparent, and has been admitted.[673] Since our own experience of debanking – in our case by PayPal in September 2022 – many others have come forward to recount their own experience of exclusion by financial services providers for which debanking appears to have become not only normalised but a tool for delivering against 'social responsibility' commitments.[674] [675]

There is also empirical evidence of State bodies and their dependents even now seeking to suppress contrarian views from being aired. Professor Karol Sikora, a leading cancer specialist of over 40 years' standing who challenged lockdowns on the basis that they would cause a backlog in cancer cases, recently found himself the victim of an attempted cancellation when a major NHS supplier threatened to pull its sponsorship of a panel discussion event if he remained a speaker.[676] On that occasion the sponsor was dropped. This is not though an isolated example; it is part of the petty yet insidious culture of suppression which is fast overrunning our public square.

We have no evidence to suggest that specific Ministers or government units were behind these particular acts of suppression. There is an inevitable opacity to these situations such that those on the receiving end have often struggled to gain a full understanding of what has occurred. In our own case, PayPal at first stonewalled our requests for information and has latterly refused to provide legally-mandated transparency of its debanking decision in response to data subject access requests[677] (a refusal which in our view has probably compounded an original breach of regulatory law with a further breach of UK and European data protection law, albeit for now at least with impunity). Knowing this, and knowing also that our debanking experience appears to have coincided with simultaneous debankings of other campaigning organisations and individuals who challenged the basis for various of the Government's pandemic policies, we feel justified in at least questioning whether PayPal acted fully on its own initiative.

There are other factors which are likely to mean this creeping censorious culture will only become more widespread and normalised. In the UK, the Online Safety Act will turbo charge the Government's ability to control and influence the information and commentary we see and read online by handing censoring powers to the communications regulator, Ofcom.

We acknowledge that a material motivation for this piece of legislation has been to protect children from harmful online content, and we agree that this is a serious harm from which children deserve to be protected. We also, though, recognise and share the concerns that free speech advocates have consistently raised about the scope for the Act as drafted, and the broad discretionary delegated powers granted under it, to be used to censor commentary and opinion far beyond that which is harmful to children.

When asked in a Select Committee hearing by Alex Davies-Jones MP whether the Act had been informed by the experience the CDU gained from managing anti-vaccine misinformation, Sarah Connolly, a senior official at the Department for Culture Media and Sports replied *"a lot"*, to which the answer was *"perfect"*.[678] The very people tasked with scrutinising the censors have become their cheerleaders. When viewed alongside the views expressed by Professor Halpern, the Government's behavioural science adviser, that *"there are times when you do need to cut through… particularly if you think people are wrongly calibrated"*, there is a clear and present risk that we shall soon discover that there is a correct way to think, and those who think differently will not be tolerated. This worrying trend may only accelerate if the WHO is successful in its current bid to secure funding and powers to ramp up its public health information control activities.[679]

Public Health

Ironically, the greatest threat may yet flow from the destabilising of public health.

By embedding mass interventions into the blueprint for forestalling future pandemics – interventions which in some cases have since been shown to have been ineffective and in other cases to have caused collateral damage of as yet unknown proportions – we are catastrophically under-recognising the role of individual responsibility for health and prevention.

As non-scientists we have chosen not to focus on a discussion of the most medically controversial pandemic topic in this work – the scale and extent of possible vaccine harms caused by the mRNA vaccine roll-out. We simply note that concerns about the extent of those harms exist, and have been raised in fora including many Parliaments, not least our own.[680]

The evidence from our own network of thousands of parents, grandparents, and other engaged individuals, both in the UK and elsewhere, reveals significant and genuine concern about this topic, emanating in many cases from their own first-hand experience, as well as an awareness of the unprecedented volume of Yellow Card adverse events reported since 2021. At the same time the UK, like many other countries which pursued a heavily interventionist pandemic response, is experiencing an excess deaths problem so severe[681] that it has become impossible for our Parliament to ignore.[682]

Yet the elevated yellow card data for this particular intervention appears to us to have been underplayed or ignored by public health institutions, regulators and the pharmaceutical industry. Instead we have seen mRNA and other novel technologies pedestalled as a victory of science over nature despite a growing volume of published studies and expert opinions casting doubt on the ostensibly unblemished official safety record for these products.[683]

One does not need to have an opinion on the safety of these products or indeed on any other pharmaceutical product to understand that restricting professional debate about safety is misguided and – when a product has been mass marketed to children – we would say, reckless. Yet, the implication of the statements made to Parliament by the Head of the CDU is that not only is the public questioning of particular vaccines problematic, but even discussion of the safety implications of *"big business and links to pharma"* – a topic to which we devoted an entire earlier chapter – is off limits as the preserve of dangerous anti-vax heretics.

Indeed, on its own terms it seems likely that the CDU would have considered Baroness Cumberlege, chair of the widely-lauded July 2020 Independent Medicines and Medical Devices Safety Review,[684] to have been peddling anti-vax content when she publicly critiqued the conflicts and outsized corporate influence of the pharmaceuticals sector, and similarly those members of the House of Commons Health Select Committee which in 2005 authored an excoriating report on the influence of the pharmaceuticals sector which cited extensive examples of conflicts and damaging corporate practices and summarised that *"[o]ur over-riding concerns are about the volume, extent and intensity of the industry's influence, not only on clinical medicine and research but also on patients, regulators, the media, civil servants and politicians"*.[685]

By the same token this work presumably stands to be flagged and if you discuss its content you might also become a dangerous heretic.

Blinded by our idolatry of vaccines we seem to have lost sight of the fact that, in the context of the pandemic at least, a novel medical product with no long-term safety record and only minimal personal benefit was rolled out to millions of healthy children. For experts, health editors, broadcasters and concerned parents to not now be able to discuss publicly whether that roll-out itself could have posed a risk to child public health is a vivid illustration of the extreme place we have reached.

More prosaically, we are reminded through news reports, docudramas and our own politicians and Select Committees the extent to which an oversized pharmaceutical industry has become a threat to our collective public health. This is an industry that is too big and too embedded in our public and private health infrastructure to be allowed to fail, but which operates astonishingly free from regulatory restraints. It took a 'black swan' banking crisis to cause global governments to recognise the societal risks of the banking sector. What greater crisis should we need to experience for governments now to recognise the societal risks of an under-regulated pharma sector?

Children

We came into this with a concern for the near-term wellbeing of our children, apparently shut out both from their schools and from consideration in pandemic policy-making. We are coming out of it despairing for the long-term health, wellbeing and prosperity not only of our own children but of generations of children to come.

That is a future we are not prepared to tolerate. Our aspiration with this work and our campaigning is to trigger the reconciliation that we believe is necessary to confront and then remedy the social damage caused by this tragic period of misgovernance, and so we turn our minds to reform.

RECONCILIATION AND REFORM

The failures we have reviewed in earlier chapters are serious, many and varied. They have included governance failures, safeguarding failures, ethical failures, failures of transparency, of integrity, of scrutiny and, more prosaically but no less importantly, of good sense and decency. There are many remedies and reforms that we could — indeed should — aspire to implement in response.

For example, the governance responsibilities of the Cabinet Secretary and of departmental secretaries for ensuring that significant decisions of Ministers, and of any sub-groups of Cabinet, are permanently documented, including the capture of all briefings and evidence relied on, could be strengthened. To achieve this, we could repurpose aspects of the regulatory regime for banks which requires significant decisions to be documented and attested by specific individuals with relevant functional responsibilities, up to the most senior responsible officer. We could also require records of ministerial decisions detailing the advice relied upon to be published, or at least made accessible under a presumption of disclosure subject to only limited exceptions, as is the case with civil service advice and briefings in New Zealand.[686]

Ministerial business should always be conducted in a format amenable to after-the-event scrutiny and audit, so communication between Ministers, and between Ministers and senior officials, by encrypted private messaging systems could be, in fact must now be, legally prohibited.

Records of ministerial decisions, including decisions of Cabinet, which effect policy in reliance on existing legislative powers should include a documented affirmation given by the responsible Minister identifying the specific power or powers being exercised (supported by the opinion of the Attorney General or a senior law officer in contentious cases). This should be buttressed by an accountability mechanism which carries the possibility of serious personal penalties for acting without proper powers.

A failsafe introduced into the procedures of Parliament could prevent legislation from being adopted if any mandatory impact assessment has not been published sufficiently in advance — a form of legislative brake which could be applied by the Speaker of the Commons, or a Committee of the House of Lords. Alternatively, the Speaker could be made responsible for policing statutory requirements for impact assessments to be published, such as for the care home workers mandate legislation, which should not have proceeded to a vote absent that information having been provided to parliamentarians.

The Cabinet Office or a new coordinating body of non-political appointees, could be given responsibility for ensuring that Ministers, Cabinet and the Prime Minister receive advice in any future health emergency situation from experts and advisory committees with expertise beyond public health and science, including for example ethical, educational and economic advice.

The Children's Minister should become a Cabinet post with explicit responsibility for ensuring that the Government's legislative and policy agenda takes into account the short and long-term needs and interests of children (recognising that children are not politically enfranchised, and are entitled to safeguarding). Principles of public policy-making should enshrine the need for Ministers to consider the impact of each of their decisions on the current and future generations of children.

To that end, Ministers should be obliged to consult with the Children's Commissioner on any legislative or new policy proposal that could be expected to impact materially on the rights or interests of children, and to publish any opinion provided by the Commissioner alongside its impact assessment. At the same time, the powers, responsibilities and resources of the Children's Commissioner need to be enhanced, including a statutory obligation to report serious safeguarding concerns promptly and directly to Parliament.

Schools should be designated as Essential Infrastructure.

The recently relaunched Better Regulation Framework should be extended to legislative and policy measures which propose any significant interference with human or civil rights, or any impact on the rights or interests of children or other vulnerable groups, so that Parliament has the benefit of a full impact assessment. MEAG, or a replacement committee of independent ethical experts, should be tasked with reviewing those categories of impact assessment, and any others which either the Regulatory Policy Committee asks it to review or which the MEAG on its own initiative asks to review.

The JCVI should be obliged to read the ethical advice of MEAG or its successor before making any mass vaccination recommendations to the Government. The Government should be bound not to override negative decisions of the JCVI unless it seeks Parliamentary approval to do so; in other words, if the JCVI recommends a mass vaccination programme the Government could choose to accept that advice or to do nothing; if however the JVCI declines to recommend a mass vaccination programme, the Government should not be able on its own initiative to override that advice.

There should be an independent inquiry into the role and extent of State and private sector censorship during the pandemic, and in any event a Select Committee should investigate the management and activities of, and the legal guardrails for, the Counter Disinformation Unit, the Rapid Response Unit and related units operated by the Government. The Government could consult on the feasibility, pitfalls and limitations of a Free Speech Act including the possibility for civil, administrative and criminal remedies for the suppression of lawful speech and comment.

Root and branch reform of the UK pharmaceutical industry regulatory framework is urgently needed, with a particular focus on conflicts, financial influence and prioritising good health outcomes and the needs of customers ahead of commercial gain. There is a ready blueprint for these concepts in the Financial Conduct Authority's Principles for Businesses. The proposed Sunshine Act on which the Government began consulting in October 2023 should be adopted with the broadest frame of reference to give transparency to all pharma industry 'payments of influence'.

This is a long list, but it is just the start of a much longer wish list. We must reluctantly recognise, however, that it is almost inconceivable that even a fraction of reforms such as these will ever seriously be discussed let alone actioned. Governments have little incentive to encumber their own powers and privileges. That said, even if all of these reform ideas were to be adopted, we believe their effectiveness would be hobbled by a deficit in probably the most critical area: a deficit of accountability.

The scale and gravity of the failings we discussed in our earlier chapters have shocked us. They speak to a hollowness at the heart of public life: hubris in place of humanity; deception in place of decency; self-interest in place of integrity; bias where there should only have been objectivity. Yet there is little chance that any Minister or official will face the awkward questions that need to be asked, less so face accountability for their decisions, actions and inactions. We may be too late for looking back now, but it is imperative to think ahead. If terrible decisions have no meaningful consequence for the decision-makers, what incentive is there to do better?

All Ministers and public officials are morally if not legally committed to observing the Seven Principles of Public Life, also known as the Nolan Principles. These are high level principles for those employed in public service of unarguable simplicity and beneficence, and so central to what it should mean to be an office holder that really they ought not to need writing down. Nevertheless in 1995 they were committed to paper by Lord Nolan as follows:

1. **Selflessness** — Holders of public office should act solely in terms of the public interest.

2. **Integrity** — Holders of public office must avoid placing themselves under any obligation to people or organisations that might try inappropriately to influence them in their work. They should not act or take decisions in order to gain financial or other material benefits for themselves, their family, or their friends. They must declare and resolve any interests and relationships.

3. **Objectivity** — Holders of public office must act and take decisions impartially, fairly and on merit, using the best evidence and without discrimination or bias.

4. **Accountability** — Holders of public office are accountable to the public for their decisions and actions and must submit themselves to the scrutiny necessary to ensure this.

5. **Openness** — Holders of public office should act and take decisions in an open and transparent manner. Information should not be withheld from the public unless there are clear and lawful reasons for so doing.

6. **Honesty** — Holders of public office should be truthful.

7. **Leadership** — Holders of public office should exhibit these principles in their own behaviour and treat others with respect. They should actively promote and robustly support the principles and challenge poor behaviour wherever it occurs.

It is sobering to reflect on how many occasions during the pandemic one or more of these principles was breached or ignored, sometimes flagrantly.

Were Ministers and officials truthful and acting solely in the public interest when they systematically and concertedly exaggerated risks and underplayed harms? Were Ministers and officials acting impartially, fairly and on the best available evidence when they closed schools in full knowledge of an array of harms predicted in the advice of SAGE? Were they acting on the best available evidence when they masked children in classrooms without having carried out a harm assessment?

Did Ministers act in an open and transparent manner and show principled leadership when they pushed through the care home workers vaccination requirement without providing Parliament with an impact assessment? Can we ever be sure that Ministers and other senior officials have acted solely in the public interest if their personal financial interests — even if disclosed — were exposed to the outcomes of their own decisions or advice? Did Ministers and officials submit to necessary scrutiny when they declined to appear before Select Committees, or provided misleading or inaccurate information to them?

We could go on.

We need collectively to acknowledge that the Seven Principles of Public Life were not adequate to restrain many serious failures involving public servants during the 'emergency' of the pandemic. Whatever the inadequacies of the status quo, and however it is achieved, it is clear that Parliament needs to reassert itself as the supreme authority to which public servants ultimately are accountable, and to restore genuine personal accountability to public office.

To this end, Parliament could sensibly give Select Committees greater powers to hold Ministers and senior civil servants accountable in the ordinary course of Parliamentary business. Senior civil servants should be held accountable by Select Committees for their role in supporting policy decisions as well as for spending decisions. Committees could also be given more flexible powers to declare any Minister or official unreasonably failing to appear, or to answer questions or provide information in a timely manner, to be in contempt of the committee with a range of meaningful adverse consequences.

It could also limit the number of MPs retained on the Government's payroll, and give consideration to other measures which might mitigate the dampening effect of the whipping system among Parliamentary parties. At the very least, Parliament, and the public, could recognise that for MPs to better perform their scrutiny and accountability role, they will need to be better resourced with professional support for the constituency aspects of their role.

But above all else, we need a stronger culture of accountability — for Ministers, for their advisors, for civil servants, for parliamentarians. We do not need a vengeful form of accountability, of seeking to catch out public servants; rather we need a reset and reaffirmation of the status of Parliament as the supreme democratic authority for scrutinising the Government's activities and for holding Ministers and officials to account. Ministers should be expected, obliged and seen to treat Parliament with deference rather than contempt, and the routine expectation of personal accountability should then have a focussing effect on the minds of those who serve the public interest.

We suggest there are at least two credible means by which this could be achieved.

First, the Nolan Principles could be overlaid by a statutory accountability regime modelled on the senior managers accountability regime for regulated banks and other financial services institutions. That regime was introduced in response to public and Parliamentary outrage that senior banking executives could not be held personally accountable for their risk-taking roles in the 2008 banking crisis.

A statutory accountability regime of this kind could apply in targeted terms specifically to Ministers, their special advisers and other senior public officials with significant influence or input into policy decision-making. It would apply binding standards of conduct and integrity at least equivalent to the Nolan Principles, but could go further. Meaningful administrative penalties (i.e. not requiring a criminal law standard of proof) would be needed to focus minds and to have a desirable deterrent effect. These could include public censure, proportionate personal financial penalties, and ultimately exclusion from public office.

Alternatively, and perhaps most simply, we could enshrine the existing Nolan Principles as binding legal obligations, and reconstitute the Committee on Standards in Public Life as a fully independent statutory body with own initiative powers (indeed duties), and access to the resources needed, to investigate potential breaches by Ministers and others.

So if we have just one message — one single call for reform — it is for the restoration of personal accountability in government. This is a cultural as well as a procedural and legal aspiration. New laws, rules and Parliamentary conventions could achieve plenty; but there needs also to be a cultural understanding among those who govern, and those who enjoy positions of unelected public authority, that with power and authority will come responsibility and, above all else, accountability.

AFTERWORD BY DANNY KRUGER MP

The British state failed the British people in 2020-22. This work details how. The authors believe that Ministers and officials were personally to blame for a series of bad decisions which inflicted what they call 'an economic, social, medical, ethical and safeguarding disaster' on the public. I also have grave concerns about many decisions the Government took. But my real concern – and indeed the authors' – goes deeper than personal culpability.

Better ministers and advisers may have made better decisions. But fundamentally what failed in 2020-22 wasn't a handful of individuals. It was the system as a whole: the British state, its outer ring of expert advisors, advisory bodies and regulators, and the wider set of supposedly independent institutions, including the media and the pharmaceutical industry, which in this crisis rallied to the State and became to all intents and purposes part of it.

And above and beneath all of them, what failed was the institution that is intended to hold the rest together and make them honest: Parliament. If we are looking for individuals to blame, look here. What failed was me, and my colleagues.

I was a late convert to scepticism about Covid policy. My view for at least the first year of the crisis was that the Government's response – mass testing, mass lockdowns, mass vaccination – was the only one that could work. I trusted the experts and, as a loyal Conservative backbencher and then Parliamentary Private

Secretary, voted for everything that Ministers put in front of us. I focused my efforts locally, in my Wiltshire constituency, where we saw both real suffering but also a remarkable spirit of neighbourliness and innovation.

In the Summer of 2020, I compiled a report for the Prime Minister exploring how we might harness the community spirit which we saw across the country to 'build back better' after the pandemic. In those early months I regarded the whole Covid episode simply as a traumatic pause in the life of the country, thankfully managed by people who knew what they were doing, and I looked forward to a brighter future beyond it.

But as time passed I became slowly radicalised by the Covid experience. Indeed what turned me into a sceptic was the corruption of the concept of 'community'. As a Conservative I have a deep respect for the institutions, formal and informal, that sustain our national life, starting with families, widening to neighbourhoods and then to the national bodies that give us identity and security. It was this respect for institutions that the Covid response relied upon for the public support it needed; and yet these institutions were its primary victims. The ties that bind us were used to throttle us.

People's love of their families was exploited by instructions to 'don't kill granny' by visiting her. The strength of local communities, so apparent in the way that neighbours came together spontaneously to look after the elderly and vulnerable, to organise pop-up grocery shops in pub car parks, to stitch (useless, as it turned out) facemasks, was ridden over by a set of diktats that drew all power to the central state. Vital local institutions like schools and churches were closed down altogether in the name of community safety, to protect the young and old. And our national institutions – Parliament most of all, but also the Church of England and the BBC – effectively suspended their independence in the name of solidarity with the Government.

AFTERWORD BY DANNY KRUGER MP

***

Now that we are out the other side of Covid we can look back and try to understand what we went through, and particularly what we MPs did to our constituents. I am sorry that so few colleagues want to do this. Like the rest of the British establishment, particularly the media which played such a central role in the saga, most politicians want to 'move on' from Covid. In this they probably reflect the views of the public. Most people would like to discuss test and trace, lockdown tiers, and the vaccine programme as much as they want to discuss Brexit.

But MPs have a duty to do the boring and the difficult stuff. In order to move on safely – and in justice to the many victims of Covid and the response to it – we need to look back, and learn the lessons.

What, then, can we learn? This account is compiled by three heroic campaigners who, like me, began the pandemic as neutral citizens, happy to trust the State, but – much quicker than me – became dismayed by the tendency of Government to reach for universal coercive measures rather than trusting in the good sense of individuals and families and the resilience of communities. My own experience, and my perspective of this period as a parliamentarian may differ from theirs, but still I agree with their overall analysis and conclusions.

Informed by their analysis, I ascribe the failures of the British state to the following factors: functional failure in Government itself; bad advice and practice from the official experts; and, most fundamentally, the failure of Parliament to do its job.

The authors have explained how the normal systems of decision-making fell apart in the pandemic. As the Public Administration and Constitutional Affairs Committee reported in 2021, official processes were more or less abandoned in the urgency of the crisis, replaced by WhatsApp groups and *ad hoc* committees of ministers, advisers and civil servants.

It is perhaps understandable that informal, relationship-based systems arose spontaneously to respond to the unfolding emergency. As Dominic Cummings has said, it turned out that the official processes had already failed. The state was utterly unprepared for the pandemic, and showed itself unable to adapt with the speed and at the scale the crisis demanded. In due course, irregular guerilla operations, on data – and, famously, on vaccine procurement – outperformed the cumbersome systems of Whitehall. But irregular forces need a regular army to form around.

The problem with guerilla government is partly one of accountability: it was unclear then, and it is unclear even with hindsight and the divulging of Whatsapp messages, who was responsible for what advice and what decision. But more profoundly the failure of proper government meant an absence of the natural balances which a good system of decision-making includes.

This is most apparent in the evidence of Professor Mark Woolhouse, a member of the Government's Scientific Advisory Group for Emergencies (SAGE), to the Science and Technology Select Committee in June 2020. The focus on modelling public health scenarios – infection and mortality predictions – to the exclusion of other considerations such as the economic and social impact of the proposed measures meant that, in Professor Woolhouse's words, 'we [were] looking literally at only one side of the equation'. The Government seems to have taken no account of the risks of harm posed by the interventions which the public health advisers recommended.

* * *

AFTERWORD BY DANNY KRUGER MP

This leads to the second failure of the British state: bad advice and practice among the experts. The modelling that the Government commissioned into the epidemiology of Covid-19, particularly from Professor Neil Ferguson of Imperial College, at the beginning of the pandemic has become notorious. Just as bad was the graph presented by Chris Whitty and Patrick Vallance in September 2020, suggesting that infections were doubling every seven days and that within a month 50,000 people a day would therefore be catching the virus.

The Covid era was defined, as cultures and civilisations tend to be, by its object of worship. During the pandemic we worshipped science – or to give it its proper name, 'the science'. The singular definitive suggests the essential error of this religion. Science involves the use of multiple facts and hypotheses. What the authors call the 'reductive simplicity' of 'the science' meant that the normal scientific processes were laid aside, and instead the clique of credentialed advisers at the top of government acquired a total supremacy.

Dominic Cummings has said that the dominance of these advisers was welcomed or encouraged by ministers who could use 'The Science' to justify their decisions and excuse any bad results. As I have written elsewhere, 'we are in thrall to a priestly class of professional scientists who, like the druids of old, reveal to the rulers the mysteries of the other world – or at least offer auguries which serve to excuse a decision. Government may be utterly bewildered but at least it can "follow the science", as in old days it heeded the flight of birds or the entrails of a chicken.'

The mysteries of science were invoked most powerfully in the case of the vaccines. Here we need to distinguish between the undoubted *operational* triumph of the vaccine programme, and the actual value of the vaccines in terms of public health and our liberation from lockdowns. The Vaccine Taskforce, led by Kate Bingham, capitalised on our new Brexit-found freedoms to procure the vaccine doses the country wanted. It was an example of effective government – probably because it took place outside the formal systems of the state. What followed, however, raises serious questions which have yet to be answered.

The vaccines were licensed by the UK's medical regulator, the Medicines and Healthcare products Regulatory Agency (MHRA), in record time in order to facilitate the end of the lockdowns. This process deserves proper scrutiny, not only because of the speed of licensing but because the technology involved in some of the vaccines was comparatively novel.

The licensing of the vaccines was the responsibility of the MHRA. The Government, advised by the Joint Committee on Vaccination and Immunisation (JCVI), then had to decide which members of the public should receive the jabs, and in which order. Initially the Government's view, expressed by Kate Bingham in October 2020, was that 'it's an adult-only vaccine, for people over 50'. Matt Hancock, the Health Secretary, reiterated in November that 'this is an adult vaccine'. Yet within 18 months the parents of children aged 5 were being encouraged to have them vaccinated.

This followed the obscure episode in September 2021 in which the JCVI refused to recommend the vaccination of healthy 12-15 year olds, and then the Government's Chief Medical Officer, Chris Whitty, overruled the advice and 'on public health grounds' recommended the vaccination of young teenagers – despite the miniscule risk of Covid for this age group. As the authors argue, this represented a very serious breach of the important ethical principle that medical treatments should be administered for the sake of the patients receiving them, not for the sake of others or 'the public' in general.

It has never been satisfactorily explained why the official advice changed so completely during 2021 – even as our understanding of the efficacy and the safety of the vaccines developed, and in the wrong direction. It was originally believed that the vaccines would stop the transmission of Covid. They turned out to do no such thing. And it gradually emerged, as more of the public was vaccinated, that for many people the jabs had significant side-effects, including serious heart conditions and in some cases death.

The licensing of the Covid-19 vaccines was the responsibility of the MHRA. This body was frequently described by ministers as 'the best in the world'; rather like 'the science', the religion in which the MHRA performed a leading priestly function, the regulator gave the Government a plausible cover to hide its decisions behind. Yet the majority of the funding for the MHRA comes from the very pharmaceutical companies whose products it is supposed to regulate.

As successive investigations over the years, including by the Health Select Committee, have found, the pharmaceutical industry exercises an excessive influence over healthcare in the UK, and is particularly influential over the regulator. In May 2022 Dame June Raine, the head of the MHRA, approvingly described the MHRA as having changed 'from a watchdog to an enabler'. This is not an appropriate description of the agency which is supposed to decide, on behalf of the public, which drugs and treatments are safe and effective for use.

When the pandemic first appeared the view of the Government, and especially of the then Prime Minister, was that the British people and its institutions would resent and even resist the degree of state control that the necessary response might entail. In the end this belief in the spirit of British liberty was disproved. People were content, even keen, to trade their freedom for what they were told was their security. And this is partly, I believe, because of the near-unanimity of establishment voices saying the same thing.

Here the role of private sector players is significant. Because it wasn't just the official agencies of the Government that recommended mass lockdowns and later mass vaccination. The mainstream media, including the major social media platforms, overwhelmingly backed the Government's position. As the authors explain, this included deliberate action to suppress the online presence of the Great Barrington Declaration, the open letter signed by eminent scientists from around the world questioning the lockdown policies. UsForThem, the authors' campaign group, found its online reach restricted by what appears to be deliberate action to mute its campaign.

The group was also subject to an early version of the 'debanking' scandal that later engulfed Coutts and Natwest when they arbitrarily terminated the account of Nigel Farage. In September 2022 Paypal suspended UsForThem's account, along with that of the Free Speech Union, apparently for the crime of being out of step with the Government's Covid policy.

* * *

I was the first MP to raise the Paypal scandal in the Commons. By then it was obvious that many of the initial assumptions about the virulence and lethality of Covid, and the interventions (pharmaceutical and otherwise) intended to combat it, were mistaken. And as an MP I share the responsibility for this. Because if the operations of Government were dysfunctional, and the advice and practice of the ecosystem of official advisers and regulators and the wider establishment (including big companies) was also at fault, the third and final body to blame for the disaster of the Covid response is the one supposed to mitigate the faults of the others and hold them to account: Parliament.

A depressing theme of this work is what the authors call the 'passivity' of the organisations theoretically supposed to defend the rights of people harmed by the Covid response, such as the children's organisations which tacitly or overtly endorsed the closure of schools and the lockdown of children in unsafe homes. But the passivity really emanated from the institution which more than any other should have held the Government to account for its decisions.

Parliament effectively went on leave for the duration of the crisis. For months we operated a 'virtual' Chamber, with speeches and questions beamed in from MPs' homes to giant screens hung over the gallery, to be met with stock pre-prepared responses from ministers. Debate was non-existent, and even Written Parliamentary Questions – the way MPs get more detailed answers from Government departments – were discouraged by the Speaker. In no way can the House of Commons or the House of Lords be said to have given Government policy the scrutiny it needed.

The legal framework for the Covid response was a set of laws, some of them already in existence and some of them hastily put together in the first phase of the crisis. As the authors explain, the Coronavirus Act – creating sweeping new powers to ban gatherings, delay elections, and organise health resources, including for quarantines – was debated for just six hours and passed in a single day on 23 March 2020. It required a vote in Parliament to renew its provisions every six months, though without the opportunity for amendments, so MPs were required to accept or reject the whole Act in full.

In the end, however, it wasn't this exceptional legislation that the Government used to order the lockdowns. Three days after the Coronavirus Bill passed the Commons, Matt Hancock signed into law the Health Protection (Coronovirus, Restrictions) Regulations 2020, using emergency powers conferred by the 1984 Public Health (Control of Disease) Act. The Public Health Act was designed to enable the Government to order the quarantine of dangerously infected, identified individuals. It was used in 2020 to order the entire country to 'stay at home'. The Regulations were not presented to Parliament until 90 minutes after they were signed and came into force; but the previous day Parliament had risen for the Easter recess, and did not get the chance to debate the measures for another six weeks.

The suspicions of the authors, and of Lord Sumption, the former Supreme Court judge who has written extensively on this episode, is difficult to dispute: the Government used the Public Health Act because it granted more sweeping powers than the Coronavirus Act or the Civil Contingencies Act (the existing vehicle for organising society in an emergency, which nevertheless entails a tight regime of Parliamentary control); and because it allowed the use of the emergency procedure to circumvent Parliamentary approval.

582 Covid-related measures were presented to Parliament in the two years of the pandemic. 100 of them followed the model of the Health Protection Regulations, being signed into law by ministers before they even came to Parliament, using the emergency procedure of the Public Health Act. A further 417 were passed using the 'negative' procedure whereby a measure becomes law automatically, without Parliamentary debate, unless the Commons actively resolves to annul it.

* * *

In September 2020 I wrote to constituents about my decision to vote for the first six-month renewal of the Coronavirus Act. It was, I said, 'an appalling situation for a free people, with a tradition of personal liberty and freedom of association going back many centuries... I am deeply uneasy about it all, but I accept the Government's leadership, based on their assessment of the scientific advice.'

As I have outlined, and as the authors make clear, that scientific advice was not adequate, and the Government's leadership, while sincerely intended to protect the public, was wanting. The official enquiry into the pandemic, led by Baroness Hallett, will, I hope, help us understand why decisions were taken and what their effect was. But we also need to make some decisions, as a society – in Parliament and in Government – about the future.

I regret that my proposals for a renewal of civil society and community responsibility, presented to an indifferent or distracted Government at the height of the first wave of Covid-19, have not been adopted. I still believe that the pandemic taught us the power and generosity of local neighbourhoods, and the capacity for innovation and flexibility in all parts of society, from universities and local government to businesses and the public services.

But it also taught us the power of the State, aided by the media and the wider establishment, to persuade the public to give up their liberty and their responsibility. The great lesson of the pandemic must be to ensure we never do that again.

The promise of Brexit was the transformation of the British state. This was the great domestic reform which was due to follow our departure from the EU, and it remains the imperative priority for the Government now. The authors show what happens when a cumbersome bureaucracy, without clear processes or the backstop of accountability, meets a dynamic and large-scale threat. More such threats are hanging over the UK: economic, ecological, military; as well as the expected next pandemic. We need a leaner, more strategic, more capable State, with more responsibility for local decisions devolved to local decision-makers and a more effective system of accountability.

And we need Parliament to do its job. I for one, with the benefit of hindsight – though some brave colleagues, and many brave people outside Parliament, were making these points at the time – recognise the mistakes that were made during the pandemic, and I apologise for the role I played in authorising them. Next time – whatever next time looks like – we need to do much, much better.

October 2023

ENDNOTES

1. https://bills.parliament.uk/bills/3063/stages
2. https://www.telegraph.co.uk/news/2022/03/20/airbrushing-childrens-lockdown-experiences-covid-inquiry-shocking/
3. https://www.telegraph.co.uk/news/2023/06/27/child-mental-health-referrals-over-million-lockdown-crisis/, https://www.gov.uk/government/publications/covid-19-mental-health-and-wellbeing-surveillance-report/7-children-and-young-people
4. https://commonslibrary.parliament.uk/research-briefings/sn03336/
5. https://cls.ucl.ac.uk/landmark-study-shows-the-impact-of-the-pandemic-on-young-people/
6. https://www.express.co.uk/life-style/health/1772647/excess-deaths-covid-nhs-investigation
7. Ibid.
8. https://news.sky.com/story/nhs-waiting-list-in-england-hits-record-high-as-7-75-million-on-hold-for-treatment-12983104
9. https://www.ons.gov.uk/economy/governmentpublicsectorandtaxes/publicsectorfinance/bulletins/publicsectorfinances/august2023
10. https://commonslibrary.parliament.uk/research-briefings/cbp-9309/
11. https://www.ons.gov.uk/peoplepopulationandcommunity/healthandsocialcare/healthcaresystem/bulletins/ukhealthaccounts/2019
12. https://assets.publishing.service.gov.uk/government/uploads/system/uploads/attachment_data/file/932898/DfE_consolidated_annual_report_and_accounts_2019_to_2020__web_version_.pdf
13. https://assets.publishing.service.gov.uk/government/uploads/system/uploads/attachment_data/file/919361/20200227_CH_UK_Defence_in_Numbers_2019.pdf
14. https://www.worldbank.org/en/news/press-release/2022/01/26/learning-loss-must-be-recovered-to-avoid-long-term-damage-to-children-s-wellbeing-and-productivity-new-report-says

15. https://news.sky.com/story/pm-asked-to-tackle-children-missing-from-schools-after-sky-report-12911176
16. https://blogs.lse.ac.uk/politicsandpolicy/the-rising-tide-of-school-absences-in-the-post-pandemic-era/
17. https://www.cypnow.co.uk/news/article/disadvantaged-children-s-life-chances-blighted-by-covid-19-and-cost-of-living-crisis
18. https://cls.ucl.ac.uk/landmark-study-shows-the-impact-of-the-pandemic-on-young-people/
19. https://www.theguardian.com/society/2021/dec/03/arthur-labinjo-hughes-timeline-of-events-that-ended-in-his
20. https://www.newsandstar.co.uk/news/19745850.child-develops-hypothermia-isolated-outdoor-classroom/
21. https://www.theguardian.com/uk-news/2021/feb/07/couple-reunited-after-year-apart-under-care-home-lockdown-rules
22. https://www.bbc.co.uk/news/uk-england-london-62001781
23. https://blogs.lse.ac.uk/politicsandpolicy/the-rising-tide-of-school-absences-in-the-post-pandemic-era/
24. https://eprints.lse.ac.uk/104673/1/Machin_covid_19_and_social_mobility_published.pdf
25. Results from a survey conducted for UsForThem in June 2023: https://jlpartners.com/s/accounatbilitydeficit.xlsx
26. https://www.spectator.co.uk/article/the-ethics-of-lockdown/
27. See our chapters on the children's vaccination programme and on ethics; also, e.g: http://blog.practicalethics.ox.ac.uk/2021/09/the-double-ethical-mistake-of-vaccinating-children-against-covid-19/
28. Ibid., Q11 and Q66.
29. https://www.theguardian.com/politics/2020/mar/05/as-chris-whit-a-dose-of-reality-boris-is-just-an-annoying-distraction
30. Ibid.
31. https://hansard.parliament.uk/Commons/2020-02-26/debates/B0FE8C31-77D5-40AA-97AF-BBA8FB620A95/Coronavirushighlight=coronavirus#contribution-75F886DC-F641-4793-AF88-86527A0929A7
32. L. Dodsworth, *A State of Fear: How the Government weaponised fear during the Covid-19 pandemic*, Pinter & Martin, 2021

ENDNOTES

33 On 8 March France had introduced restrictions on mass gatherings, and on 10 March the devolved executive in Scotland indicated that it would move to ban big sporting events, with Hancock reporting a conversation to the effect that "... there is little epidemiological benefit, but [they] think there's value in public reassurance". https://www.telegraph.co.uk/news/2023/03/07/messages-reveal-how-britain-plunged-lockdown/

34 https://www.theguardian.com/world/2020/mar/13/uk-to-ban-mass-gatherings-in-coronavirus-u-turn

35 https://www.imperial.ac.uk/media/imperial-college/medicine/sph/ide/gida-fellowships/Imperial-College-COVID19-NPI-modelling-16-03-2020.pdf

36 https://hansard.parliament.uk/commons/2020-03-16/debates/235689EC-0A18-4488-BFCF-9F012A1A0C1B/Covid-19

37 https://www.gov.uk/government/speeches/pm-statement-on-coronavirus-17-march-2020

38 https://www.gov.uk/government/speeches/pm-statement-on-coronavirus-20-march-2020

39 https://www.bbc.co.uk/news/uk-52011928

40 https://www.reuters.com/article/uk-factcheck-italy-coffins-idUSKBN21F0XL

41 https://www.theguardian.com/world/2020/mar/19/chinas-coronavirus-lockdown-strategy-brutal-but-effective?CMP=Share_iOSApp_Other

42 Ibid.

43 Classification as a HCID would have placed Covid alongside infections such as Ebola, Lassa Fever and Avian Flu, and (according to healthcare protocols at the time) would have meant only specialist treatment facilities could provide Covid-related care.

44 https://webarchive.nationalarchives.gov.uk/ukgwa/20201130171946/https://www.gov.uk/guidance/high-consequence-infectious-diseases-hcid

45 https://app.box.com/s/uolyuc1tmjarix61b93xtsd9z731k549/file/805732339388; in September 2020

46 https://www.whatdotheyknow.com/request/708513/response/1713448/attach/4/Letter%20JVT%20March13th%20Redacted.pdf?cookie_passthrough=1

47 https://web.archive.org/web/20200330090938/https://www.gov.uk/guidance/high-consequence-infectious-diseases-hcid

48 A review of Hansard records for the period between 13 March and 25 March when the Coronavirus Act became law.
49 https://assets.publishing.service.gov.uk/government/uploads/system/uploads/attachment_data/file/887467/25-options-for-increasing-adherence-to-social-distancing-measures-22032020.pdf
50 See https://committees.parliament.uk/oralevidence/113/html/, response to Q12, including "It is clear that the risk is very heavily weighted towards older people…"
51 https://covid19.public-inquiry.uk/wp-content/uploads/2023/10/16195035/2023-10-16-Module-2-Day-10-Transcript.pdf
52 At the time of writing, a narrative is being developed at the official Covid Inquiry that in 2020 the UK's existing pandemic plans were somewhere between poor and non-existent. See, e.g., https://www.rcn.org.uk/news-and-events/news/uk-rcn-expert-declares-pandemic-preparedness-inadequate-in-evidence-to-covid-inquiry-260623 and https://www.theguardian.com/uk-news/2023/jul/19/uk-covid-inquiry-pandemic-planning. We dispute that narrative. Although there was not a single set of convenient instructions, years of planning was captured in thoughtful framework documents.
53 https://assets.publishing.service.gov.uk/government/uploads/system/uploads/attachment_data/file/213717/dh_131040.pdf
54 https://www.telegraph.co.uk/news/2023/03/04/project-fear-covid-variant-lockdown-matt-hancock-whatsapp/
55 https://hansard.parliament.uk/commons/2021-12-14/debates/8034393B-C568-4DE6-8695-1D63F957537E/PublicHealth#contribution-7AA842CB-A98D-4458-B58C-1E454F11B08E
56 The debate lasted a little under 5 hours before votes were called: https://hansard.parliament.uk/commons/2021-12-14/debates/8034393B-C568-4DE6-8695-1D63F957537E/PublicHealth
57 https://www.theguardian.com/politics/live/2020/sep/09/uk-coronavirus-live-matt-hancock-covid-testing-shortage-boris-johnson?CMP=Share_iOSApp_Other
58 Ibid.

ENDNOTES

59 https://www.reuters.com/article/uk-health-coronavirus-britain-vaccines-idUSKBN28A24R
60 https://inews.co.uk/news/health/covid-vaccines-immunity-passport-admission-pubs-restaurants-sporting-venues-778251
61 https://news.sky.com/story/covid-19-michael-gove-rules-out-vaccine-passports-for-pub-theatre-and-sport-stadium-visits-12147819
62 https://www.independent.co.uk/news/uk/politics/test-trace-app-vaccine-covid-b1763831.html
63 https://www.independent.co.uk/news/uk/politics/covid-vaccine-passport-nadhim-zahawi-b1798785.html
64 https://www.bbc.co.uk/news/av/uk-56082530
65 https://assets.publishing.service.gov.uk/government/uploads/system/uploads/attachment_data/file/969427/TORs_-_Certification_Review.pdf
66 https://www.bbc.co.uk/news/uk-politics-56605598
67 https://www.telegraph.co.uk/politics/2021/03/31/exclusive-covid-vaccine-passports-would-un-british-sayssir-keir/
68 https://petition.parliament.uk/petitions/569957
69 https://www.bbc.co.uk/news/uk-56755161
70 https://dhexchange.kahootz.com/MEAGpublications/view?objectId=128443781
71 https://covid19.public-inquiry.uk/documents/inq000214216_0052-extract-of-whatsapp-messages-sent-in-a-group-chat-titled-pm-updates-between-no-10-colleagues-including-henry-cook-and-boris-johnson-dated-21-02-2021/
72 https://inews.co.uk/news/government-id-cards-stealth-vaccine-passports-contract-1023897
73 Ibid.
74 https://committees.parliament.uk/publications/6264/documents/69158/default/
75 Ibid., paragraph 7.
76 Ibid., page 3.
77 Ibid., paragraph 64.
78 https://twitter.com/NHSuk/status/1407372299968393216?s=20
79 https://twitter.com/BigBrotherWatch/status/1407313043458080774?s=20

80 https://assets.publishing.service.gov.uk/government/uploads/system/uploads/attachment_data/file/999408/COVID-Status-Certification-Review-Report.pdf
81 Ibid., paragraph 4.
82 Ibid., paragraphs 7 and 8.
83 Ibid., paragraphs 14 and 15.
84 https://www.gov.uk/government/speeches/pm-statement-at-coronavirus-press-conference-19-july-2021#:~:text=Let%20me%20stress%20%2D%20we%20want,of%20our%20massive%20vaccination%20campaign.
85 https://committees.parliament.uk/publications/7176/documents/75707/default/
86 https://www.telegraph.co.uk/news/2021/09/01/uk-school-closures-second-longest-europe-past-18-months/
87 https://committees.parliament.uk/publications/7176/documents/75707/default/
88 https://assets.publishing.service.gov.uk/government/uploads/system/uploads/attachment_data/file/100807/file47158.pdf
89 https://researchbriefings.files.parliament.uk/documents/CBP-9288/CBP-9288.pdf pg 23
90 https://www.reuters.com/world/africa/safrican-doctor-says-patients-with-omicron-variant-have-very-mild-symptoms-2021-11-28/
91 Sir Graham Brady MP: https://www.mirror.co.uk/news/politics/breaking-mps-back-new-covid-25582791
92 https://www.itv.com/news/2021-12-07/no-10-staff-joke-in-leaked-recording-about-christmas-party-they-later-denied
93 https://www.gov.uk/government/news/prime-minister-confirms-move-to-plan-b-in-england
94 The Health Protection (Coronavirus, Wearing of Face Coverings) (England) (Amendment) Regulations 2021 had come into force on 10 December; the Health Protection (Coronavirus, Restrictions) (Self-Isolation) (England) (Amendment) (No. 6) Regulations 2021 had come into force on 14 December.
95 The Health Protection (Coronavirus, Restrictions) (Entry to Venues and Events) (England) Regulations 2021.

ENDNOTES

96 https://hansard.parliament.uk/commons/2021-12-14/debates/8034393B-C568-4DE6-8695-1D63F957537E/PublicHealth
97 All extracts, Ibid.
98 https://www.independent.co.uk/news/uk/home-news/covid-vaccine-uk-government-jobs-discrinimation-b1799273.html
99 https://www.thetimes.co.uk/article/18f619e4-7824-11eb-9d58-b0b1ea096ce7?shareToken=d8db90e520dca4862054a6bdf184be94
100 https://www.telegraph.co.uk/news/2021/07/21/third-covid-deaths-england-care-homes/
101 INQ000214216_0052.pdf (covid19.public-inquiry.uk)
102 https://www.theguardian.com/society/2021/mar/23/englands-care-home-operators-warn-against-compulsory-covid-jabs
103 https://www.thetimes.co.uk/article/18f619e4-7824-11eb-9d58-b0b1ea096ce7?shareToken=d8db90e520dca4862054a6bdf184be94: 'Robert Buckland, the justice secretary, said that the government would not be taking a "blanket approach" to mandating immunisation among care home workers, but he defended providers who say that they will only employ vaccinated staff.'
104 https://www.telegraph.co.uk/politics/2021/03/22/care-home-staff-face-compulsory-covid-vaccination/
105 https://www.thetimes.co.uk/article/18f619e4-7824-11eb-9d58-b0b1ea096ce7?shareToken=fa8d4f9bc8ce76c954d2cb2b45c48178
106 https://dhexchange.kahootz.com/MEAGpublications/view?objectId=128443621
107 https://edition.cnn.com/2021/04/02/europe/italy-vaccines-health-workers-decree-intl-cmd/index.html
108 https://www.gov.uk/government/consultations/making-vaccination-a-condition-of-deployment-in-older-adult-care-homes/making-vaccination-a-condition-of-deployment-in-older-adult-care-homes
109 Ibid., paragraphs 2 and 6.
110 https://www.gov.uk/government/consultations/making-vaccination-a-condition-of-deployment-in-older-adult-care-homes/outcome/making-vaccination-a-condition-of-deployment-in-care-homes-government-response

111 Ibid.
112 https://www.england.nhs.uk/statistics/wp-content/uploads/sites/2/2021/06/COVID-19-weekly-announced-vaccinations-24-June-2021.pdf
113 https://www.gov.uk/government/news/everyone-working-in-care-homes-to-be-fully-vaccinated-under-new-law-to-protect-residents
114 https://www.bma.org.uk/bma-media-centre/mandatory-vaccination-for-nhs-staff-is-incredibly-complex-issue-says-bma
115 https://www.legislation.gov.uk/ukdsi/2021/9780348224993/contents
116 https://hansard.parliament.uk/commons/2021-07-13/debates/BD25E3D7-6EFB-48A9-A564-966D3898D8FC/NationalHealthService
117 https://committees.parliament.uk/publications/6644/documents/164355/default/
118 https://committees.parliament.uk/committee/255/secondary-legislation-scrutiny-committee/news/156531/lords-summon-minister-to-address-concerns-about-proposed-vaccination-of-care-home-staff-as-a-condition-of-employment/
119 https://publications.parliament.uk/pa/ld5802/ldselect/ldsecleg/40/4003.htm
120 Ibid., paragraphs 39 to 41.
121 Ibid., paragraph 41.
122 https://committees.parliament.uk/oralevidence/2542/pdf/
123 https://committees.parliament.uk/publications/6810/documents/72255/default/
124 Ibid., paragraphs 6 and 8.
125 Ibid., paragraphs 9 and 10.
126 Ibid., paragraph 20.
127 https://hansard.parliament.uk/commons/2021-07-13/debates/BD25E3D7-6EFB-48A9-A564-966D3898D8FC/NationalHealthService#
128 Ibid.
129 For example, https://hansard.parliament.uk/commons/2021-07-13/debates/BD25E3D7-6EFB-48A9-A564-966D3898D8FC/NationalHealthService#contribution-A85805A1-BA7D-475E-BFC1-8B4DCEBEE2C3 and https://hansard.parliament.uk/commons/2021-07-13/debates/BD25E3D7-

ENDNOTES

6EFB-48A9-A564-966D3898D8FC/NationalHealthService#contributi
on-00C06475-5A1E-4B96-BC87-CE502CB7B1A3 and https://hansard.
parliament.uk/commons/2021-07-13/debates/BD25E3D7-6EFB-48A9-A564-
966D3898D8FC/NationalHealthService#contribution-B7A6583D-2306-
48FD-B106-DDAC2D743586

130 https://hansard.parliament.uk/commons/2021-07-13/debates/BD25E3D7-
6EFB-48A9-A564-966D3898D8FC/NationalHealthService#contribution-
05EA16D8-2841-4727-AC6C-7FF5E943296E

131 https://hansard.parliament.uk/commons/2021-07-13/debates/BD25E3D7-
6EFB-48A9-A564-966D3898D8FC/NationalHealthService#contribution-
5B1F8B50-0CD7-4167-BC3B-B72377316A50

132 https://hansard.parliament.uk/commons/2021-07-13/debates/BD25E3D7-
6EFB-48A9-A564-966D3898D8FC/NationalHealthService#contribution-
2E0CC234-409A-4991-8383-B22C15AC901F

133 https://hansard.parliament.uk/commons/2021-07-13/debates/BD25E3D7-
6EFB-48A9-A564-966D3898D8FC/NationalHealthService#contribution-
2CF2D60A-9B42-4BD1-AAFF-36E1AF42C4A1

134 https://hansard.parliament.uk/commons/2021-07-13/debates/BD25E3D7-
6EFB-48A9-A564-966D3898D8FC/NationalHealthService#contribution-
08834773-E158-40DF-BB33-D089BA382BC7

135 https://www.gov.uk/government/news/regulatory-policy-committee-
statement-on-the-draft-health-and-social-care-act-2008-regulated-
activities-amendment-coronavirus-regulations-2021

136 https://www.parliament.uk/business/news/2021/july/lords-considers-new-
regulations/

137 https://www.legislation.gov.uk/uksi/2021/891/pdfs/uksi_20210891_en.pdf

138 https://news.sky.com/story/thousands-of-care-home-staff-to-lose-their-
jobs-as-mandatory-covid-19-vaccine-deadline-passes-12465668

139 https://www.legislation.gov.uk/ukia/2021/83/pdfs/ukia_20210083_en.pdf

140 https://assets.publishing.service.gov.uk/government/uploads/system/
uploads/attachment_data/file/1032152/making-vaccination-a-condition-
of-deployment-in-older-adult-care-homes-impact-assessment.pdf,
paragraph 124.

141 Ibid., page 3.

142 Ibid., page 1.
143 https://www.unison.org.uk/news/press-release/2021/11/staffing-levels-in-care-dangerously-low-with-dying-residents-denied-dignified-end-says-unison-survey/#:~:text=Commenting%20on%20the%20findings%2C%20UNISON,fed%20up%20with%20low%20wages.
144 https://www.theguardian.com/society/2021/oct/13/nhs-faces-beds-crisis-as-care-homes-stop-taking-patients-from-hospitals?CMP=Share_iOSApp_Other; and https://www.itv.com/news/2021-10-22/burnt-out-and-exhausted-social-care-staff-quit-to-fill-hospitality-shortage
145 https://www.gov.uk/government/news/consultation-on-removing-vaccination-as-a-condition-of-deployment-for-health-and-social-care-staff
146 https://www.gov.uk/government/news/regulations-making-covid-19-vaccination-a-condition-of-deployment-to-end
147 https://pubsonline.informs.org/doi/abs/10.1287/mnsc.2023.4832
148 https://www.nottingham.ac.uk/news/mandatory-covid-vaccines-care-home-workers-reduction-in-staff#:~:text=Home-,Mandatory%20Covid%20vaccines%20for%20care%20home%20workers,in%20staff%2C%20new%20research
149 https://inews.co.uk/news/government-id-cards-stealth-vaccine-passports-contract-1023897
150 Ibid.
151 Ibid.
152 https://committees.parliament.uk/publications/6810/documents/72255/default/, para 19.
153 https://www.zahawi.com/parliament/covid-vaccine-passports
154 https://reuters.com/article/idUSKBN26P0YX
155 https://www.facebook.com/skynews/videos/Hancock-vaccine-will-not-be-used-on-children/408529806968441/
156 https://www.telegraph.co.uk/news/2023/03/07/covid-not-deadly-enough-fast-track-vaccines-chris-whitty-advised/
157 https://www.gov.uk/government/publications/jcvi-update-on-advice-for-covid-19-vaccination-of-children-aged-5-to-11/jcvi-statement-on-vaccination-of-children-aged-5-to-11-years-old#:~:text=million%20young%20children.-,Advice,least%2012%20weeks%20between%20doses

ENDNOTES

158 https://covid19.public-inquiry.uk/documents/inq000214216_0052-extract-of-whatsapp-messages-sent-in-a-group-chat-titled-pm-updates-between-no-10-colleagues-including-henry-cook-and-boris-johnson-dated-21-02-2021/
159 https://news.sky.com/story/covid-19-uk-vaccine-rollout-should-turn-to-children-as-fast-as-we-can-says-sage-expert-12224817
160 https://committees.parliament.uk/oralevidence/1748/pdf/, Q 2141.
161 https://news.sky.com/story/morally-wrong-to-offer-covid-jabs-to-children-while-poorer-nations-suffer-says-oxford-expert-12310101
162 https://www.thetimes.co.uk/article/e1fc5352-c6b3-11eb-b6f5-fed739e7c1ca?shareToken=7a581e7dc8a75adf5b4e1f5ce4694859
163 https://www.telegraph.co.uk/news/2021/05/02/schools-back-mass-vaccinations-children-headteachers-say-peer/
164 https://news.sky.com/story/morally-wrong-to-offer-covid-jabs-to-children-while-poorer-nations-suffer-says-oxford-expert-12310101
165 https://www.thetimes.co.uk/article/e1fc5352-c6b3-11eb-b6f5-fed739e7c1ca?shareToken=47e042a1f7563203ada408a46b3ec4ab
166 https://app.box.com/s/acvlrtpiom6l7krf7szzl2jg5da69sm9/file/1313434629385
167 https://www.gov.uk/government/publications/covid-19-vaccination-of-children-and-young-people-aged-12-to-17-years-jcvi-statement/jvci-statement-on-covid-19-vaccination-of-children-and-young-people-aged-12-to-17-years-15-july-2021
168 https://app.box.com/s/1lo4032vy09krs6cma1rcbf39vhht8mu/file/1312151634843
169 Ibid.
170 A concern which appears to have been born out by reality: https://www.independent.co.uk/news/uk/mmr-nhs-england-gp-surgery-world-health-organisation-england-b2420260.html
171 https://www.thetimes.co.uk/article/e1fc5352-c6b3-11eb-b6f5-fed739e7c1ca?shareToken=7a581e7dc8a75adf5b4e1f5ce4694859
172 https://app.box.com/s/acvlrtpiom6l7krf7szzl2jg5da69sm9/file/1313432054361

173 For example, https://www.telegraph.co.uk/news/2021/06/14/children-may-need-get-covid-jabs-avoid-disruption-education/; https://www.bbc.co.uk/news/uk-58338481; and https://inews.co.uk/news/politics/nicola-sturgeon-jabs-children-12-up-schools-prepare-return-1143239

174 https://www.gov.uk/government/publications/jcvi-statement-august-2021-covid-19-vaccination-of-children-and-young-people-aged-12-to-17-years/jcvi-statement-on-covid-19-vaccination-of-children-and-young-people-aged-12-to-17-years-4-august-2021

175 Ibid.

176 Ibid.

177 https://app.box.com/s/acvlrtpiom6l7krf7szzl2jg5da69sm9/file/1313432054361, paragraph 30.

178 Ibid., paragraph 34.

179 https://twitter.com/SkyNews/status/1422940774522572804

180 https://www.theguardian.com/society/2021/aug/07/jcvi-largely-opposed-to-covid-vaccination-for-children-under-16

181 https://www.gov.uk/government/publications/jcvi-statement-september-2021-covid-19-vaccination-of-children-aged-12-to-15-years/jcvi-statement-on-covid-19-vaccination-of-children-aged-12-to-15-years-3-september-2021

182 Covid: What do parents think about vaccinating children? https://www.bbc.co.uk/news/uk-58447040

183 https://www.telegraph.co.uk/news/2021/09/05/teenagers-can-overrule-parents-take-covid-vaccine-says-minister/

184 https://www.gov.uk/government/publications/universal-vaccination-of-children-and-young-people-aged-12-to-15-years-against-covid-19/universal-vaccination-of-children-and-young-people-aged-12-to-15-years-against-covid-19

185 https://committees.parliament.uk/oralevidence/2767/pdf/, Q31.

186 https://www.gov.uk/government/publications/jcvi-update-on-advice-for-covid-19-vaccination-of-children-aged-5-to-11/jcvi-statement-on-vaccination-of-children-aged-5-to-11-years-old

187 https://www.thetimes.co.uk/article/jcvi-refuse-to-back-covid-vaccine-for-children-m993bgt09

188 https://petition.parliament.uk/petitions/594272

ENDNOTES

189 https://questions-statements.parliament.uk/written-statements/detail/2021-09-14/hcws287
190 Interview on Talk Radio, 13 September 2021.
191 https://www.telegraph.co.uk/columnists/2021/09/08/unseemly-rush-give-children-vaccine-dont-need/
192 https://hansard.parliament.uk/commons/2021-09-21/debates/62D8784D-4D15-42BE-9912-72EED73A40D0/Covid-19VaccinationOfChildren
193 https://committees.parliament.uk/oralevidence/2767/pdf/
194 The JCVI's statement had noted as a key benefit that "vaccinating children and young people could have some impact on hospitalisations and deaths in older adults".
195 Ibid.
196 Ibid.
197 https://committees.parliament.uk/oralevidence/3205/pdf/, Q2678.
198 https://www.england.nhs.uk/2021/09/nhs-rolls-out-covid-19-jab-to-children-aged-12-to-15/
199 Soon after the BBC interview aired, UsForThem submitted a complaint to the PMCPA. The complaint cited the overtly promotional nature of the BBC's reports and challenged the compliance of Dr Bourla's comments about children with the apparently strict rules governing the promotion of medicines in the UK. See https://usforthem2020.substack.com/p/pfizer-sales-before-child-safety.
200 https://www.gov.uk/government/news/uk-regulator-approves-use-of-pfizerbiontech-vaccine-in-5-to-11-year-olds
201 https://www.gov.uk/government/publications/jcvi-update-on-advice-for-covid-19-vaccination-of-children-aged-5-to-11/jcvi-statement-on-vaccination-of-children-aged-5-to-11-years-old
202 Ibid.
203 https://www.gponline.com/covid-19-vaccine-uptake-children-stalls-less-10-5-11s-jabbed/article/1789274
204 https://www.huffingtonpost.co.uk/entry/chris-whittys-letter-to-ministers-on-why-covid-jabs-for-over-12s-can-go-ahead_uk_613f4f94e4b090b79e86d53d

205 https://www.england.nhs.uk/2021/09/nhs-rolls-out-covid-19-jab-to-children-aged-12-to-15/
206 https://twitter.com/educationgovuk/status/1473194055433654274
207 https://unherd.com/thepost/nhs-england-deletes-misleading-covid-stats-video/
208 https://www.gov.uk/government/publications/universal-vaccination-of-children-and-young-people-aged-12-to-15-years-against-covid-19
209 https://inews.co.uk/inews-lifestyle/travel/travel-spain-announces-children-aged-12-and-over-must-have-both-covid-vaccinations-for-holidays-from-december-1325649
210 https://www.dailymail.co.uk/news/article-9850193/Coffee-cinema-tickets-new-incentives-beat-Covid-vaccine-hesitancy-youngsters.html
211 https://www.huffingtonpost.co.uk/entry/cash-covid-encourage-young-people-jab-jcvi_uk_610a3c84e4b0e882ab64b122
212 https://www.telegraph.co.uk/news/2022/05/22/nhs-trusts-wrote-letters-directly-young-children-urging-get/
213 https://jlpartners.com/s/accountabilitydeficitchildvaccines.xlsx
214 https://www.huffingtonpost.co.uk/entry/chris-whittys-letter-to-ministers-on-why-covid-jabs-for-over-12s-can-go-ahead_uk_613f4f94e4b090b79e86d53d
215 https://www.telegraph.co.uk/news/2021/08/25/nhs-draws-plans-vaccinate-12-year-olds
216 https://uk.news.yahoo.com/teenagers-able-overrule-parents-covid-142913640.html
217 https://www.standard.co.uk/news/politics/children-covid19-vaccine-consent-final-say-health-secretary-sajid-javid-b954328.html
218 https://www.dailymail.co.uk/news/article-10123999/Education-Minister-send-teenagers-vaccine-letter.html
219 https://hansard.parliament.uk/commons/2021-09-21/debates/62D8784D-4D15-42BE-9912-72EED73A40D0/Covid-19VaccinationOfChildren
220 https://www.telegraph.co.uk/news/2021/09/22/virtually-children-will-get-covid-dont-get-vaccinated-warns/
221 https://jlpartners.com/s/accountabilitydeficitchildvaccines.xlsx
222 Ibid.

223 https://www.telegraph.co.uk/news/2021/05/03/healthy-children-simply-do-not-need-covid-jab/ and https://www.telegraph.co.uk/news/2021/06/07/education-should-not-conditional-children-having-jab/
224 Witness Statement for the UK Covid Inquiry of Susannah Storey, Director General for Digital, Technology and Telecoms at DCMS, paragraph 1.1: https://covid19.public-inquiry.uk/wp-content/uploads/2023/07/21175218/INQ000183331.pdf
225 https://hansard.parliament.uk/Commons/2020-02-26/debates/B0FE8C31-77D5-40AA-97AF-BBA8FB620A95/Coronavirushighlight=coronavirus#contribution-D4A7BE0B-3E29-4151-9F31-6F50DD645C79
226 Ibid., paragraph 1.11.
227 https://www.gov.uk/government/news/fact-sheet-on-the-cdu-and-rru. Following departmental reorganisations the CDU now sits within the Department for Science, Innovation and Technology.
228 https://committees.parliament.uk/publications/1494/documents/13607/default/
229 https://committees.parliament.uk/oralevidence/300/pdf/
230 Ibid.
231 https://committees.parliament.uk/committee/378/culture-media-and-sport-committee/news/132812/committee-to-call-in-social-media-companies-on-covid19-vaccine-misinformation/
232 https://committees.parliament.uk/oralevidence/1448/pdf/
233 Given that the Government would inevitably have been following mainstream print and broadcast media coverage of its policies there is a reasonable question to be asked about whether print and broadcast media were ever encouraged to limit or drop critical coverage of lockdown policies and particularly of the child vaccination programme during the Summer of 2021. Big Brother Watch describes correspondence unearthed among officials in November 2020 following social media coverage of an article in The Daily Mail newspaper which had questioned some of the modelling data used by the Government to justify lockdowns, which ends by encouraging DHSC press officers to contact the Daily Mail to 'make them aware of the public health impact' and ask them to put a government line in

THE ACCOUNTABILITY DEFICIT

the piece. This is justified by a Cabinet Office official claiming that the article could undermine compliance with coronavirus restrictions.

234 https://www.telegraph.co.uk/news/2023/06/09/covid-disinformation-unit-hourly-tech-lockdown-dissent/

235 https://committees.parliament.uk/oralevidence/1448/pdf/

236 https://www.dailymail.co.uk/news/article-12498527/Biden-Amendment-ruling.html; Opinion of the 5th US Circuit Court of Appeals in New Orleans as reported: "... the White House, the Surgeon General, the CDC, and the FBI likely coerced or significantly encouraged social-media platforms to moderate content, rendering those decisions state actions. In doing so, the officials likely violated the First Amendment".

237 https://bigbrotherwatch.org.uk/wp-content/uploads/2023/01/Ministry-of-Truth-Big-Brother-Watch-290123.pdf

238 https://www.telegraph.co.uk/education/2020/09/07/overzealous-social-distancing-turning-return-school-tragedy/

239 https://www.telegraph.co.uk/news/2023/06/10/twitter-refused-removal-requests-covid-spy-unit/

240 https://hansard.parliament.uk/commons/2020-03-16/debates/235689EC-0A18-4488-BFCF-9F012A1A0C1B/Covid-19#contribution-29840E4E-4D9D-4C9E-B171-2561021C5BBA

241 https://hansard.parliament.uk/commons/2020-03-16/debates/235689EC-0A18-4488-BFCF-9F012A1A0C1B/Covid-19#contribution-603C9865-C384-4944-9A47-800ACD4DB22E

242 https://committees.parliament.uk/oralevidence/1448/pdf/, Q.20.

243 Ibid., Q.14 et seq.

244 https://dhexchange.kahootz.com/MEAGpublications/view?objectId=113919749

245 C-19 Inquiry 161023 Module 2 Day 10 (covid19.public-inquiry.uk), pages 56 and 62

246 https://www.gov.uk/government/news/fact-sheet-on-the-cdu-and-rru

247 https://covid19.public-inquiry.uk/wp-content/uploads/2023/07/21175218/INQ000183331.pdf, paragraphs 1.19 and 1.20.

248 https://covid19.public-inquiry.uk/wp-content/uploads/2023/07/21175218/INQ000183331.pdf, paragraph 1.20.

ENDNOTES

249 https://bigbrotherwatch.org.uk/wp-content/uploads/2023/01/Ministry-of-Truth-Big-Brother-Watch-290123.pdf, page 12.

250 Ibid., see for example pages 13 to 15.

251 https://hansard.parliament.uk/commons/2021-02-04/debates/4AC33846-AB60-45FD-B23E-7C0DD70CFAB0/Covid-19VaccineUpdate#contribution-66833166-99C0-4A3F-A027-8CDDCDA2F015

252 https://hansard.parliament.uk/Commons/2022-01-06/debates/484ECC23-71D8-4C01-AFC9-906BF093326A/OnlineSafetyBill#contribution-7CAA38F6-96EF-49FD-86EC-A15206532DFC

253 https://committees.parliament.uk/oralevidence/1448/pdf/, Q.8.

254 Ibid., Q.10.

255 Ibid., Q.11.

256 https://committees.parliament.uk/oralevidence/1448/pdf/, Q.107.

257 Robert F Kennedy Jnr, July 2023, https://www.youtube.com/watch?v=QOFYdIiiMIs

258 See for example https://hansard.parliament.uk/commons/2020-10-19/debates/9BA8B5B2-9473-40A0-86C3-92E0EF00ADED/VaccineMisinformationOnline

259 https://www.thetimes.co.uk/article/the-unvaccinated-must-be-persuaded-to-do-what-is-right-p0fd03cjn

260 https://www.conservativewoman.co.uk/mrna-vaccines-must-be-banned-once-and-for-all/

261 https://www.telegraph.co.uk/world-news/2023/09/24/china-lab-wuhan-leaking-covid-loses-us-funding-experiments/

262 Comments provided directly to UsForThem by Richard Tice in October 2023.

263 https://www.kingsfund.org.uk/sites/default/files/2022-01/The%20Covid-19%20Vaccination%20Programme%20online%20version_3.pdf, page 77.

264 https://www.gov.uk/government/news/rule-of-six-comes-into-effect-to-tackle-coronavirus#:~:text=The%20new%20%E2%80%9Crule%20of%20six,will%20be%20against%20the%20law

265 https://www.thetimes.co.uk/article/affluent-youth-are-catching-coronavirus-most-says-matt-hancock-qvbpxw2nk

266   L. Dodsworth, *A State of Fear: How the Government weaponised fear during the Covid-19 pandemic*, Pinter & Martin, 2021.
267   https://www.telegraph.co.uk/news/2023/03/05/project-fears-psychological-warfare-must-never-repeated-say/
268   https://www.telegraph.co.uk/politics/2020/11/04/theresa-may-launches-commons-broadside-boris-johnsons-covid/
269   The now infamous presentation given in September 2020 in which Sir Patrick warned that if Covid cases continued to double every seven days, by mid-October there would be 50,000 new cases of Covid each day. https://www.gov.uk/government/speeches/chief-scientific-advisor-and-chief-medical-officer-briefing-on-coronavirus-covid-19-21-september-2020--2
270   https://www.ft.com/content/d2e00128-7889-4d5d-84a3-43e51355a751
271   https://www.telegraph.co.uk/news/2023/03/05/matt-hancock-kate-bingham-clive-dix-covid-vaccines/
272   https://www.pfizer.com/news/press-release/press-release-detail/pfizer-and-biontech-announce-vaccine-candidate-against
273   https://www.telegraph.co.uk/news/2023/03/05/matt-hancock-triumph-covid-vaccine-lockdown-files-whatsapp/
274   https://hansard.parliament.uk/commons/2020-11-10/debates/FB5296EC-628D-4C17-9C28-4863AC8C07C9/Covid-19Update
275   https://assets.publishing.service.gov.uk/government/uploads/system/uploads/attachment_data/file/938052/SR20_Web_Accessible.pdf, at page 28.
276   https://www.telegraph.co.uk/politics/2020/12/08/matt-hancock-fights-back-tears-television-watches-first-patients/
277   https://www.telegraph.co.uk/news/2023/03/05/matt-hancock-triumph-covid-vaccine-lockdown-files-whatsapp/
278   https://hansard.parliament.uk/commons/2020-12-08/debates/9B72D51F-0542-4BAB-9ADE-A70195F52064/Covid-19VaccineRoll-Out#contribution-7A84FA04-9580-4169-85BC-54BE6475546C
279   https://hansard.parliament.uk/commons/2020-12-08/debates/9B72D51F-0542-4BAB-9ADE-A70195F52064/Covid-19VaccineRoll-Out#contribution-38846219-74B6-4006-988D-0641413A3875

ENDNOTES

280 https://www.theguardian.com/uk-news/2020/jul/31/hands-face-space-boris-johnson-unveils-new-coronavirus-slogan
281 https://committees.parliament.uk/oralevidence/1448/pdf/
282 Paragraph 6.6 of the MHRA's Blue Guide prohibits the use of the word 'safe' to advertise any medicine: https://assets.publishing.service.gov.uk/media/6012d7f2d3bf7f05b92f6cfc/BG_2020_Brexit_Final_version.pdf
283 https://committees.parliament.uk/oralevidence/1448/pdf/
284 Ibid.
285 Ibid.
286 Ibid.
287 https://www.gov.uk/government/news/leading-social-media-platforms-unite-to-support-covid-19-vaccine-drive
288 Ibid.
289 For example, according to the UK pharmaceutical industry's ABPI financial disclosure database, between 2019 and 2021, the London School of Hygiene and Tropical Medicine, home of the Vaccine Confidence Project which partnered with YouTube "to reach people with credible information about the COVID-19 vaccine in accessible and culturally relevant ways", received more than £1 million from the vaccine manufacturers Pfizer and AstraZeneca, Janssen and GSK
290 https://www.ft.com/content/69e43380-dd6d-4240-b5e1-47fc1f2f0bdc
291 https://www.gatesfoundation.org/about/committed-grants?q=bbc#committed_grants
292 https://committees.parliament.uk/oralevidence/1448/pdf/
293 https://www.youtube.com/watch?v=h4ubjd_Asko; we do not question the accuracy of Dr Ranj's account of his experience, we use it as an example of a broadcaster presenting vaccination as an essentially inconsequential step for any individual to take, and without downsides to consider.
294 https://www.gov.uk/government/publications/social-media-endorsements-guide-for-influencers/social-media-endorsements-being-transparent-with-your-followers#:~:text=must%20be%20clearly%20labelled%20as,endorse%20or%20review%20a%20product.
295 https://www.netmums.com/life/what-this-gp-wants-every-parent-to-know-about-the-covid-vaccine-and-their-child

296 https://www.mirror.co.uk/news/uk-news/its-incredibly-safe-everything-you-25110465.amp
297 https://www.mirror.co.uk/news/health/two-doses-not-give-you-26066790.amp
298 https://www.mirror.co.uk/news/uk-news/delays-between-vaccine-doses-provide-23471787.amp and https://www.netmums.com/pregnancy/the-covid-vaccine-your-questions-about-fertility-and-pregnancy-answered
299 https://www.rsph.org.uk/our-work/policy/vaccinations/public-attitudes-to-a-covid-19-vaccine.html
300 https://www.theguardian.com/world/2021/aug/06/third-adults-unvaccinated-parts-london-data-shows-covid?CMP=Share_iOSApp_Other
301 https://data.london.gov.uk/dataset/coronavirus--covid-19--cases
302 https://www.telegraph.co.uk/politics/2021/03/23/exclusive-children-line-covid-vaccines-august/
303 https://www.dailymail.co.uk/news/article-9395467/Children-vaccinated-August-11m-18s-inoculated-start-term.html
304 https://hansard.parliament.uk/commons/2020-11-10/debates/FB5296EC-628D-4C17-9C28-4863AC8C07C9/Covid-19Update#contribution-7C95F0C3-04C2-4649-8311-8021912CE6B3
305 https://www.gov.uk/guidance/advertise-your-medicines#:~:text=claim%20a%20medicine's%20safety%20or,part%20of%20promoting%20the%20product.
306 https://ico.org.uk/for-organisations/uk-gdpr-guidance-and-resources/childrens-information/children-and-the-uk-gdpr/what-if-we-want-to-target-children-with-marketing/#:~:text=Advertising%20standards%20stipulate%20that%20marketing,vulnerability%20or%20lack%20of%-20experience.
307 https://www.local.gov.uk/our-support/coronavirus-information-councils/covid-19-service-information/covid-19-vaccinations/behavioural-insights/resources/encouraging-vaccine-take-among-younger-people
308 Ibid.
309 https://www.bbc.co.uk/news/av/world-us-canada-57147328
310 https://www.bbc.co.uk/news/world-57201111

ENDNOTES

311 https://www.gov.uk/government/news/leading-social-media-platforms-unite-to-support-covid-19-vaccine-drive
312 https://www.decisionmarketing.co.uk/news/youtube-targets-youngsters-with-pro-covid-jab-ad-blitz
313 https://www.spectator.co.uk/article/vaccine-passports-for-university-are-a-dreadful-mistake/
314 https://www.gov.uk/government/news/more-leading-businesses-join-vaccine-uptake-drive
315 https://www.huffingtonpost.co.uk/entry/cash-covid-encourage-young-people-jab-jcvi_uk_610a3c84e4b0e882ab64b122
316 https://www.thesun.co.uk/news/15793643/vaccine-buses-premier-league-gigs-teens-jabbed/
317 https://inews.co.uk/news/health/tiktok-influencers-help-boost-covid-vaccine-uptake-young-teens-half-want-jab-1220423
318 https://www.telegraph.co.uk/news/2021/09/05/teenagers-can-overrule-parents-take-covid-vaccine-says-minister/
319 https://www.dailymail.co.uk/news/article-10123999/Education-Minister-send-teenagers-vaccine-letter.html
320 https://twitter.com/educationgovuk/status/1473194055433654274
321 https://jlpartners.com/s/accounatbilitydeficit.xlsx
322 https://www.theguardian.com/commentisfree/2021/may/20/unvaccinated-covid-patients-bolton-matt-hancock-virus
323 https://www.bbc.co.uk/news/uk-politics-57987016
324 https://news.sky.com/story/covid-19-downing-street-seeks-to-play-down-significance-of-boris-johnsons-mandatory-jabs-comment-12490971
325 https://www.theguardian.com/world/2021/dec/19/sajid-javid-hits-out-at-unvaccinated-for-taking-up-hospital-beds
326 https://www.telegraph.co.uk/politics/2021/12/11/unvaccinated-should-forced-covid-lockdown-one-three-people-believe/
327 https://www.dailymail.co.uk/news/article-10344567/Door-door-Covid-jab-teams-sent-homes-five-million-unvaccinated-Britons.html
328 https://twitter.com/statsjamie/status/1475778041498550278?s=20
329 https://www.reuters.com/world/uk/uks-johnson-says-people-without-covid-boosters-ending-up-hospital-2021-12-29/

330 https://www.bmj.com/content/376/bmj.o5
331 https://www.theguardian.com/world/2021/dec/28/unvaccinated-uk-covid-dilemma-vaccine-refusers
332 https://www.campaignlive.co.uk/article/nhs-get-vaccinated-named-emotionally-effective-ad-2021/1749745
333 https://hansard.parliament.uk/commons/2020-12-02/debates/FE328933-735C-48E9-9BF0-ED692E9CF8C4/CoronavirusVaccine
334 https://hansard.parliament.uk/commons/2021-02-02/debates/D93C0613-D241-4A12-BC9B-6CD23955DE7D/Covid-19Update
335 https://assets.publishing.service.gov.uk/government/uploads/system/uploads/attachment_data/file/876043/Moral_and_Ethical_Advisory_Group_-_terms_of_reference.pdf
336 Ibid., paragraph 8.
337 Those former members were not asked to review this chapter in advance of publication.
338 https://dhexchange.kahootz.com/MEAGpublications/view?objectId=113919653
339 https://dhexchange.kahootz.com/MEAGpublications/view?objectId=113919973#
340 Ibid.
341 https://dhexchange.kahootz.com/MEAGpublications/view?objectId=113919877
342 https://dhexchange.kahootz.com/MEAGpublications/view?objectId=113920005#
343 https://dhexchange.kahootz.com/MEAGpublications/view?objectId=113919909#
344 https://dhexchange.kahootz.com/MEAGpublications/view?objectId=113920165
345 https://app.box.com/s/acvlrtpiom6l7krf7szzl2jg5da69sm9/file/1313427986353
346 Ibid., paragraph 92.
347 https://dhexchange.kahootz.com/MEAGpublications/view?objectId=113919781

348 https://dhexchange.kahootz.com/MEAGpublications/view?objectId=128443557
349 https://dhexchange.kahootz.com/MEAGpublications/view?objectId=128443813
350 Cabinet Office and Department of Health, *Responding to pandemic influenza, The ethical framework for policy and planning*, 2007.
351 https://dhexchange.kahootz.com/MEAGpublications/view?objectId=128443525
352 https://dhexchange.kahootz.com/MEAGpublications/view?objectId=128443717
353 Ibid.
354 Ibid.
355 https://dhexchange.kahootz.com/MEAGpublications/view?objectId=113919749
356 https://dhexchange.kahootz.com/MEAGpublications/view?objectId=113919685
357 https://dhexchange.kahootz.com/MEAGpublications/view?objectId=128443781
358 Ibid.
359 Ibid.
360 https://dhexchange.kahootz.com/MEAGpublications/view?objectId=128443685
361 SAGE meeting of 10 December 2020: https://assets.publishing.service.gov.uk/government/uploads/system/uploads/attachment_data/file/999169/S0969_Seventy-second_SAGE_meeting_on_COVID-19.pdf, page 4
362 https://committees.parliament.uk/oralevidence/1936/pdf/, https://committees.parliament.uk/oralevidence/2223/pdf/, and https://committees.parliament.uk/oralevidence/2266/pdf/
363 https://committees.parliament.uk/publications/6264/documents/69158/default/
364 https://dhexchange.kahootz.com/MEAGpublications/view?objectId=128443685
365 https://dhexchange.kahootz.com/MEAGpublications/view?objectId=128443653

366 https://dhexchange.kahootz.com/MEAGpublications/view?objectId=128443589
367 https://dhexchange.kahootz.com/MEAGpublications/view?objectId=128443621
368 https://dhexchange.kahootz.com/MEAGpublications/view?objectId=128443749
369 https://www.telegraph.co.uk/politics/2021/06/15/exclusive-no-green-light-start-vaccinating-children-ministers/
370 https://www.telegraph.co.uk/news/2021/06/28/end-madness-isolating-children-government-warned/
371 https://www.express.co.uk/life-style/health/1400450/coronavirus-testing-children-schools-covid-19-march-8-schoolchildren-england
372 https://www.theguardian.com/education/2021/jun/29/children-are-not-guinea-pigs-parents-and-teachers-on-plans-to-stop-self-isolation-in-england
373 https://app.box.com/s/iddfb4ppwkmtjusir2tc/file/941427434013
374 https://www.gov.uk/government/publications/jcvi-statement-september-2021-covid-19-vaccination-of-children-aged-12-to-15-years/jcvi-statement-on-covid-19-vaccination-of-children-aged-12-to-15-years-3-september-2021
375 https://dhexchange.kahootz.com/MEAGpublications/view?objectId=144395429
376 https://www.gov.uk/government/publications/universal-vaccination-of-children-and-young-people-aged-12-to-15-years-against-covid-19/universal-vaccination-of-children-and-young-people-aged-12-to-15-years-against-covid-19
377 https://dhexchange.kahootz.com/MEAGpublications/view?objectId=144395493
378 https://dhexchange.kahootz.com/MEAGpublications/view?objectId=144395685
379 https://covid19.public-inquiry.uk/wp-content/uploads/2023/06/22124739/C-19-Inquiry-21-June-23-Module-1-Day-7-Amended.pdf
380 https://covid19.public-inquiry.uk/wp-content/uploads/2023/06/26190702/C-19-Inquiry-26-June-23-Module-1-Day-9.pdf

381 https://bristoluniversitypressdigital.com/view/journals/evp/19/2/article-p236.xml
382 https://assets.publishing.service.gov.uk/government/uploads/system/uploads/attachment_data/file/213717/dh_131040.pdf
383 M. Woolhouse, *The Year The World Went Mad*, Sandstone, 2022, page 110.
384 https://www.gov.uk/government/publications/spi-m-o-consensus-view-on-the-impact-of-mass-school-closures-10-february-2020/spi-m-o-consensus-view-on-the-impact-of-mass-school-closures-10-february-2020
385 https://www.gov.uk/government/publications/spi-m-o-consensus-view-on-the-impact-of-mass-school-closures-19-february-2020/spi-m-o-consensus-view-on-the-impact-of-mass-school-closures-19-february-2020
386 Matt Hancock on Wednesday 26 February 2020 https://hansard.parliament.uk/Commons/2020-02-26/debates/B0FE8C31-77D5-40AA-97AF-BBA8FB620A95/Coronavirus?highlight=coronavirus#contribution-75F886DC-F641-4793-AF88-86527A0929A7
387 See, e.g., Lucy Easthope quoted in L. Cole and M. Kingsley, The Children's Inquiry, 2022, Pinter & Martin, page 64.
388 https://assets.publishing.service.gov.uk/government/uploads/system/uploads/attachment_data/file/873726/04-spi-b-insights-on-combined-behavioural-and-social-interventions.pdf
389 https://www.gov.uk/government/publications/spi-m-o-consensus-view-on-the-impact-of-mass-school-closures-17-march-2020/spi-m-o-consensus-view-on-the-impact-of-school-closures-on-covid-19-17-march-2020
390 https://www.ucl.ac.uk/news/2020/apr/school-closures-play-marginal-role-containing-covid-19-are-key-restarting-society
391 https://www.gov.uk/government/publications/sage-minutes-coronavirus-covid-19-response-18-march-2020/sage-17-minutes-coronavirus-covid-19-response-18-march-2020
392 https://covid19.public-inquiry.uk/wp-content/uploads/2023/10/10191531/2023-10-10-Module-2-Day-6-Transcript.pdf
393 https://hansard.parliament.uk/commons/2020-03-18/debates/FCD4DEB2-86A8-4F95-8EB8-D0EF4C752D7D/EducationalSettings
394 Ibid.

395 https://www.manchestereveningnews.co.uk/news/greater-manchester-news/been-more-900-calls-childline-17986993
396 https://www.theguardian.com/world/2020/apr/02/coronavirus-lockdown-raises-risk-of-online-child-abuse-charity-says
397 https://amp.theguardian.com/society/2020/apr/16/mps-call-for-action-over-expected-rise-in-child-sexual-abuse-during-coronavirus-pandemic
398 https://www.bmj.com/content/bmj/369/bmj.m1669.full.pdf
399 https://adc.bmj.com/content/106/3/e14, for the period between 23 March and 23 April 2020.
400 https://researchbriefings.files.parliament.uk/documents/CBP-8915/CBP-8915.pdf, page 23.
401 https://www.bbc.co.uk/newsround/55033768
402 https://schoolsweek.co.uk/coronavirus-schools-have-legal-duty-to-provide-remote-education/
403 https://committees.parliament.uk/oralevidence/299/pdf/
404 https://www.gov.uk/government/publications/spi-m-the-role-of-children-in-transmission-16-april-2020/spi-m-the-role-of-children-in-transmission-16-april-2020--2#fn:3
405 Ibid.
406 Ibid.
407 https://www.bbc.co.uk/news/in-pictures-52370968
408 https://committees.parliament.uk/oralevidence/299/pdf/, Q16
409 https://www.childrenscommissioner.gov.uk/resource/were-all-in-this-together/
410 https://committees.parliament.uk/oralevidence/380/pdf/
411 https://committees.parliament.uk/oralevidence/299/pdf/
412 https://committees.parliament.uk/oralevidence/438/pdf/
413 https://www.theguardian.com/society/2021/dec/03/arthur-labinjo-hughes-vulnerable-children-slipped-from-view-in-pandemic
414 https://www.bbc.co.uk/news/health-55863841
415 https://committees.parliament.uk/oralevidence/627/pdf/
416 https://www.childrenscommissioner.gov.uk/blog/news/changes-to-send-duties/
417 https://committees.parliament.uk/oralevidence/627/pdf/

418 https://www.theguardian.com/uk-news/2021/feb/11/olga-freeman-uk-woman-who-killed-disabled-son-detained-in-hospital-indefinitely
419 https://www.instituteforgovernment.org.uk/publication/schools-and-coronavirus
420 https://www.telegraph.co.uk/news/2020/07/01/revealed-new-coronavirus-guidelines-schools-open-september/
421 Ibid.
422 https://www.mirror.co.uk/news/uk-news/schools-could-go-part-time-22697331 and https://www.telegraph.co.uk/news/2020/09/10/plans-get-children-back-classroom-derailed-lack-tests-headteachers/
423 https://www.telegraph.co.uk/news/2020/10/21/overcautious-teachers-sending-entire-year-groups-home-unnecessarily/
424 https://covid19.public-inquiry.uk/wp-content/uploads/2023/10/09184407/INQ000083851_7.pdf
425 https://www.telegraph.co.uk/news/2020/10/26/six-ten-pupils-getting-full-education-despite-schools-reopening/
426 https://www.telegraph.co.uk/news/2020/11/18/lockdown-did-not-just-put-childrens-lives-hold-meant-went-backwards/
427 https://assets.publishing.service.gov.uk/government/uploads/system/uploads/attachment_data/file/935192/SPi-B-dfe-benefits-remaining-education-s0861-041120.pdf
428 Ibid. page 5 et seq.
429 https://assets.publishing.service.gov.uk/government/uploads/system/uploads/attachment_data/file/968945/Covid-19_SAGE_65_minutes_footnote.pdf
430 https://hansard.parliament.uk/commons/2020-11-02/debates/6AF57346-80F3-491D-AA67-9EF31B9B3B26/Covid-19Update
431 Ibid.
432 https://www.telegraph.co.uk/news/2020/12/15/remote-learning-no-substitute-classroom-ofsted-chief-says/
433 https://www.standard.co.uk/news/education/greenwich-schools-legal-challenge-stay-open-government-b310672.html
434 https://www.standard.co.uk/news/uk/schools-coronavirus-tests-gavin-williamson-b590868.html

435 https://www.tes.com/magazine/archived/school-mass-testing-plans-undeliverable-warn-heads
436 https://assets.publishing.service.gov.uk/government/uploads/system/uploads/attachment_data/file/999169/S0969_Seventy-second_SAGE_meeting_on_COVID-19.pdf
437 Core UK Decision-making and Political Governance (Module 2) – Public Hearings - UK Covid-19 Inquiry (covid19.public-inquiry.uk)
438 https://committees.parliament.uk/oralevidence/1496/pdf/, Q.1101.
439 https://www.independent.co.uk/news/uk/politics/schools-close-national-lockdown-boris-johnson-b1782295.html
440 https://www.gov.uk/government/speeches/prime-ministers-address-to-the-nation-4-january-2021
441 Ibid.
442 https://committees.parliament.uk/oralevidence/1496/pdf/
443 https://www.telegraph.co.uk/news/2023/03/01/matt-hancock-gavin-williamson-whatsapp-exchange-school-closures/
444 https://committees.parliament.uk/oralevidence/1531/pdf/
445 Ibid.
446 Ibid.
447 https://educationhub.blog.gov.uk/2021/01/28/prime-minister-announces-that-schools-and-colleges-will-return-from-8-march-at-the-earliest/
448 https://assets.publishing.service.gov.uk/government/uploads/system/uploads/attachment_data/file/963347/S1061_SAGE__78_minutes__1_.pdf, paragraph 31.
449 https://www.mirror.co.uk/news/uk-news/breaking-more-1m-kids-england-24574647
450 https://www.telegraph.co.uk/news/2021/06/30/exclusive-schools-must-return-normal-july-19-tory-mps-warn-boris/
451 https://www.gov.uk/government/news/self-isolation-removed-for-double-jabbed-close-contacts-from-16-august
452 https://www.telegraph.co.uk/news/2023/03/05/matt-hancock-rejected-covid-self-isolation-advice/
453 https://www.telegraph.co.uk/news/2021/11/11/six-healthy-children-died-covid-year/

ENDNOTES

454 https://www.dailymail.co.uk/news/article-12213895/George-Osborne-insists-austerity-policies-meant-Britain-BETTER-able-respond-Covid.html#:~:text=The%20ex%2DChancellor%20claimed%20it,eight%2Dyear%2Dold'.

455 https://www.ucl.ac.uk/news/2023/jun/pandemic-policies-overlooked-long-term-needs-children

456 See https://media.ed.ac.uk/media/Moray+House+Online+Conversations+-+Mark+Woolhouse%2C+Professor+of+Infectious+Disease+Epidemiology/1_manc94er; and https://www.thetimes.co.uk/article/8f4a3cd8-cb9a-11ea-979f-ba077cfea17c?shareToken=3248a6a7b72b9cf9e14bc1933afb7d26; and https://www.medrxiv.org/content/10.1101/2020.09.21.20196428v1; and https://publications.aap.org/pediatrics/article/146/2/e2020004879/36879/COVID-19-Transmission-and-Children-The-Child-Is

457 https://www.sportengland.org/news/reopening-schools-vital-boost-childrens-activity-levels

458 https://www.ox.ac.uk/news/2020-06-16-children-show-increase-mental-health-difficulties-over-covid-19-lockdown

459 https://assets.publishing.service.gov.uk/government/uploads/system/uploads/attachment_data/file/933490/COVID-19_series_briefing_on_schools_October_2020.pdf; and https://ukedchat.com/2020/08/26/attainment-gap-widens/

460 https://news.sky.com/story/county-lines-gangs-have-changed-tactics-during-covid-and-their-victims-are-getting-even-younger-12258744; and https://www.crestadvisory.com/post/county-lines-after-covid-a-new-threat

461 https://www.theguardian.com/education/2023/mar/16/one-in-five-pupils-in-england-were-persistently-absent-in-past-school-year?CMP=Share_iOSApp_Other

462 https://www.centreforsocialjustice.org.uk/wp-content/uploads/2022/01/CSJ-Lost_but_not_forgotten-2.pdf

463 https://www.theguardian.com/society/2021/aug/21/serious-child-harm-cases-in-england-rose-by-20-during-pandemic

464 https://explore-education-statistics.service.gov.uk/find-statistics/school-pupils-and-their-characteristics#:~:text=There%20are%20almost%209.1%20million,primary%20schools%20and%20nursery%20schools.

465 https://schoolsweek.co.uk/coronavirus-schools-have-legal-duty-to-provide-remote-education/
466 https://www.gov.uk/government/news/billion-pound-covid-catch-up-plan-to-tackle-impact-of-lost-teaching-time
467 https://schoolsweek.co.uk/boris-johnson-promises-huge-amount-of-catch-up-for-pupils-to-be-announced-next-week/
468 https://www.gov.uk/government/news/new-education-recovery-package-for-children-and-young-people
469 https://news.sky.com/story/woeful-schools-recovery-plan-slammed-as-education-secretary-gavin-williamson-gets-12bn-less-than-asked-for-12322989
470 https://www.theguardian.com/politics/2021/jun/02/education-recovery-chief-kevan-collins-quit-english-schools-catch-up-row
471 https://publications.parliament.uk/pa/cm5802/cmselect/cmeduc/940/report.html
472 https://appgpandemic.org/news/mass-testing-of-children
473 https://www.theguardian.com/education/2020/dec/18/covid-unions-say-mass-testing-of-englands-pupils-undeliverable?CMP=Share_iOSApp_Other
474 https://www.instituteforgovernment.org.uk/publication/schools-and-coronavirus
475 Mark Woolhouse: *The Year The World Went Mad*: Sandstone Press: 2022
476 Interview given to UsForThem, June 2023.
477 https://www.dailymail.co.uk/news/article-9186711/Schools-closures-risk-calamitous-impact-childrens-mental-health-paediatricians-warn.html
478 See, for example, https://www.ncbi.nlm.nih.gov/pmc/articles/PMC7412780/ and more recently, https://ebm.bmj.com/content/28/3/175
479 https://www.bmj.com/content/369/bmj.m2439/rr
480 https://www.tandfonline.com/doi/full/10.1080/10854681.2022.2167423
481 https://committees.parliament.uk/oralevidence/3098/pdf/; and https://appgpandemic.org/news/mass-testing-of-children; and see L. Cole and M. Kingsley, *The Children's Inquiry*, Pinter & Martin, 2022, page 52, for a summary of facemask harms to children

ENDNOTES

482 Letter from Children's Minister Vicky Ford MP to Robert Halfon MP, Chair of the Education Select Committee https://committees.parliament.uk/publications/919/documents/6822/default/

483 https://assets.publishing.service.gov.uk/government/uploads/system/uploads/attachment_data/file/609903/PU2077_code_of_practice_2017.pdf

484 https://www.telegraph.co.uk/news/2023/03/04/michael-gove-matt-hancock-covid-lockdown-files-whatsapp/

485 https://hansard.parliament.uk/commons/2021-07-13/debates/BD25E3D7-6EFB-48A9-A564-966D3898D8FC/NationalHealthService#contribution-08834773-E158-40DF-BB33-D089BA382BC7

486 https://twitter.com/educationgovuk/status/1473194055433654274

487 https://www.huffingtonpost.co.uk/entry/chris-whittys-letter-to-ministers-on-why-covid-jabs-for-over-12s-can-go-ahead_uk_613f4f94e4b090b79e86d53d

488 https://www.itv.com/news/2020-08-26/england-follows-scotland-with-changed-guidance-over-masks-for-pupils

489 https://www.thenational.scot/news/23170063.matt-hancock-says-nicola-sturgeon-forced-tories-face-mask-u-turn/

490 https://www.dailymail.co.uk/news/article-11821671/Matt-Hancock-discussed-deploying-new-virus-variant-frighten-pants-everyone.html

491 https://www.telegraph.co.uk/politics/2022/01/28/grossly-unethical-downing-street-nudge-unit-accused-scaring/

492 Government transparency and accountability during Covid 19: The data underpinning decisions; https://publications.parliament.uk/pa/cm5801/cmselect/cmpubadm/803/80302.htm

493 https://publications.parliament.uk/pa/cm5801/cmselect/cmpubadm/803/80306.htm, paragraph 83

494 https://www.telegraph.co.uk/news/2023/03/06/jacob-rees-mogg-covid-lockdown-self-isolation/

495 https://www.independent.co.uk/news/uk/politics/covid-inquiry-whatsapp-sunak-b2351473.html, and https://www.thetimes.co.uk/article/the-three-vital-whatsapp-groups-no10-used-to-beat-the-pandemic-xx57fcvxb

496 https://www.independent.co.uk/news/uk/home-news/rishi-sunak-whatsapp-texts-covid-inquiry-b2422937.html

497 WhatsApp chats vanish — and take the possibility of scrutiny with themhttps://www.thetimes.co.uk/article/9a753874-017f-11ee-96f6-54413087455a?shareToken=59d686ca99596697219cf3031f768465
498 https://www.legislation.gov.uk/ukpga/2006/46/part/10/chapter/9/crossheading/records-of-meetings-of-directors
499 https://committees.parliament.uk/publications/5076/documents/50285/default/
500 https://publications.parliament.uk/pa/cm5801/cmselect/cmpubadm/803/80306.htm
501 Ibid.
502 https://www.theguardian.com/law/2020/may/16/government-legal-action-refusal-to-publish-sage-minutes-lockdown
503 https://goodlawproject.org/we-won-government-commits-to-publishing-248m-missing-covid-contracts-after-breaching-transparency-guidelines/
504 https://www.telegraph.co.uk/news/2023/03/02/matt-hancock-simon-case-quarantine-hotel-covid-whatsapp/
505 Ibid.
506 https://www.telegraph.co.uk/news/2023/02/28/whatsapp-messages-matt-hancock-care-homes-testing-target/
507 https://www.telegraph.co.uk/news/2023/03/06/matt-hancocks-plan-block-funding-disabled-children-mp-opposed/
508 https://www.independent.co.uk/life-style/lockdown-anniversary-uk-covid-rules-b2041525.html
509 https://www.theguardian.com/world/2021/jan/11/derbyshire-police-withdraw-two-womens-200-fines-for-lockdown-walk
510 https://www.walesonline.co.uk/news/politics/coronavirus-supermarket-lockdown-non-essential-19159319
511 https://insights.doughtystreet.co.uk/post/102g80l/did-dominic-cummings-act-responsibly-and-legally
512 M. Woolhouse, *The Year the World Went Mad*, Sandstone, 2022; T. Green and T. Fazi, *The Covid Consensus*, 2nd ed., Hurst, 2023; L. Cole and M. Kingsley, *The Children's Inquiry*, Pinter & Martin, 2022.
513 Prime Minister's statement of 16 March 2020: https://www.gov.uk/government/speeches/pm-statement-on-coronavirus-16-march-2020

ENDNOTES

514 https://committees.parliament.uk//oralevidence/539/html, Q823.
515 https://usforthem2020.substack.com/p/responses-to-freedom-of-information
516 https://www.thetimes.co.uk/article/c7b7aee4-741b-11ed-be91-363346a310de?shareToken=48ce9fd1fb3f8f895479547463aa5e3d
517 https://usforthem.co.uk/wp-content/uploads/2021/05/UsforThem_Potential-Harms-of-Face-Coverings-in-Schools_v3-1.pdf
518 https://covid19.public-inquiry.uk/wp-content/uploads/2023/10/18193417/C-19-Inquiry-18-October-23-Module-2-Day-12.pdf
519 https://www.telegraph.co.uk/news/2020/11/10/headache-pm-dozens-conservative-mps-set-covid-recovery-group/
520 That infamous paper predicted more than 500,000 deaths from Covid in the UK without action, and advocated for "epidemic suppression" as the only viable strategy. https://www.imperial.ac.uk/media/imperial-college/medicine/sph/ide/gida-fellowships/Imperial-College-COVID19-NPI-modelling-16-03-2020.pdf
521 https://www.aier.org/article/the-failure-of-imperial-college-modeling-is-far-worse-than-we-knew/; though there were also at that time academic defences of the Imperial College modelling, such as https://blogs.lse.ac.uk/covid19/2021/05/06/bad-data-and-flawed-models-fact-checking-a-case-against-lockdowns/
522 https://www.telegraph.co.uk/technology/2020/05/16/coding-led-lockdown-totally-unreliable-buggy-mess-say-experts/
523 https://www.nature.com/articles/s41586-020-2405-7
524 https://www.aier.org/article/professor-lockdown-now-claims-to-have-saved-3-1-million-lives/
525 M. Woolhouse, *The Year The World Went Mad*, Sandstone Press, 2022; and D. Axe, W. Briggs and J. Richards, *The Price of Panic*, Regnery Publishing, 2020 https://www.telegraph.co.uk/technology/2020/05/16/coding-led-lockdown-totally-unreliable-buggy-mess-say-experts/
526 https://dailysceptic.org/2020/04/04/how-reliable-is-imperial-colleges-modelling/
527 https://www.spectator.co.uk/article/my-twitter-conversation-with-the-chairman-of-the-sage-covid-modelling-committee/

528 Ibid.
529 https://www.telegraph.co.uk/news/2023/03/04/matt-hancock-lockdown-files-covid-10-things-learnt/
530 https://www.telegraph.co.uk/news/2023/03/02/britain-failed-pro-lockdown-clique-incapable-admitting-errors/
531 https://www.cebm.net/covid-19/masking-lack-of-evidence-with-politics/
532 https://covid19.public-inquiry.uk/wp-content/uploads/2023/06/29175003/C-19-Inquiry-29-June-23-Module-1-Day-12.pdf
533 https://news.sky.com/story/there-was-no-plan-cummingss-key-claims-on-early-pandemic-strategy-12317238
534 https://covid19.public-inquiry.uk/documents/inq000147810-witness-statement-of-sir-patrick-vallance-dated-11-04-2023/
535 Ibid.
536 L. Dodsworth, *A State of Fear: How the Government weaponised fear during the Covid-19 pandemic*, Pinter & Martin, 2021, page 92.
537 https://www.hansardsociety.org.uk/blog/the-care-home-covid-vaccination-regulations-a-case-study-in-problems-with
538 https://hansard.parliament.uk/commons/2021-07-13/debates/BD25E3D7-6EFB-48A9-A564-966D3898D8FC/NationalHealthService
539 Sir Christopher Chope on Tuesday 13 July 2021: https://hansard.parliament.uk/commons/2021-07-13/debates/BD25E3D7-6EFB-48A9-A564-966D3898D8FC/NationalHealthService#contribution-05EA16D8-2841-4727-AC6C-7FF5E943296E
540 https://news.sky.com/video/speaker-lindsay-hoyle-demands-matt-hancock-apologise-over-commons-statement-12067371
541 https://hansard.parliament.uk/Commons/2020-03-16/debates/4748cf75-300a-430f-a802-65963409b523/CommonsChamber
542 https://www.itv.com/news/2020-09-30/covid-government-has-shown-a-total-disregard-for-parliament-says-speaker-sir-lindsay-hoyle
543 https://www.youtube.com/watch?v=va8KveK5ko8
544 https://www.miriamcates.org.uk/news/debate-vaccination-children
545 https://hansard.parliament.uk/commons/2021-09-21/debates/62D8784D-4D15-42BE-9912-72EED73A40D0/Covid-19VaccinationOfChildren
546 https://twitter.com/EstherMcVey1/status/1617874878379565057

ENDNOTES

547 https://publications.parliament.uk/pa/cm5801/cmselect/cmpubadm/803/80306.htm, paragraph 98.
548 See, e.g. https://committees.parliament.uk/publications/2992/documents/28476/default/, and https://www.dailymail.co.uk/news/article-11009249/Priti-Patel-REFUSES-appear-Home-Affairs-Committee-Rwanda-policing.html
549 https://committees.parliament.uk/publications/5815/documents/66352/default/; and https://www.independent.co.uk/news/uk/politics/dominic-cummings-defence-committee-boris-johnson-security-armed-forces-a9610036.html
550 https://www.independent.co.uk/news/uk/politics/kemi-badenoch-speaker-brexit-eu-laws-b2336975.html
551 Euzebiusz Jamrozik of The Wellcome Centre for Ethics and Humanities at University of Oxford, wrote in a September 2022 article: "The global response to the recent coronavirus pandemic has revealed an ethical crisis in public health...The "new normal" of police-enforced lockdowns, border closures with bans on citizens leaving and returning home, prolonged school closures, and, in general, restrictive public health policies with large penalties for non-compliance, diverges from the "old normal" of public health pandemic response planning, which generally recommended against widespread, prolonged, and/or punitive policies because the harms of such policies would likely outweigh any benefits in terms of reduced infectious disease transmission (and the harms would often be inequitably distributed)...Many policies would be considered unacceptable according to pre-pandemic norms of public health ethics". https://link.springer.com/article/10.1007/s40592-022-00163-7
552 Further commentary on this topic appears in our chapter on ethics.
553 https://www.spectator.co.uk/article/the-ethics-of-lockdown/
554 https://www.telegraph.co.uk/news/2023/07/06/britain-drilled-to-accept-lockdown-in-future-pandemics/;; For example: https://www.gov.uk/government/news/get-boosted-now; https://educationhub.blog.gov.uk/2021/10/25/education-secretary-writes-to-parents-about-vaccinations-for-12-to-15-year-olds/;

555 For example: https://www.bbc.co.uk/newsround/57389353. amp, https://twitter.com/educationgovuk/status/1493586270567677953?s=20; https://twitter.com/nhsuk/status/1471160600495640576?s=61&t=5jXbzYYBZ9pPegEW0v5Xhg; https://twitter.com/sheffieldhcp/status/1536045673488990209?s=61&t=5jXbzYYBZ9pPegEW0v5Xhg

556 https://pubmed.ncbi.nlm.nih.gov/32767271/

557 Jay Bhattacharya, Professor of medicine, Economics, and Health Research at Stanford University, interview given to UsForThem.

558 https://appgpandemic.org/news/mass-testing-of-children

559 Ibid.

560 https://usforthem.co.uk/open-letters/no-masks-in-class/

561 https://www.telegraph.co.uk/politics/2022/01/15/tory-mps-back-legal-challenge-against-masks-classroom/

562 More commentary on this topic appears in our chapter on ethics.

563 Revenue and profit figures for 2022 taken from Pfizer's 2022 Full Year Results: https://s28.q4cdn.com/781576035/files/doc_financials/2022/q4/Q4-2022-PFE-Earnings-Release.pdf. See also https://www.newsweek.com/pfizer-obscene-covid-pandemic-profits-record-revenues-1778513. Even now that the pandemic is officially over, Pfizer has predicted that its vaccine and Paxlovid sales will generate a further US$21 billion of revenue in 2023.

564 Revenue and profit figures for 2021 taken from Pfizer's 2021 Full Year Results: https://s28.q4cdn.com/781576035/files/doc_financials/2021/q4/Q4-2021-PFE-Earnings-Release.pdf

565 https://databankfiles.worldbank.org/public/ddpext_download/GDP.pdf

566 All figures taken from Moderna's 2022 and 2021 Full Year Results: https://news.modernatx.com/news/news-details/2022/Moderna-Reports-Fourth-Quarter-and-Fiscal-Year-2021-Financial-Results-and-Provides-Business-Updates/default.aspx and https://news.modernatx.com/news/news-details/2023/Moderna-Reports-Fourth-Quarter-and-Fiscal-Year-2022-Financial-Results-and-Provides-Business-Updates/default.aspx

567 https://publications.parliament.uk/pa/cm200405/cmselect/cmhealth/42/42.pdf, paragraph 276.

ENDNOTES

568 Letter to shareholders from Pfizer's Chairman and Chief Executive Officer, introduction to Pfizer Inc's 2023 Proxy Statement, https://s28.q4cdn.com/781576035/files/doc_financials/2022/sr/Proxy-Statement-2023.pdf

569 Pfizer Inc., 2023 Proxy Statement, page 1, https://s28.q4cdn.com/781576035/files/doc_financials/2022/sr/Proxy-Statement-2023.pdf

570 https://www.theguardian.com/science/2023/jul/22/revealed-drug-firms-funding-uk-patient-groups-that-lobby-for-nhs-approval-of-medicines

571 https://www.theguardian.com/business/2023/mar/12/revealed-experts-who-praised-new-skinny-jab-received-payments-from-drug-maker, and https://www.theguardian.com/business/2023/apr/02/revealed-maker-of-wegovy-skinny-jab-is-funding-nhs-weight-loss-services

572 One such insight was captured in 2013 when, as a contributor to a documentary about the HPV vaccine Gardasil, Dr Peter Rost, a former Pfizer marketing executive turned whistleblower, gave an interview in which he explained how he believed Big Pharma used its influence and marketing budgets to procure favourable research and coverage from academic and medical institutions: https://www.youtube.com/watch?v=TrCizlAOBAo

573 For a detailed exploration of the workings of the pharmaceuticals industry, see B. Goldacre, *Bad Pharma: how medicine is broken and how we can fix it*, Fourth Estate, 2013.

574 Fourth Estate, 2013.

575 https://publications.parliament.uk/pa/cm200405/cmselect/cmhealth/42/42.pdf, paragraph 338

576 Ibid., paragraphs 155 and 158.

577 Ibid., paragraph 282 et seq.

578 Ibid, paragraphs 191, 195 and 221.

579 https://www.standard.co.uk/news/uk/patrick-vallance-vaccine-shares-denies-conflict-interest-a4555141.html

580 https://www.gov.uk/government/news/new-global-partnership-launched-to-fight-future-pandemics

581 https://www.telegraph.co.uk/news/2020/09/23/revealed-sir-patrick-vallance-has-600000-shareholding-firm-contracted/

582 https://www.gov.uk/government/speeches/chief-scientific-advisor-and-chief-medical-officer-briefing-on-coronavirus-covid-19-21-september-2020--2
583 For more commentary on this episode, see our chapter on propaganda.
584 https://www.independent.co.uk/news/uk/home-news/jonathan-van-tam-job-moderna-vaccine-b2395006.html
585 https://www.gov.uk/government/news/moderna-to-open-vaccine-research-and-manufacturing-centre-in-uk
586 https://www.gov.uk/government/news/uk-cements-10-year-partnership-with-moderna-in-major-boost-for-vaccines-and-research
587 https://www.independent.co.uk/news/uk/home-news/jonathan-van-tam-job-moderna-vaccine-b2395006.html
588 https://www.theguardian.com/politics/2020/nov/17/rishi-sunak-refuses-to-say-if-he-will-profit-from-moderna-covid-vaccine
589 Although blind trust arrangements are commonly used by Ministers to navigate the Ministerial Code requirement that Ministers ensure that no conflict could arise, or be perceived to arise, between their Ministerial position and their private interests, critics of the system point out that beneficiaries tend to be aware of the assets they are putting into the trust.
590 https://www.theguardian.com/politics/2023/mar/22/rishi-sunak-publishes-long-awaited-personal-uk-tax-returns
591 https://assets.publishing.service.gov.uk/government/uploads/system/uploads/attachment_data/file/1145059/PM_Rishi_Sunak_Tax_Summary_.pdf
592 Ed Davey MP, leader of the Liberal Democrats, quoted in the Guardian: https://www.theguardian.com/politics/2020/nov/17/rishi-sunak-refuses-to-say-if-he-will-profit-from-moderna-covid-vaccine
593 https://www.dailymail.co.uk/news/article-8776339/Test-tsar-770-000-shares-firm-sold-13million-pointless-antibody-screening-kits.html
594 Ibid.
595 This can be confirmed by means of a LinkedIn search.
596 https://www.express.co.uk/comment/expresscomment/1796281/covid-vaccine-taskforce-brexit-britain?int_source=amp_continue_reading&int_medium=amp&int_campaign=continue_reading_button#amp-readmore-

ENDNOTES

target; and https://conservativehome.com/2023/09/15/nadhim-zahawi-and-stuart-carroll-whitehall-needs-another-injection-of-the-vaccines-taskforce/

597 https://twitter.com/mrstuartcarroll/status/1684987294845939724?s=12
598 https://www.bmj.com/company/newsroom/conflicts-of-interest-among-the-uk-governments-covid-19-advisers-are-not-transparent/
599 https://www.abpi.org.uk/reputation/disclosure-uk/about-disclosure-uk/im-a-member-of-the-public/
600 https://www.kingsfund.org.uk/about-us/who-we-are/independence
601 https://www.kingsfund.org.uk/sites/default/files/2022-01/The%20Covid-19%20Vaccination%20Programme%20online%20version_3.pdf
602 https://twitter.com/rcgp/status/1356629683325046784
603 https://twitter.com/rcgp/status/1367775903950987264
604 https://www.gov.uk/government/publications/myocarditis-and-pericarditis-after-covid-19-vaccination/myocarditis-and-pericarditis-after-covid-19-vaccination-guidance-for-healthcare-professionals
605 https://www.britishcardiovascularsociety.org/resources/editorials/articles/covid-19-implications-cardiologists
606 https://static1.squarespace.com/static/62416ca389785537abb9dea3/t/639348b2042b2d3f94fcaf32/1670596787381/BSH+Postion+Statement+-+CoViD-19+Vaccinations+-+18-12-2020.pdf
607 Ibid.
608 https://www.bmj.com/content/382/bmj.p1658
609 We have relied here on the accuracy and completeness of the ABPI database search facility accessible via https://www.abpi.org.uk/reputation/disclosure-uk/ and all of our data analysis and calculations have been carried out in good faith to the best of our abilities; we cannot therefore categorically vouch for the accuracy of these figures, which are included for illustrative purposes only.
610 https://www.imperial.ac.uk/news/197017/imperial-covid-19-vaccine-team-secures-225/
611 https://www.imperial.ac.uk/media/imperial-college/medicine/sph/ide/gida-fellowships/Imperial-College-COVID19-NPI-modelling-16-03-2020.pdf

612 https://www.imperial.ac.uk/news/197017/imperial-covid-19-vaccine-team-secures-225/
613 https://www.rcm.org.uk/media/4395/caffeine-in-pregnancy-oct2020-003.pdf
614 https://www.rcm.org.uk/media/5550/should-iget-the-covid-vaccine.pdf
615 See for example: https://ec.europa.eu/research-and-innovation/en/horizon-magazine/five-things-you-need-know-about-mrna-vaccine-safety
616 https://search.disclosureuk.org.uk/
617 https://questions-statements.parliament.uk/written-questions/detail/2023-01-09/119065#:~:text=The%20MHRA%20is%20primarily%20funded,Treasury's%20Managing%20Public%20Money%20guidelines (which suggests 75%), and https://www.bmj.com/content/377/bmj.o1538 (which suggests 86%)
618 We know that the MHRA has also received funding from other private sources; for example it received grants of US$3m funding from the Bill and Melinda Gates Foundation over several years: https://www.gov.uk/government/publications/freedom-of-information-responses-from-the-mhra-week-commencing-23-may-2022/freedom-of-information-request-on-funding-and-contributions-from-pharmaceutical-companies-foi-22702
619 https://www.youtube.com/watch?v=xUQfzTqPUm4, starting at 31:00 minutes.
620 https://yellowcard.mhra.gov.uk/information
621 https://www.bmj.com/content/373/bmj.n1283?ijkey=54bd5d861fdb-471041f50ace169bb6b70d90a36c&keytype2=tf_ipsecsha
622 https://onlinelibrary.wiley.com/doi/10.1111/1468-0009.12073
623 https://www.bmj.com/content/373/bmj.n1283?ijkey=54bd5d861fdb-471041f50ace169bb6b70d90a36c&keytype2=tf_ipsecsha
624 https://publications.parliament.uk/pa/cm200405/cmselect/cmhealth/42/42.pdf, paragraph 282 et seq.
625 According to the ABPI's financial disclosures database, between 2019 and 2022, pharmaceutical companies paid NHS bodies more than £169 million; www.abpi.org.uk/reputation/disclosure-uk/
626 The Prescriptions Medicine Code of Practice Authority: https://www.pmcpa.org.uk/

627 The PAGB is the consumer healthcare association for Great Britain, representing the manufacturers of branded over-the-counter medicines: https://www.pagb.co.uk/about-us/
628 Ibid.
629 https://www.bmj.com/content/377/bmj.o1538
630 https://careappointments.com/care-news/england/164232/government-urged-to-halt-drastic-job-cuts-at-medicines-regulation-agency/; see also this September 2021 early day motion from Labour Party MPs: https://edm.parliament.uk/early-day-motion/58955/staffing-reductions-at-the-medicines-and-healthcare-products-regulatory-agency
631 https://www.pmcpa.org.uk/about-us/meet-the-team/
632 https://www.pmcpa.org.uk/cases/completed-cases/auth35911221-a-complaint-on-behalf-of-usforthem-v-pfizer/
633 https://usforthem2020.substack.com/p/pfizer-sales-before-child-safety
634 Most financial services firms in the UK are subject to regulation and supervision by the Financial Conduct Authority. The financial services regulatory framework comprises both conduct regulation (controlling the nature of the products offered and the manner in which regulated firms market and sell their products) and prudential regulation (overseeing the manner in which those businesses organise themselves and manage their business affairs)
635 The existence of those arrangements has been made public but the detail of them has remained private: https://questions-statements.parliament.uk/written-statements/detail/2020-12-08/hcws630
636 https://www.transparency.org.uk/sites/default/files/pdf/publications/29-06-2016-Corruption_In_The_Pharmaceutical_Sector_Web-2.pdf
637 B. Goldacre, *Bad Pharma: how medicine is broken and how we can fix it*, Fourth Estate, 2013.
638 A. Wagner, Emergency State, The Bodley Head, 2022, pages 49-50.; J.Sumption, *Government by Decree: Covid 19 and the Constitution*, Cambridge Freshfields Lecture, 2020. https://resources.law.cam.ac.uk/privatelaw/Freshfields_Lecture_2020_Government_by_Decree.pdf
639 https://www.instituteforgovernment.org.uk/article/explainer/eu-withdrawal-act-2018

640 L. Dodsworth, *A State of Fear: How the Government weaponised fear during the Covid-19 pandemic*, Pinter & Martin, 2021; https://www.telegraph.co.uk/news/2023/07/06/britain-drilled-to-accept-lockdown-in-future-pandemics/
641 https://www.gov.uk/government/speeches/pm-address-to-the-nation-on-coronavirus-23-march-2020
642 https://www.legislation.gov.uk/ukpga/2020/6/enacted, read with s.86 of the Coronavirus Act 2020
643 J. Sumption, *Law in a Time of Crisis*, Profile Books, 2022, page 226
644 Boris Johnson has since admitted in his evidence to the official Covid Inquiry that the Government's to rely on powers derived from the Public Health Act, which required less regular engagement between the Government and Parliament, had not ultimately been for the best: "Looking back, I think the arguments deployed against a pan-UK Civil Contingencies Act based approach are weak. For sheer scale, horror and urgency Covid-19 easily met the tests of the Act. I believe that it would have been useful, in retrospect, to have regular parliamentary review, as prescribed, and it would have saved a lot of argument later with MPs who wanted more scrutiny"; https://covid19.public-inquiry.uk/wp-content/uploads/2023/10/09184412/INQ000255836_303745.pdf, paragraph 155.
645 J. Sumption, *Law in a Time of Crisis*, Profile Books, 2022
646 https://committees.parliament.uk/publications/1281/documents/11348/default/, see para 15.
647 https://www.theguardian.com/commentisfree/2021/jan/17/id-love-to-ignore-covid-sceptics-and-their-tall-tales-but-they-make-a-splash-and-have-no-shame
648 https://www.politico.eu/article/covid19-coronavirus-twitter-warrior-neil-obrien-brexit-leveling-up/
649 https://www.thetimes.co.uk/article/the-tory-mp-taking-on-the-covid-sceptics-tweet-by-toxic-tweet-czmkmr9cp
650 https://www.theguardian.com/commentisfree/2021/jan/17/id-love-to-ignore-covid-sceptics-and-their-tall-tales-but-they-make-a-splash-and-have-no-shame?CMP=Share_iOSApp_Other
651 https://www.hansardsociety.org.uk/publications/data/coronavirus-statutory-instruments-dashboard

ENDNOTES

652 Ibid.
653 https://www.instituteforgovernment.org.uk/explainer/secondary-legislation-scrutiny, known as the 'made negative' procedure.
654 https://committees.parliament.uk/publications/9356/documents/160933/default/, page 3.
655 https://hansard.parliament.uk/commons/2021-12-14/debates/8034393B-C568-4DE6-8695-1D63F957537E/PublicHealth
656 https://assets.publishing.service.gov.uk/government/uploads/system/uploads/attachment_data/file/1032203/making-vaccination-a-condition-of-deployment-in-the-health-and-wider-social-care-sector-government-response.pdf, Chapter 6.1, Figure 1.
657 A report published by the Hansard Society in 2000 commented presciently that "the workload of the MP is greater at the beginning of the 21st century than at any time in the history of the House of Commons. Public expectations of our elected representatives have also grown.....[Without reform] the alternative is a growing disparity between expectation and reality, which can only lead to a further erosion of support for Parliament". Since then the pressure of 24/7 news, social media and 'always on' communication has only increased that workload, and the public and media scrutiny of MPs; https://www.hansardsociety.org.uk/publications/reports/under-pressure-are-we-getting-the-most-from-our-mps
658 https://www.hansardsociety.org.uk/blog/the-first-100-days-a-survival-guide-for-new-mps
659 https://hansard.parliament.uk/commons/2020-03-23/debates/5C09B7DC-BD70-4306-979C-DB59C02D0529/Speaker%E2%80%99SStatement
660 https://publications.parliament.uk/pa/cm5801/cmselect/cmcumeds/correspondence/Chair-to-Twitter-Covid-misinformation.pdf
661 https://publications.parliament.uk/pa/cm5801/cmselect/cmcumeds/correspondence/Chair-to-Google-Covid-misinformation.pdf
662 https://publications.parliament.uk/pa/cm200910/cmselect/cmpubadm/457/457.pdf
663 https://www.instituteforgovernment.org.uk/article/explainer/parliamentary-private-secretaries
664 Ibid.

665 https://www.hansardsociety.org.uk/publications/reports/proposals-for-a-new-system-for-delegated-legislation-a-working-paper
666 See further, L. Cole and M. Kingsley, The Children's Inquiry, Pinter & Martin, 2022.
667 https://www.telegraph.co.uk/news/2023/06/27/britain-harder-lockdowns-covid-inquiry-matt-hancock/
668 https://www.covid19.public-inquiry.uk/documents/inq000182610-witness-statement-of-jeremy-farrar-chief-scientist-at-the-world-health-organisation-dated-10-03-2023/
669 https://www.telegraph.co.uk/news/2023/07/06/britain-drilled-to-accept-lockdown-in-future-pandemics/
670 https://twitter.com/SKyriakidesEU/status/1665684950111211526?s=20
671 https://usforthem.co.uk/briefing-paper-the-who-pandemic-treaty-and-ihr-amendments/
672 https://thehill.com/opinion/judiciary/4198285-missouri-v-biden-and-the-crossroads-of-politics-censorship-and-free-speech/
673 Coutts Bank has admitted this in relation to its debanking scandal in 2023. The major social media platforms had earlier admitted this to Parliament in December 2020.
674 https://www.smh.com.au/world/europe/australian-at-centre-of-nigel-farage-debanking-controversy-resigns-20230728-p5drvt.html
675 https://www.dailymail.co.uk/news/article-12253081/Vicar-accuses-Yorkshire-Building-Society-bullying-closing-account-trans-protest.html
676 https://www.telegraph.co.uk/news/2023/10/03/tory-party-conference-nhs-karol-sikora-cancel-criticism/
677 As of the time of writing, in mid-October 2023.
678 https://committees.parliament.uk/committee/378/digital-culture-media-and-sport-committee/news/114660/impact-of-covid19-coronavirus-digital-inclusion-examined/
679 https://usforthem.co.uk/briefing-paper-the-who-pandemic-treaty-and-ihr-amendments/
680 https://hansard.parliament.uk/commons/2022-12-13/debates/EAB2E8A2-A721-47DD-A79C-4EFD10F10C2D/VaccinesPotentialHarms
681 https://www.bbc.co.uk/news/health-64209221

ENDNOTES

682 As of the date of writing, a short debate is scheduled to take place in Parliament on the topic of excess deaths.

683 We do not attempt to summarise the extensive scientific literature on this topic, but two examples of concerns having been raised by eminent experts are https://pubmed.ncbi.nlm.nih.gov/36055877/ and https://www.conservativewoman.co.uk/mrna-vaccines-must-be-banned-once-and-for-all/

684 https://www.immdsreview.org.uk/Report.html

685 https://publications.parliament.uk/pa/cm200405/cmselect/cmhealth/42/42.pdf, paragraph 338.

686 https://www.kcl.ac.uk/policy-institute/assets/fixing-whitehalls-broken-policy-machine.pdf

Printed in Great Britain
by Amazon